THE GOOD NEWS CLUB

—— *The* ——

GOOD NEWS CLUB

THE CHRISTIAN RIGHT'S
STEALTH ASSAULT
ON AMERICA'S CHILDREN

KATHERINE STEWART

PUBLICAFFAIRS
New York

PublicAffairs books are available at special discounts for bulk purchases in the U.S. by corporations, institutions, and other organizations. For more information, please contact the Special Markets Department at the Perseus Books Group, 2300 Chestnut Street, Suite 200, Philadelphia, PA 19103, call (800) 810-4145, ext. 5000, or e-mail special.markets@perseusbooks.com.

Some of the names of individuals mentioned in the book have been changed to protect their privacy.

Book Design by Trish Wilkinson
Text set in 11.5 point Goudy Old Style

Library of Congress Cataloging-in-Publication Data

Stewart, Katherine.
    The Good News Club : the Christian right's stealth assault on America's children / Katherine Stewart.—1st ed.
        p.   cm.
    Includes bibliographical references and index.
    ISBN 978-1-58648-843-7 (hardcover : alk. paper)—ISBN 978-1-61039-050-7 (e-book) 1. Religion in the public schools—United States. I. Title.
LC111.S69 2011
379.2'80973—dc23   2011032271

First Edition

10 9 8 7 6 5 4 3 2 1

For my family

Contents

INTRODUCTION

THIS BOOK HAD its beginnings in one of those events that at first seems too small to matter, until suddenly it becomes too big to ignore. When a program called the "Good News Club" showed up on a roster of after-school activities at my daughter's public elementary school in Santa Barbara, California, I didn't give it much thought. The Club advertised itself as a nondenominational "Bible study" program for children of kindergarten age and older, and it required parental consent for children to participate. I soon found out, however, that the Good News Club is very different from what it appears to be. More importantly, I discovered that the Club is really just one small part of a much larger story that should be of concern to anyone who cares about the future of public education—or indeed the future of secular democracy—in the United States.

We have been told, mostly by religious conservatives, that US public schools are devoid of religion. Following the Supreme Court decisions concerning school prayer in the 1960s, the usual story goes, God was kicked out of the classroom. I believe that this story grossly misrepresents reality. In conducting research for this book, I traveled to dozens of cities and towns across the country. I visited regions famous for their piety, like west Texas and Alabama, and others known for the opposite, like Seattle and New York City. Everywhere I found religion-driven programs and initiatives inserting themselves into public school systems with unprecedented force and unexpected consequences. I saw student athletic programs turned into vehicles for religious recruiting. I attended services at a dozen of the hundreds of school facilities that double as taxpayer-financed houses of worship. I heard the stories of children who have been subject to proselytizing in classrooms and school yards, and I spoke with other children who have been instructed to proselytize their friends at school. I met with school board officials who are busy rewriting textbook standards to conform to their own religious agendas. I interviewed the people promoting and attending "Bible Study" courses that turned out to be programs of sectarian indoctrination. And I sat in on training sessions with instructors for the Good News Club, which now operates in nearly 3,500 public elementary schools around the country. Today, there is more religious activity in American public schools than there has been for the past 100 years.

Like the Good News Club that appeared one day in my California town, many of the religious initiatives in public schools present themselves as spontaneous expressions of faith by members of local communities. But they are not. The labor behind the initiatives may be local, but the ideas, the money, and the legal firepower that make them possible are national. The movement is coordinated and given strategic direction by extremely well financed groups whose leaders write the scripts that are followed in classrooms, playgrounds, and courtrooms from New York to California. Some of the most powerful forces in public education today are groups that you may never have heard of—the Alliance Defense Fund (ADF), the Liberty Counsel, the American Center for Law and Justice (ACLJ), and other conservative legal groups—that, with combined budgets totaling over $100 million per year, have masterminded the religious assault on public education.

Many religions are represented to some degree in initiatives that have inserted themselves in public schools, but evangelical Christianity accounts for the overwhelming majority of the programs. Although the evangelical programs often present themselves as nondenominational, they tend to represent a very conservative, even fundamentalist form of religion. Most of the activists I met believe that the Bible is the literal and inerrant word of God; that conversion to their form of faith is the only path to salvation; and that they are engaged in a daily struggle with Satan. They also believe that most people who call themselves Christian are not. Many of them are confident that United Methodists, liberal Congregationalists, US Episcopalians, the "wrong kind" of Presbyterians,[1] and Roman Catholics, for example, will not be among the saved.

The largest and most active programs at work in the public schools are associated with groups that should be called Christian Nationalists. These groups maintain that the United States was founded as a Christian nation, and that it is the right of Christians to take it back. They see their efforts in the schools as a part of a plan to bring the nation's children back to its founding religion and thereby lay the basis for Christian control of all the important parts of government and society. Many of the activists I met believe that the United States has a special role to play in preparing for the imminent end of the world. Of course, many social conservatives who are also Christians are not members of the Christian Right, and many supporters of the Christian Right are not Christian Nationalists; however, to a degree that many social conservatives fail to appreciate, it is the Christian Nationalists who are driving the agenda in the public schools.

In my research, I was surprised to see, over and over again, that one of the distinguishing features of the public school initiatives involving religion—and one of the reasons they have failed to attract the attention they should—is that they rely on misdirection and deceit. Programs that advertise themselves as Bible "study" from a historical or nondenominational perspective, for example, routinely turn out to be thinly disguised sectarian training. Programs presented as initiatives arising from students are instead conceived, coordinated, and funded by adults who may live in a different state. Programs that were described to school administrators and legal staff as entirely independent of the schools in which they operate turn around and seek to convey exactly the opposite message to the children who participate in them. Programs that reassure parents that their aim is to reinforce the religion of their families make it part of their mission to convert children to beliefs that differ from those of their parents. Programs that ostensibly limit their attention to students whose parents have explicitly permitted their participation seek to use those students to reach the children of parents who have not given their consent.

Although the programs aim at all age groups, a surprising number are directed at the very young—children in the first years of school. Among many of the modern missionary groups, it is now accepted wisdom that the most fruitful targets of conversion efforts are children between the ages of four and fourteen—a cohort that they refer to as "the 4/14 Window." Schools are especially attractive because small children are easily swayed by representatives of authority, such as teachers and school officials, and typically can't distinguish between schoolteachers and the people who teach them in school classrooms after hours.

I was surprised to discover that the damage caused by these initiatives did not always take the form one might expect. In the usual narratives about religion in the schools, the unstated premise is that the religious activity in question represents the will of a majority, and minorities within the community are harmed. But in many instances, the programs enter the schools from outside the community altogether, and are at odds with it from the beginning. And, while minorities frequently bear a special burden, the greatest harm often falls on the school and its populace in general. The insertion of programs with blatantly sectarian agendas into public schools causes intense conflict among formerly harmonious groups of parents, students, and school staff. It imposes a substantial and inappropriate burden on school administrators and teachers. Communities that once rallied around the school begin to withdraw their support. And representatives of all religious groups—including those that sought to insert themselves in the schools in the first place—feel unfairly treated. In short, these initiatives produce precisely the kind of undesirable outcomes that always result when individual sects within pluralistic societies attempt to commandeer common resources for their own purposes.

It would be nice to believe that this cost to the community and to public education is an unintended by-product of efforts by religious groups to express their views. With respect to the Christian Nationalist groups most closely and intensively involved in school programs, however, such a comforting assumption would be inaccurate. Here was perhaps the greatest surprise for me in my research, and the most important reason for writing this book. The activists with whom I met, by and large, see the weakening of support for public education as a desirable side effect or even a goal of their work. Indeed, the national groups most active in supporting religious initiatives in public schools see our system of public education as a bad thing. These are the same groups that sponsor efforts to undermine, defund, and perhaps ultimately destroy the system altogether. If they can't "break down the doors" to the public schools, as some of them describe their efforts, they will be happy just to break the schools.

It is often difficult for people who are not close to this movement to accept that its aims with respect to public education are so destructive. And yet if one simply listens to what the leaders of the movement say and take them at their word, that is clearly the case. In 1979, Jerry Falwell made the agenda transparent: "I hope to see the day when, as in the early days of our country, we don't have public schools," he said. "The churches will have taken them over again and Christians will be running them."[2] Robert Thoburn, a member of the

Council for National Policy—a "little-known group of the most powerful conservatives in the country" according to the *New Yorker*—
repeated the message a few years later: "I imagine every Christian
would agree that we need to remove the humanism from the public
schools. There is only one way to accomplish this: to abolish the public schools." He urged Christians to run for school boards wherever
possible, explaining that "Your goal must be to sink the ship."[3] The
founder of the influential and deeply conservative megachurch, Coral
Ridge Ministries (recently renamed Truth in Action Ministries),
D. James Kennedy, continued the drumbeat of hostilities against public schools, asserting that "the modern, public education system was
begun in an effort to deliver children from the Christian religion," and
alleging that "our public education system has been engaged in a vir-
tual act of war on America and has placed the very survival of this nation at risk."[4]

As my research progressed, I found myself asking how the present
level of involvement of religion in public schools is possible in the
United States, given our vaunted separation of church and state.
There are many complicated answers that stretch back through history and across contemporary society, politics, and culture. And then
there is one simple answer that covers much of the same ground: the
Supreme Court. We have been told for a long time, mostly by conservatives, that activist judges are necessarily liberals, and that these
activist liberal judges took God out of the schools. In fact, it was the
collective wisdom of the American people, not the arbitrary mandates of judges, that secularized US schools, mainly because we discovered over long and bitter experience that introducing sectarian
agendas into public schools is divisive and unsustainable. Conversely,
it has been activist judges of a conservative stripe who are in large
measure responsible for, in effect, legislating the mandatory inclusion
of religious programming in the schools. The Good News Club was a
comparatively small operation until 2001, when the Supreme Court
all but made it law that every school should have one. There were

few churches operating rent-free in New York City's public schools until the courts handed down a related set of decisions that all but required that every school building in the city should become a house of worship on Sunday.

Religious nationalism has now become part of American political theater, and we take notice of it mostly during election campaigns. When it shows up in our backyard, in our schools and local communities, we reach instinctively for our First Amendment, interpreting the whole matter in terms of whose rights are being respected and whose feelings are being hurt. The most important issue before us, however, is not just a question of the rights or feelings of individuals. The fact is that there is a movement in our midst that rejects the values of inclusivity and diversity, a movement that seeks to undermine the foundations of modern secular democracy. It has set its sights on destroying the system of public education—and it is succeeding. Unless we confront that fact directly, we may well keep our rights but lose the system of education that has long served as the silent pillar of our democracy.

1

THE GOOD NEWS CLUB
COMES TO TOWN

> Think not that I am come to send peace on earth: I came not to
> send peace, but a sword. For I am come to set a man at variance
> against his father, and the daughter against her mother.
>
> MATTHEW 10:34–35

THE BALLARD NEIGHBORHOOD evolved as the center of Seattle's ethnically Scandinavian seafaring community, its inhabitants originally lured to the area by salmon-fishing opportunities. From the sky, it is a straightforward grid of tree-lined streets with neat rows of wood-and-brick homes. It is populated with lawyers and graphic designers, government workers and engineers, and, above all, the kind of families that value welcoming backyards and good schools.

It's hard not to notice the abundance of churches. Local lore has it that the Scandinavian immigrants built so many saloons that the town elders, in a bid to allow salvation to keep pace with sin, mandated the construction of a church for every new bar. If you query Google for its churches, the map of Ballard lights up with forty-one bright red dots. In the Loyal Heights neighborhood alone—the neighborhood

9

where more than two hundred youngsters attend the Loyal Heights Elementary School—there are fifteen Christian houses of worship.

The arrival of the Good News Club in Loyal Heights is a tale of two of these churches. Both take a great interest in the religious instruction of the young people in their communities. One of them has followed the time-honored path of encouraging parents to bring their school-age children to a house of worship. The other, pushing through the door opened by the Supreme Court in its 2001 decision *Good News Club v. Milford Central School*, decided to bring the church to the school.

RICH LANG, THE pastor at Trinity United Methodist Church, is a solidly built man with wide-set hazel eyes and a full beard. He speaks in a reassuring baritone that still carries the flat vowels of his Midwestern origins. On this brisk fall day, he drapes his ecclesial white-and-purple robe over a fuzzy sweater and pleated khaki trousers before describing the circumstances that put him on his path to faith.

He was born in the deep end of life, with nothing to hold on to. His father was an alcoholic and his mother married five times. The divorces began when he was in kindergarten. He spent first grade in an orphanage. "My father couldn't handle kids," he explains, "and my mother's new husband didn't want us around." His high school years drifted by in a haze of mescaline, hash, Quaaludes—anything that took him out of his pain.

At nineteen, he underwent a drugs-to-Jesus conversion, and everything changed. "If you had a video camera that day, all you would have seen [was] a long-haired, skinny kid, weeping, and twenty minutes later he would get off his knees. There was a huge emotional purging, a tearful dump, all of it wrapped in prayer, asking Jesus to help me. At that moment I lost the will to get high. It was lifted from me. It was very powerful, and I knew I had to get to a church."

He started delving into his faith at the conservative Moody Bible Institute, in Chicago, and very soon he became, in his own words, a

"Christian fundamentalist." But his spiritual path took him to new and different places—to Trinity College in Hartford, Connecticut, and ultimately to a more moderate worldview, "theocentric and Christocentric, but not afraid of questions, not afraid of the world," he says. "It was a godsend. I never lost my faith, but it was there at Trinity that I gave up fundamentalism, that I realized it was a dead-end road." In 1983, he got married, and he is now the father of two sons.

Drawn to the teachings of the eighteenth-century Anglican spiritual leader John Wesley, an open-air preacher who advocated a relationship with God that is less dependent on clerical mediation, Lang eventually found his place at the helm of Trinity United Methodist. The brick edifice was built during the Depression. With its vaulted ceilings and three-story bell tower, it has an understated working-man's elegance. The church's message revolves significantly around the "Social Gospel" movement, which calls on adherents to address social problems including poverty and injustice, and Lang devotes much of his time to the local soup kitchen.

One day in the spring of 2009, Lang sat down with John Lederer, a member of the congregation whose two daughters receive religious instruction at Trinity. Curly haired, with a jovial face, Lederer is usually a pretty happy-go-lucky guy. He's a somewhat atypical congregant, as he is Jewish, but he finds a spiritual home at Trinity, where both he and his wife are involved in church life. They were also active in their local public school, the Loyal Heights Elementary School, where his wife served on the PTA and he did volunteer work when his job at the State Board of Education allowed. But on this day, Lederer seemed genuinely alarmed. In fact, as long as the pastor had known Lederer, he had never seen him so anxious.

In a scene that has played out in similar ways in so many places around the United States, Lederer had come to his pastor in pressing need of advice about an after-school program of Bible study at the public elementary school. Lederer was still grappling with the odd fact that a group with the innocuous name of the Good News Club had become the source of so much conflict for his children, his family, and their school. Lederer directed Lang's attention to a blog entry posted by Mark Wheeler, the pastor at the United Evangelical Free Church, located a short walk north of Trinity United. Rather than expressing dismay about the religious tensions emerging in the community or attempting to help resolve them, Wheeler's post seemed to revel in them. It was the discovery of this post that had unnerved Lederer and sent him to Lang this morning.

Lang perused the document and turned to Lederer calmly. "And this surprises you how?" he asked.

THE ELEGANT, CONTEMPORARY main structure of the United Evangelical Free Church was erected in 1957. Extensions were added in the 1960s, and an office annex dates from 2001. The modern-looking entryway has freshly painted walls and new carpeting.

The church's pastor, Mark Wheeler, is about the same age as the church building. A married father of three, he has a résumé strong on religious schooling—a degree from Biola University in La Mirada, California, in 1977; advanced training at the Dallas Theological Seminary; and a PhD from the Talbot School of Theology at Biola. He is a large man with wavy, thick hair, a full mustache, and intense focused eyes, and he has a tendency to sit back in his chair with arms crossed.

His church is just over a dozen blocks away from Rich Lang's church, but in terms of theology they are worlds apart. The United Evangelical Free Church, Wheeler makes clear, is "Bible believing." Only a certain kind of faith alone, they say, offers the keys to God's kingdom. There is a movement among contemporary conservative Christian churches to distinguish their core beliefs from the teachings of "do-good," "Social Gospel" churches of yesteryear—a form of the religion they often deride as "feminized"[1]—and United Evangelical is emphatically a part of this movement. Its newsletter boasts a tough-guy name: "Body Builder: Uniting and Strengthening the

Body of Christ." Its website sports images of muscles, barbells, and fitness equipment.

Citing Tullian Tchividjian, the grandson of Billy Graham and newly anointed leader of Fort Lauderdale's Coral Ridge Presbyterian Church, which has been one of the most active and politically influential evangelical churches in the United States, Wheeler explains that there are two kinds of Christians. On the one hand, there are "'Sink' Christians," who "view salvation as something to soak up. It fills the sink and they soak in the benefits (heaven, peace, Jesus, and so on)." On the other hand, there are "'Faucet' Christians." They "see salvation as something that comes to them in order to flow out through them to the rest of the world as a blessing to others, as a pipe carries water from its source to a parched land."

To judge from church photos, the Faucet Christians don't look very different from the Sink ones. Photos on United Evangelical's website reveal a largely gray-haired population, a majority of them women, indistinguishable from the crowd at Trinity United. Among the United Evangelical congregation, Margo Widmark would not appear at all remarkable. In her midfifties, heavy-set, with a ruddy complexion and small eyes that retreat into her face, she is regularly cited in church newsletters for her service.

Sometime in the spring of 2008—the year before John Lederer had his meeting with Rich Lang at Trinity United—Widmark and other members of Wheeler's congregation decided to set up a Good News Club at the local public elementary school.

Good News Clubs bill themselves as "Bible study" programs and are aimed principally at children from kindergarten through sixth grade. The Clubs typically meet after school, in classrooms, and require that children have parental permission to attend. They are sponsored by the Child Evangelism Fellowship (CEF), a worldwide organization founded in Warrenton, Missouri, more than seventy years ago. The declared mission of the CEF is to produce conversion experiences in very young children and thus equip them to "witness" for other children. "I was told that a child at five, if properly in-structed, can as truly believe as anyone," said Mr. J. Irvin Over-holtzer, the founder of the CEF, in 1937. "I saw that if there was any truth in this statement, there was a door of opportunity lying open before us."

For much of its history, the CEF had only a small presence in the nation's public schools; instead, it organized programs of religious instruction in private homes and churches. Education authorities by and large tended to exclude the group out of concern that its pres-ence would represent an undesirable and possibly unconstitutional mixing of church and school. The Supreme Court changed all of that dramatically in 2001. By 2010, as a direct consequence of the Milford ruling, there were 3,439 Good News Clubs, nearly all in public K–6 schools around the country.

To Wheeler, the Good News program must have seemed like an excellent opportunity for "outreach." It was Faucet Christianity in action.

Over at Trinity United, on the other hand, Rich Lang saw the situation differently, and perhaps as less aboveboard. "Churches are struggling for membership," says Lang laconically. "By supporting the CEF, he's probably hoping the kids will draw the parents. He's hoping he'll lure families away from their liberal churches or get nonchurchgoers to join his church. It's marketing, pure and simple. And these days we all have to do it. Of course, it's framed around the language of 'We have life and light and want to share life and light with people.'"

THE ANNOUNCEMENT OF the impending arrival of the Good News Club at Loyal Heights Elementary could hardly have passed with less notice. "I got a posting on Facebook that there was a religious club happening at our school," says Lederer. "My first thought was, 'That's interesting, some nice Bible club, they sing Kumbaya songs, it's no big deal.'"

Loyal Heights residents Maile and David initially agreed. Maile is Christian, David is Jewish. When Maile heard about the new club, she gave the matter little thought. As a rule, she believed that the more activities available to kids, the better off the school would be. At about the same time that she learned about the Club, Maile volunteered to teach a yoga class in the school. It would require a lot of commitment on her part, of course, but she felt the children would benefit from physical fitness activities.

Joseph Rockne, another dad, asked the PTA president about the Club when he ran into her in the hallways. "You just have to meet them," he recalls her saying. "They are harmless."

Among the families who are members of Wheeler's congregation or sympathetic to its religious perspective, the announcement of the Good News Club's approach seemed like good news indeed. Why not have the kids stay after school for some religious instruction?

When the Good News Club at last appeared in the school, however, heads turned with surprise. "They came in like a bunch of gangbusters," recalls one mother who prefers to remain anonymous. "They started putting a Statement of Faith in kids' mailboxes. They distributed flyers. They were doing everything they could to have as big a presence on campus as possible."

"The Club would put huge signs up on top of an easel during school hours announcing the club," adds Rockne. "They were three feet high, right by the two main entrances, with great big eagles on them."

In preparation for its after-school meetings, the Club also seemed to make a point of displaying a supply of candy and cookies to as many passing students as possible.

Margo Widmark, the Good News leader, soon became a constant presence on campus. She volunteered as an aide in a first-grade classroom, then in a kindergarten. She supervised children during lunchtime, stuffed PTA packets, and participated in school grounds clean-up events. She set up a table during the Loyal Heights "Welcome Back

Night," an event intended to help parents connect with new teachers. Every week, she posted large flyers announcing the CEF activities on the community bulletin board. Parents said she also developed a habit of leaving Bibles behind as she moved from one classroom to the next.

"She was a more visible presence at the school than any parent or grandparent," says Lederer. Another parent, who also wishes to remain unidentified, was dismayed to learn that his daughter was having contact with Widmark four days a week. "There was a lot of religious talk at the school," he adds. "Some of the Christian kids who were involved in the club started to put down other kids' faiths."

Disconcerted, Lederer, Rockne, and a number of other parents began to research the Club and its parent organization. Their findings dramatically increased their level of concern.

Because the Good News Club seeks to reach children who in many cases are not old enough to read, a centerpiece of its program is the "wordless book," a simple picture book intended to convey religious doctrine. The "Gold Page," with a picture of a church and a cross, accompanies a lesson about heaven. The "Dark Page," depicting the Garden of Eden, teaches children that they are born sinners. The "Green Page" details the methods children can use for personal growth, which include prayer, studying the Bible, and sharing their beliefs with other children. The CEF itself makes quite clear that the purpose of these exercises is not to educate, but to convert. Indeed, it forthrightly declares that its goal is "to evangelize boys and girls with the Gospel of the Lord Jesus Christ, disciple them in the Word of God, and establish them in a Bible-believing church for Christian living."

In the fine lawyering supplied by the CEF's well-funded defenders, the Good News Club is characterized as a form of "moral instruction" from a "religious viewpoint." It is that, too, but that is hardly the whole truth. The CEF teaches not just "morals," but also religious doctrines. In the CEF's own literature, public schools are "mission fields," and evangelizing in public schools is characterized as "harvest work." Children of other faiths are "unreached" and need to be "counseled for Salvation." The unreached include many who are, in the view of the CEF and its members, insufficiently Christian, by which they mean anyone who isn't "born again"—that is, most Roman Catholics, Unitarians, liberal Congregationalists, United Methodists, Mormons, mainline Episcopalians, and liberal and moderate members of the United Church of Christ and of the Presbyterian Church of the USA, among others too numerous to mention. Children who attend the clubs are emphatically told that "nonbelievers" are going to hell, to be "separated from God forever."

At Loyal Heights, some parents found it alarming that the school should have allowed such a prominent place to a group that teaches children to view people of different faiths and backgrounds as "other." "The gay and lesbian families with kids were especially worried," says one parent. "With the CEF operating in the school, people started to feel that they were not included. The administration had to respond, so they put a policy in place and issued a statement saying, 'This school welcomes all families, and if you don't feel welcome, call this number.' That happened as a direct result of the CEF."

Jeanne had particularly strong feelings on the issue, since her child, as a member of an ethnic minority, was already sensitive to issues of acceptance by his peers. Then Jeanne came across an article in a CEF-related publication titled "Rice Bowl Communication" that struck her as overtly racist. "How can we better understand and teach Asian-American children in our classes?" author Karin Fleegal wanted to know. The answer, apparently, lay in "relating message content to the Asian mind." "Confused and out of balance, many [Asian Americans] live with extraordinary tensions including dependency, crowded living conditions, lack of steady employment, language barriers, and little of normal social disciplines," Fleegal continued. "It is difficult for children of Hindu, Buddhist, or Taoist background to recognize lying as a sin for they do not have moral absolutes."[2]

Another CEF-produced pamphlet, *Reaching Children in Public Schools*, features a young African American child holding up a sign with the words from an old Baptist hymn: "What can wash away my sin? What can make me whole again? Nothing but the blood of Jesus." Readers familiar with the traditional tune will know that the next, unprinted lines are: "Oh! Precious is the flow / that makes me white as snow."

For Jeanne, as for a growing group of concerned parents at Loyal Heights, the religious message of the Good News Club, as well as its casual bigotry, seemed to run directly counter to the school's interest in fostering a harmonious, inclusive environment for all students and families.

For Rich Lang, the impending culture clash between the Good News Club and at least some of the parents of the Loyal Heights community was eminently foreseeable. "When people see or hear about a little Bible club starting after school, they assume it's kind of neutral, that there will be shared values there," he says. "They don't realize that the Child Evangelism Fellowship, which is in the fundamentalist strand of Christianity, is in a sense a purity cult. It is intentionally exclusive. There is not an openness to Muslims or Jews, not even to liberal Methodists or Catholics. All of those people and more are the harvest; they need to be converted."

ACCORDING TO THE most powerful minds of the United States judicial system, entities like the Good News Club can be allowed into public schools because they are clearly not part of the school system. Since their meetings take place after school and require parental permission for participants, the theory goes, no reasonable person would have the perception that the school in any way endorses their religious teaching.

On the ground at Loyal Heights, things looked very different. "Does a six-year-old child understand the difference between a school-sponsored group and an outside group when he sees adults going from the classroom to the GNC and back, which happened last year, or when he sees the GNC meeting in the lunchroom alongside all the school-sponsored after-school groups?" Joseph Rockne asks. "No. They don't see the difference."

The school principal, Wayne Floyd, cautiously echoes the same concern. "If you're talking about a seven-year-old, how do you tell a kid it's separate from the school, rather than one endorsed by the school?" he asks. "A seven-year-old is not equipped to ward off the advances of a more sophisticated organization. . . . It can be sticky. I can see this becoming a real complicated situation."

The problem of misperceptions, however, isn't limited to the six- and seven-year-olds. While the Good News Club was launching its program, as it happens, Maile got her yoga program going. But suddenly she ran into resistance. Some of the Good News Club families, she says, "seemed to freak out." They demanded that she not use Hindi names for any of the poses, which she hadn't planned on doing anyhow. And they told, her, "No 'Om.'" Maile did not have a problem with the requests in principle. "Yoga is just a method of physical fitness," she says, so she agreed. But the families watched her, monitoring her for signs of religious content in her classes, and she became offended. "I was putting a lot of time into teaching the class, and this just didn't make sense."

To be clear, Maile's yoga program, unlike the Good News Club, occurred during school hours. But such distinctions seemed irrelevant to her. "If they think religious content is so horrible and inappropriate for kids, how do they justify supporting religious fundamentalism in the school? It just seemed so hypocritical. And I wasn't teaching religion or philosophy, while that's what they are doing so blatantly."

Among the parents at Loyal Heights, Maile is far from alone in the perception that the CEF receives hands-off treatment simply because it is linked (at least nominally) with the majority religion. As Rockne observes, "If someone brought in an atheist group that goes after 'churched' kids, they'd go nuts."

When I visited the Good News Club at Loyal Heights in November 2009, the group was gathering in the spacious auditorium that doubles as the school's lunchroom. A number of other clubs happened to be meeting around tables in other areas of the same room—a science club, an art club, and so on. At the Good News table, Joyce and Bob Butcher, an older couple who are members of Wheeler's church, piled paper plates high with Double Stuf Oreos, vividly colored Fruit Gusher gummy candies, and boxes of Capri Sun Pacific Cooler juice blend drink. They were the only group laying out snacks of any kind. As children trickled in to the large room, they wandered slowly to their various destinations, rubbernecking the junk food as they paused to chat with one another. Some of the clubs meeting that day were school sponsored. Others, such as the Good News Club, were not. I had no way of distinguishing one set from the other. There can be little doubt that if any of the children present had been asked to distinguish between the groups sponsored by the school and those not sponsored by the school, they would have found the distinction unintelligible.

At Loyal Heights, there was ample evidence that the leaders of the Good News Club efforts were aware that they might be perceived as a school-sponsored group—and were pleased about it. Indeed, it is certain that their very purpose in being in the school was to be perceived as part of the school. As Lederer points out, there are eight churches within a two-block radius of Loyal Heights Elementary School. "Several times we suggested, 'May we help move you off school grounds?'" he recalls. "We even had a church next to the school that was offering them free space. But they didn't want to talk about it. It was clear that the public school is where they wanted to be."

The pattern of the CEF's behavior at Loyal Heights is representative of its practice throughout the country. In my child's elementary school in Santa Barbara, California, the discussion about using neighboring church space in Loyal Heights replayed itself exactly.

When the presence of the Club in the school became a cause for concern, parents secured free space for the group at a church immediately next door to the school. But the CEF refused to consider the move. When parents requested that the Club delay the start of its meetings in order to allow nonparticipants to clear the area, the CEF again refused.

As a rule, the Good News Club seeks to convey the impression to students that it is in some way a part of the school. For example, it aims to use after-school facilities as soon as possible after the bell rings, and club leaders regularly lay out balloons and treats well in advance in order to maximize their visibility with nonparticipating students. In Valencia, California, a parent of a kindergartner reported that the Good News Club actually started fifteen minutes prior to the end of her child's school day. The instructor, she said, would enter the classroom as kindergarten was winding down and perform a roll call, cementing the impression that the Club was a school activity and effectively using that implied authority to segregate the children by religious affiliation. In one Wisconsin school, cheerful flyers announcing Good News Club–sponsored "parties" were posted three feet from the floor, at children's eye level. "There was a tremendous feeling of peer pressure to attend, and parents get that," said a father at the school. At Santa Barbara's Foothill Elementary School, an administrator said, the Good News instructor was found approaching students and distributing leaflets just outside school grounds.

There is plenty of anecdotal evidence to suggest that young children do in fact form the strong impression that the Good News Club is just another school program. In Will County, Illinois, a Unitarian couple tells an interesting story about what happened when an eight-year-old Good News Club attendee told their second-grade daughter that "being Christian" was "the only way" to get to heaven. When their daughter voiced her disagreement, the other girl replied, "It is true! I learned it in school and they don't teach things in school that are not true."

At the Vieja Valley Elementary School in Hope Ranch, California, parents reported an incident that began on the playground, when Ashley, a sprightly six-year-old, approached her first-grade classmate Chloe, near the swing sets and delivered the bad news: "You can't go to heaven."

Ashley had already figured out that Chloe, the only Jewish girl in her class, did not believe in Jesus.

Chloe protested, but Ashley persisted. "If you don't believe in Jesus, you are going to hell."

Their teacher overheard the increasingly heated exchange. When class resumed, she asked everyone to pay attention. People from different religious backgrounds, she explained, have very different perspectives on certain kinds of issues and beliefs.

Chloe, feeling good that she had stood her ground, seemed content with the result. But Ashley was crushed.

"You mean they lied to me right here in school?" she began to cry. "Because that's what they taught me here! How can they teach me things that aren't true?"

IMPLICIT IN THE reasoning of the US Supreme Court majority in its Milford decision is the notion that the Good News Club is an activity aimed at serving the interests and concerns of those children whose parents authorize their participation. Yet it takes only a little experience with the CEF to understand that its primary intended target is not just the children whose parents sign them up, but also the children of parents who do not volunteer for their children to participate. More to the point, the children who sign up are the means to reach the ones who do not. At Loyal Heights, as in hundreds of similar situations across the nation, the concentrated effort by the CEF to use participating kids as instruments with which to reach nonparticipating kids rapidly became the most contentious aspect of its program and the source of greatest anxiety among a significant number of the school's families.

"They had their club meetings next door to my daughter's class-room," says Rockne. "There are accordion walls and you can hear that it's all about, 'If you recruit your friends you'll get candy and prizes.' They coach the kids to exert pressure on other kids."

One of the CEF leaders in Santa Barbara, Si Ishimaru, confirms the practice. "We are not allowed to approach the children who aren't in the club," he concedes. "But we can't stop the children from ap-proaching other children," he adds with a smirk and a shrug of feigned helplessness. Since the group's stated target is indeed converting "unchurched" children to its form of Christianity, it is hardly surpris-ing that Good News Clubs throughout the country employ systems of "points" and prizes to reward children who recruit their friends.

The children inevitably respond to the rewards plan by seeking to draw other children into the group, as they are told to do. "One girl who attended the club started saying to a Jewish boy in her class, 'Jesus is the best, Jesus is great, don't you want to be with Jesus?'" continues Rockne. "It's that whole thing, they tell you how bad you are."

For David and especially Maile, fresh from her irritation over the yoga class, the coordinated peer pressure on their son was particu-larly distressing. "The thing that concerned me the most [was] it was very clear that the kids at the club were proselytizing him," says David. "He'd come home and say, 'You're a bad person if you don't believe in Jesus.' It started happening mid-year, around when the Good News Club got going. As a Jew, I found this really upsetting—that he's getting this stuff in the public school, [where] we are man-dated by law to send him."

As he talks, Maile becomes noticeably agitated. "He said to me, 'Mommy, are we bad people because we don't believe in Jesus?' I think another little girl, who attends the Good News Club, was talking to him about it. That really bothered me."

In setting children against children, as Maile and David's experi-ence makes clear, the CEF is also setting children against their own parents. As Rockne said, "The part that gets to my core is they undermine parental authority. You go after my kid, you're going after me. And they do it through fear and intimidation."

"I grew up Christian, and I definitely believe in God," adds Jeanne. "My problem with the CEF is that they undermine parental authority. They are predators. This is not about a division between the believers and the nonbelievers. It's stay away from my kid!

"My son is a little bit different than most of the other kids in the school and is already very sensitized to difference," she continues, alluding to his ethnic identity. "I think it would destroy him if he was told that he was not the 'right' faith. Our family teaches our child about God and faith, and the other families are free to do that as we do, in our homes and churches. Why do they have to use the schools?"

From the CEF perspective, of course, setting children against their parents is part of the process, too, for the ultimate aim is to bring the parents into the fold. "They are all about getting into the public schools in order to recruit kids, who will then recruit their parents into a 'Bible-believing' church," says Lederer, echoing the thoughts of Rich Lang.

For Lang, the course of events is not surprising: "So what happens in schools is what you can predict. Little Sammy and Mary go to the Bible club, and the next day they are telling little Jill, who is Jewish, that she's going to hell."

THE FEELINGS AT Loyal Heights reached fever pitch when the CEF, through Margo Widmark, sought to donate $500 to sponsor the annual school fund-raiser.

"All hell broke loose," says Lederer.

"Can you imagine being at the auction with the CEF logo on the video screen, and a little card from them on your table?" asks Jeanne. "I am trying to convey the level of frustration and anger we experienced. And then to have to send your children to that school?!"

Margo Widmark, for her part, was clearly aware of parental concerns about her presence. Like many CEF instructors, however, she seemed to take a perverse delight in the stir she was causing. It seemed, in fact, that she was having the time of her life. She reported in the CEF newsletter that she had already saved one boy's soul. "'I am a very, very bad boy,'" she recounted him saying. After he accepted Jesus, she reported, he was no longer seen "pushing and shoving in the cafeteria line."

About forty concerned parents joined together to form a mailing list to share information, observations, and news about the Good News Club. They called it the Good News Watch at first, but then changed the name to Seattle Schools Free From Proselytizing (SSFFP). They decided to have one of their number sit in on Good News Club meetings whenever possible, to watch and observe. They soon began to take action to limit those activities of the Club that they considered inappropriate.

Joseph Rockne decided to take aim at the massive posters that the CEF was placing in the school during school hours. "I spent two weeks digging around school documents on school policy until I found the document that says you can't do that. So Margo got called in and was told to take the signs down." The Club agreed to wait until the end of the academic school day to put up its signs.

The flyers proved a more complicated issue. In order to avoid disputes about what may or may not be included in information packets that students bring home from school, Loyal Heights no longer sends home any flyers from groups other than the PTA.

The SSFFP parents had particularly strong concerns about Widmark's dual role as teacher's aide by day and CEF instructor after school. Just as young children cannot readily distinguish between school-sponsored groups and outside groups, they maintained, so too they fail to grasp the difference between a school employee, like a teacher, and an outside volunteer, like an aide. When parents of the first-grade class complained, Widmark was removed from the class—and was then placed in the classroom of kindergarten teacher Tricia Lepse, who happens to be a member of Mark Wheeler's Evangelical Free Church. When parents in that class objected in turn, Widmark was placed in a different kindergarten class. Soon, those parents objected as well.

Widmark was eventually removed as an aide altogether, but only because she made a mistake. In her article about the young boy whose improved behavior in the cafeteria line she took as proof of his salvation through her efforts, Widmark inadvertently described the child with enough detail that his identity could be readily discerned by members of the school community. Her article therefore counted as an invasion of the boy's privacy. The principal at that time, a woman named Cashel Toner, then gave her a "warning," justifying her decision with "Everyone is entitled to a warning." When parents pressed the issue, however, and pointed to the clear violation of school policy, Toner finally dismissed Widmark as a volunteer teacher's aide. Widmark nonetheless continued to involve herself in the life of the school via her role as a Good News Club instructor.

With tensions mounting, the principal and the PTA president organized a meeting for Widmark to present herself and discuss the Club's activities with interested members of the community. The meeting, however, only exacerbated the situation. "There was so much anger on both sides," recalls David.

"I saw the face of CEF, and it wasn't harmless," adds Rockne. "It was litigious." Instead of talking to the community on her own, Rockne recalls, "Margo brought a 'friend' with her." The friend, a lawyer named Jan Linville, carried a packet from the CEF's legal backer, the Liberty Counsel. "The message was crystal clear," says Rockne. "If you push us too far, there will be legal consequences."

The CEF soon resolved to exclude members of the SSFFP from sitting in on Club meetings. When parents who did not have children in the program appeared at meetings, Widmark asked them to leave. Not willing to push the matter further, the SSFFP obliged and stopped attending.

The most vexing issue for many of the SSFFP parents remained the CEF's proposed sponsorship of the school auction. About twenty parents wrote letters to the PTA protesting the idea. One woman, a lesbian parent of a fifth grader, wrote a letter suggesting a boycott of the event. "I called the PTA and said that if they sponsored the fundraiser, they could forget about us attending," reports another mother.

Jan Linville, Widmark's legal-minded friend, weighed in on the dispute. She claimed that the Loyal Heights PTA was required to accept funds from the CEF as they would from any other group.

Facing an insurrection among an appreciable group of parents, however, the PTA members decided to take their chances. They gave the CEF back its $500.

THE INCREASINGLY STRIDENT opposition to the Good News Club at Loyal Heights inevitably gave rise to an equal and opposite reaction from those parents at the school who did support the program and its objectives. Those families—some of whom were active members of Wheeler's United Evangelical Church and others who were not particularly religious themselves, but welcomed the opportunity to give their children some free religious instruction in such a convenient setting—found the hostility to the group astonishing and deeply dismaying. They began to feel that the opposition was "targeting Christians." Even the fact that the majority of the Club's opponents were themselves Christians could not dislodge from its supporters the feeling that they were being persecuted for their religious beliefs.

One, a mother whom I'll call Esme, seemed especially hurt about the protests. Esme took an active role in the school community, donating many hours a week to its various programs. Now, the fact that other parents were monitoring, or attempting to monitor, what happened at the Good News Clubs made her feel that her privacy, and her children's, was being violated. In telling her story, Esme broke down in tears several times. Her sense of persecution was so strong that she started to wonder whether Loyal Heights was an appropriate school for her children.

Once vibrant and harmonious, the Loyal Heights Elementary School community was now angrily divided. "When parents were picking up their kids, you could see that groups divided along faith lines had formed," says Jeanne. "Parents weren't intermingling anymore. Parents who supported the GNC were sticking together, and parents who opposed it stuck together."

The tension within the Loyal Heights community rose to the point at which, at least for some people, it all snapped.

In the spring of 2009, Lederer decided it was important to let the other parents in his child's first-grade class know what he had learned about the CEF. "I sent out what I thought was an innocuous e-mail saying, in case you're not aware, this group CEF is operating in our school. Then I attached an FAQ about the CEF and said, 'If you want to learn more about who they are and what they believe in, see attached.'"

Many of the classmates' parents, however, thought that the message was anything but innocuous. "How is this group different from any other group?" one demanded. "Why would a group like this get more scrutiny than any other? I'm glad you sent this message out so that I know I need to protect my kids from people like you," wrote another. Still other parents were furious to learn of the CEF's existence: "I didn't know you could do this in public schools!" wrote an outraged father. "I thought the Constitution prohibited it!"

Various correspondents hit "reply all," and others added "ccs" and "bccs." The result was a giant snowball of hate, rolling through the school community. Lederer tried to respond to the hostile e-mails one by one, hoping to calm things down, but to little avail.

With the anger came a good deal of mutual suspicion. The SSFFP mailing list was supposed to be a closed list, reaching about forty people. But some of its internal communications leaked out. Then people began to send anonymous messages. "I got some scary e-mails from people I didn't know," says Lederer. "I asked them to ID themselves and they didn't reply."

The cold fury coursing through the Loyal Heights network reached an ominous climax, in the eyes of many parents, in one particular e-mail.

"There was a guy who supported the Good News Club who frightened me," says one mother, her voice trailing off uncertainly. The e-mail in question reads, in part, as follows:

> *There is a rumor flying around ballard that your school is harassing and persecuting christians. I was VERY surprised to hear this, even more surprised that immediate action has not been taken to expel the offending bigots! . . . What is at the center of this hatred and clear discrimination? The hatred of Jesus Christ. . . . Have you ever thought what that date is based on? The birth of Christ!! Do you teach that? Have you ever wondered the source of the 7 day week? The bible! Do you teach that? Why not? My simple answer is that you hate the judeo-christian heritage that gives freedom to us all! All of our laws are based on Christian laws. The first capital of our country was named after a church (Philadelphia) in the book of revelation. What do you think the founding fathers were thinking there? God was to be the center of our Nation! Do you teach that? Christ and His church are the reason for the equality and acceptance we all have here in this country! Obama took his oath on "a bible"!! Now because of peoples hatred of Christ, christians must endure persecution and be stamped on because of your political correctness and fear of teaching the truth, which might offend some people!*

"In the letter there wasn't an actual threat of physical violence," Lederer says. "But there was a sense of outrage, and the bizarre idea that Christians are the victims here."

In my conversations at Loyal Heights, however, it was clear that, whatever the intentions behind this and similar messages, many parents were grappling with an emotion that they likely never imagined they would feel in connection with the local elementary school: fear.

"It was frightening," said one mother who declined to be identified. "I was scared for my safety."

"Please don't mention our names—that is very important, I don't want to get blowback from this, we've had to deal with enough hostility already," says another parent.

"I can't allow you to use my name," says a third mom, repeating the point for emphasis. "I'm scared of what he might do. There have been times that I've actually been afraid for my safety. When you get into these extreme forms of religion, it always brings out the crazies. You just don't want them fixating on you in any way. I've been trying to stay under the radar. I don't speak openly about this issue—I only talk about it with people one at a time, and only when I have been given the signal that they share my concerns."

"Please don't reveal our identities," a dad confides. "This might sound melodramatic, but there were times when we actually feared for our lives."

IN MARCH 2009, Lederer and his fellow parents at the SSFFP decided on a fresh approach. They agreed to seek the help of the pastor at United Evangelical, Mark Wheeler. They hoped that he might be able to defuse the tensions that had arisen between some members of the school community and some members of his church.

On a Saturday morning, Loyal Heights mothers Laura Blumhagen and Jennifer Carrell met with Wheeler at his church. "It went really well," Laura reported back in a cheerful e-mail to the SSFFP. "The conversation lasted for about half an hour. Pastor Wheeler was very friendly and seemed to understand our intentions."

A few days after the meeting, however, one of the parents of the SSFFP discovered that Mark Wheeler was keeping a blog. And in an entry posted the day after the meeting, Wheeler revealed a strikingly different take on the significance of that encounter. Citing

Matthew 10:35—in which Jesus says, "I have not come to bring peace, but a sword"—Wheeler wrote:

> *Rather than bringing peace on earth and making everyone happy, sometimes the gospel brings division. Because some believe the message and others do not, lines get drawn, sides are chosen, and weapons are reached for. . . . A Christian organization wanted to start an after school Bible class at one of the local schools. . . . Not surprisingly, some parents objected to having a "religious" group meeting at a public school. Rumors were started, complaints were filed, decisions were questioned, and bad feelings escalated. As I have watched the drama from afar, I realized I was watching Jesus' promise being lived out in real life. Sometimes the gospel divides because some choose not to believe.*

Lederer and his fellow parents were stunned. "We couldn't believe it," says Jeanne. "We thought it went well. We thought we had communicated well, that we were taking steps to really mend fences and understand one another better. And here he was, with his hostile reaction. It was really surprising and disappointing."

I visited Mark Wheeler in the fall of 2009 and asked for his view on the matter. He remembered the encounter with the SSFFP parents in detail. "I wrote on my blog that I had met with the mothers, these two women." He sighs. "It had something to do with the truth of what Jesus said, that when his message is communicated, it will sometimes cause conflict. And that this was being played out in our community in that there are people that are for that particular club and people that are against that particular club. It wasn't a comment against what was said at the meeting, just an illustration of here's what scripture says."

I asked Wheeler if he thought Jesus intended to divide people.

"I think based on what scripture says, his message does," he replied. "Our role is not to cause division to but to teach what Jesus taught. And as people accept that message or reject that message it will divide. . . . It has to do with the nature of teaching a particular belief. Whenever it's a belief about anything, you will unite some people around that belief and others that reject that belief, it will cause division. I don't know if I would say it's our role to do that, but it is the aftereffect."

"IT ASTONISHES ME that people don't get it, that ideas have consequences," Lang tells me one afternoon over a cup of tea in his church office. "And that putting these ideas in your public school is going to have consequences.

"When I was born again, faith was something inside of you, something you were supposed to reflect through your life," says Lang. "But in the 1980s, something happened. Fundamentalist Christianity jumped back into the public square with the intention to reshape the country as a Christian nation as defined by them. That revolution now is thirty years old. It's not gone away. People who think it's defeated are fooling themselves."

His frustration is palpable now, raising his pitch a half-tone higher. In Lang's view, the American public remains inexcusably ignorant about the new religion in its midst. The new fundamentalism, he insists, is not "historic Christianity." In fact, it's not uniquely Christian, nor is it uniquely American. "Fundamentalism is a global phenomenon, and it has come back on steroids since the 1970s and 1980s. Whether you're talking Buddhism, Hinduism, Judaism, Christianity, or Islam, all forms of fundamentalism are on the rise," he says.

"And they all want the kids," he adds, looking at me meaningfully. "Kids are so, so vulnerable at that age, just like little sponges. They don't talk back to adults, they are not in dialogue. So it's clear why the children are being targeted. It's no different than the Lord's Army in Africa. It's no different than the Nazis wanting to start with the Hitler Youth. That is where you'd want to start if you were trying to build a fascist movement."

He pauses to make sure I've heard him correctly. "That's the word, 'fascism,'" he repeats. "Nobody likes to use it in this country. But I believe that in this country, underneath the appearances, that is exactly the great temptation of our time. The CEF is part of a movement, and you have to call it what it is—'Christian Fascism.'"

In Lang's mind, the defining features of this new movement are the same ones that distinguish it from historical Christianity. Modern fundamentalism, like fascism in earlier times, he says, involves a strong feeling of persecution, typically at the hands of godless liberals or a religious "other"; the belief that one belongs to a pure race or national group that is responsible for past greatness, suffers unjust oppression in the present, and is the rightful ruler of the world; the impulse to submit unquestioningly to absolute authority; and the relentless drive for power and control. It is, he says, a kind of supremacist movement, with religion rather than race at its core.

"It's very scary and it's totally under the radar," says Lang. "People have no idea it's going on. I think there is this notion that groups like the CEF are kind of neutral, that it's not important, that if we can get our kids to behave right, if they are nice and courteous, what is the big deal? But those who view Good News Clubs as benign are deluding themselves."

Lang pauses to collect himself while he refreshes his cup of tea. He has dedicated his life to spreading the word of Jesus, he reminds me. For him, that word is love.

"Ask yourself," he tells me as I get ready to leave, "What does it mean that the conservative church that's growing in America is an end-times church? What does it mean that we are raising a generation of children to believe that they are the last generation? What is going to happen if we keep on telling them, 'Don't care about the environment, and bring on the war, because we're going to be lifted out of here, and you can forget about loving your neighbors, because they're just going to get blown away'?"

MAILE AND DAVID pulled their son out of the school at the end of the year. "There were additional reasons why we felt he would thrive in a different school environment," Maile says cautiously. "But the fear and the hostility that were generated by the Child Evangelism Fellowship were major motivations for us."

On the other side of the cultural divide, the battle also claimed a casualty. Esme pulled her children out of school, too. On a website she wrote that she had left the school because she "found the persecution and intolerance of the presence of the club too overwhelming."

Esme's departure made matters worse. "When she left, her friends were upset, and there were a lot of very hard feelings," says Jeanne.

"I can say that the presence of the CEF in our school ripped it apart," says another Loyal Heights parent. In fact, the damage to the fabric of trust and respect upon which the community had earlier prided itself was substantial enough that it could be measured in dollars not donated and hours not volunteered. In the aftermath of the conflict, a number of families have decided not to donate money to the PTA.

"We send our money to Americans United for the Separation of Church and State," reports Rockne.

"I don't want to be as involved with the community anymore," Jeanne says. "With those people from the Child Evangelism Fellowship hanging around, I want to take a step back. Before, I used to volunteer for the science fair, to work in the classrooms, et cetera. I don't volunteer anymore."

In any assessment of the contribution of the Good News Club to Loyal Heights Elementary School, its impact must surely enter on the negative side of the ledger. The Club compromised the ability of the school in its most important function: teaching academic subjects to children. The principal, administrators, and teachers devoted an unmeasured but manifestly inordinate amount of time to the conflict— time that was necessarily taken away from other school business. "The presence of the CEF interferes with the mission of the school," says one of the parents who insisted on anonymity. "It interferes with instruction, and it interferes with the culture of the school."

Principal Wayne Floyd shoots me a look of frustration as I press him on the matter. "This is not an issue we should be spending a lot of time on," he says with more than a hint of exasperation. "We have enough things to focus on in terms of instruction and management."

In the winter of 2010, as I talk with the survivors of the episode, the overwhelming feeling is one of battle fatigue. "Since our kids started school it's by far the most intense issue that's come up for me," says Jeanne. "It gets to the core of people, and is definitely a polarizing thing. It takes an emotional toll. This issue consumed me last year. I spent so much time and emotional energy, and I'm burned out. There are people at school who won't say hello to me in the halls anymore."

"Before, we were all Loyal Heights parents together," sighs Rockne. "Now we're divided into groups and labels: you're a Christian; you're the wrong kind of Christian; you're a Jew; you're an atheist."

John Lederer is weary and discouraged. "I see that other parents in the group lost energy around the issue. I've seen more apathy or acceptance among the parents. I don't see this group going away, and I don't see them laying low for very long. I worry more about some sort of repercussion for my kid, rather than for myself. Last year my daughter didn't get invited to a birthday party for a good friend of hers, and her parents are supportive of the Good News Club. I have no way of knowing whether that was a factor or not, but we were really very surprised she didn't get invited."

I visited Loyal Heights in the fall of 2009, a year after the Good News Club's initial arrival in the school community. As I wandered into the lunchroom that is shared by the Good News Club and other school groups that meet after school, the tension was silent but palpable. At the Good News Club table, a mother arrived with an additional box of chocolate chip cookies. The treats seemed hardly necessary, given the extraordinary volume of candy already on the table, but the show of support was clearly welcome. Widmark entered the room briefly, then left to attend to some Club-related business. Joyce, a friendly woman with gray hair, ruddy cheeks, and an excited, ready smile who was also representing the Club, distributed the cookies with delight, adding them to the existing piles of Oreos and candy on the kids' paper plates. Her husband, Bob, tall and un-smiling, waved at some of the parents passing by. A Loyal Heights dad came over and said, with a nod of satisfaction, "I see you guys are here."

"Yep," said Bob with a significant look.

IF YOU THROW a baseball about two hundred feet from the play-ground of the Loyal Heights Elementary School, you might just hit a supersize, twenty-four-hour neon sign with gothic vertical lettering in lipstick pink that transmits the message "Jesus Saves." The sign belongs to the Philadelphia Church of Seattle.

The Philadelphia Church, an independent member of an associa-tion of Pentecostal Evangelical churches, has long prided itself on its missionary work. One of its missionary couples, for example, works on audio programs that promise to "broadcast the Gospel to every Muslim man, woman, and child on the planet in their language." The church has recently discovered a new means to reach the youth closer to home. Walk ten blocks to the east of the church and you will come across Whittier Elementary School. The Philadelphia Church is pro-moting a Good News Club there.

2

ALL PART OF THE PLAN

LOYAL HEIGHTS ELEMENTARY School is just one of thousands of public schools across the nation to host a Good News Club, and the Good News Club is just one of over a dozen initiatives of the Child Evangelism Fellowship. Headquartered in Warrenton, Missouri, the CEF is a genuinely national—indeed global—organization, boasting an astonishingly ambitious plan for carrying out its mission to "disciple" children as young as five years of age. Aside from its highly successful Good News Clubs, the CEF also offers ministries targeted at the children of military personnel, "5-Day Clubs" in public parks, Camp Good News summer programs, a ministry for the children of prisoners, and the CEF Mailbox Club, an evangelizing correspondence program. The Child Evangelism Fellowship also runs children's ministries in more than 150 countries around the globe and operates training centers for adults who wish to staff them.

Watching Margo Widmark, the Good News Club instructor in Loyal Heights, in action, it was clear that she wasn't making it up as she was going along. She was following a carefully scripted plan, and at key moments she was able to call in reinforcements. At one end of the movement are the foot soldiers on the ground who run individual clubs and raise local money for them; at the other end are the national leaders. These national leaders, it was clear to me, exercise a tremendous amount of power in shaping the curriculum, establishing the tactics, and providing support at crucial junctures.

Who were these leaders, and what were their ambitions and aims? To find out, I attended the CEF's triennial National Convention, which was held in 2010 at the Shocco Springs Baptist Convention Center in Talladega, Alabama. After registering with the convention center directly, I was soon on the ground, among the CEF elite.

THE BUMPER STICKERS plastering the SUVs in the parking lot are defiant: "Evolution is a Big, Fat, Lie," "Abortion Stops a Beating Heart," "Marriage = 1 Man + 1 Woman," "Obama is not Jesus: Jesus Could Build a Cabinet." I wonder if I stand much chance of blending in with this crowd. I spent some time the previous evening considering just what one should wear to a National Convention of the Child Evangelism Fellowship. I've chosen a knee-length skirt and pale pink sweater, and I have my hair pulled back in a prim braid.

It's late May in Alabama, and the air smells of white cedar trees and the spicy bloom of wild geraniums. The walkways are lined with forsythia, columbine, and Virginia pine. Neat cinder-block buildings dot the hills of the 600-acre wooded campus. Along the hiking trails that snake throughout the property are rest stops outfitted with benches for contemplation and ten-foot-tall crosses. A tranquil pond is stocked with floats and rowboats. I find my way to the large, multi-use building that serves as one of the convention center's main gathering spots, as does the large, cathedral-like chapel.

This year, the convention has attracted about 450 attendees. Everybody appears to be affiliated with the CEF in some official capacity. Most are higher-ups on the totem pole: senior staff of the Warrenton headquarters and regional leaders from all over the country. Other attendees head up the CEF's youth, military, and prison ministries, write CEF textbooks, act as area coordinators, and serve other important roles in the organization's functioning.

Every morning of the convention starts with a 7 a.m. prayer session for CEF workers in a room designated as one of the convention center's smaller chapels. This morning, about fifty attendees take their seats, ready for prayer. From my spot toward the back of the room, I can smell coffee and fried breakfast foods being prepared elsewhere in the convention building.

The first thing that strikes me about the crowd is the large number of men in attendance. Most conventions organized around education and children—gatherings of curriculum experts, school volunteers, even Sunday school teachers or other religious education employees—are heavily dominated by women. Here at the national convention of CEF, however, the men equal or outnumber the women.

"How's it going at that school you were telling me about? The one where the principal was . . . you know . . . uncooperative?" a gray-haired gentleman in a plaid button-down shirt asks a younger friend in a white vest. "We slaughtered 'em!" the younger man replies. They both nod, satisfied. Throughout the convention, a phrase that I keep hearing is "kicking in the doors"—as in "We're going to kick in the doors of every public school in the country!" The men are uniformly dressed, as though from a dated edition of *The Preppy Handbook*, in khakis, plaid shirts, and crew-neck sweaters, and most are in middle or late middle age, though there is a sprinkling of younger men. Some of the men are accompanied by wives; others appear to be single.

I notice with alarm that my efforts to blend in are an abysmal failure. My subdued pastel getup is no match for the boisterous prints and separates that dominate the group. Even more atypical, of course, are my Semitic features. Naturally, I would have answered a pointed question about my religion truthfully—I am Jewish—but I do not want to be asked; I do not want my interactions to devolve into a forum on my ethnicity, which would not be productive for my research. I am resolved to simply say as little as possible and allow people to make their own assumptions.

On my way in, a participant suspiciously asks me what church I belong to, and I answer that our family is affiliated with an Episcopalian church. (In fact, at the time our son was attending an Episcopalian preschool.) "Is that a Bible church?" she sniffs disparagingly. Strangely, I have spotted more than one Star of David worn around the necks of fair, Germanic types—which I take to be either an appropriation of the notion of "chosen people" (several Baptists have told me that they consider themselves to be "ingrafted" as the "new chosen") or an expression of Christian Zionism in which the State of Israel is the linchpin for ushering in the end-time.

Near the chapel entrance I bump into Joan, who flew into Birmingham on the same plane I did. Joan is based in Los Angeles. Pale blond hair falls in soft waves to her shoulders; she wears a black T-shirt with silver sequins around the collar and white clam-diggers. In her early sixties, she seems friendly and curious.

Joan wasn't saved until her forties. By then she was divorced, with two young boys. "My life was a mess," she says, offering few details. They don't matter anymore because faith has provided her with a brand-new direction, a clean and certain future. But it hasn't completely extinguished her suffering.

Joan believes firmly that we are living in the last days on earth before the Second Coming. "In these End Times, you never know what's going to happen," she says, commenting on a dramatic volcanic eruption in Iceland that has clouded parts of Europe. For Linda, signs of the End Times are everywhere: earthquakes in Chile and Indonesia, an oil spill in the Gulf of Mexico, a failed bombing attempt in Times Square.

"Isn't it just awful how much the terrorists have changed our lifestyle?" she says.

Before joining CEF, she had never taught children before. Now she instructs a class of up to forty kids every week. She was nervous about teaching at first. But the behind-the-scenes support for her and others like her, courtesy of the CEF, is so substantial and so expertly coordinated and delivered that it gave her the confidence she needed. Indeed, it leaves almost no room for novice teachers such as Joan to fail.

Joan and I are joined by David, a wide-framed, bearded man, probably in his forties, who has been working for CEF for twenty-three years and currently runs CEF Military Ministries. The night before, he met us at the airport and took us by minivan to the convention center.

He and Joan trade stories about the CEF classes they teach. Joan acknowledges how all-consuming work with CEF can be. Teaching a Good News Club, she says, requires as much personal commitment as a full-time job. "I'm in awe of how much effort they put into it, and what they do to prepare us," she says, then offers enviously: "I know one lady who recruited a bunch of homeschooled kids to teach her clubs in the public schools. Now she barely teaches at all, just spends her time helping to train them!"

"It's important to get young people involved," David assures her, "[like] homeschooled kids who are willing to step up and volunteer." He tells us that there are up to 120 kids in some of his classes. "But some doors are harder to open than others," he says darkly, "so we partner with Cadence International [a large, evangelical Christian military ministry] and say, 'You pry open those doors and we will do the work in the harvest fields.'"

"That's great," says Joan. "This one superintendent in L.A., she was telling the teachers she was going to run us out of the school."

David responds with a relaxed laugh. He knows he is on the winning side of this war.

I SIT DOWN in the chapel pews next to Karlie, a CEF worker from Texas. In a purple shirt and midi-length skirt, she appears to be in her late twenties. She has long honey-colored hair and eyebrows so pale they are practically invisible.

"My cat reads the Bible!" she quips. "On my Facebook page I have a picture of my cat reading the Bible. My cats are saved."

For Karlie, however, the salvation of others is no joking matter. It weighs on her so heavily that she brings it up constantly, no matter the circumstance. "When I meet a stranger I don't say good-bye to them without learning whether they are saved or not," she confides.

"I share the gospel wherever, whenever. On the airplane coming here, I was praying for a half hour on the flight. Luckily, the two guys I was sitting with, they were both believers." She nods approvingly: two more souls to check off her list.

Karlie was born in Germany; her father was in the military. When her parents returned to the United States, they divorced. I gather that her upbringing was complicated and imperfect, and that her faith gave her a much craved road map to righteousness and order. Converting little children to belief in that same order confirms her belief in the path she has chosen for herself.

"We are in a spiritual battle," she says in a conspiratorial tone. "Satan disguises himself. When I meet someone I can always tell if there is something off about them. You always have to be on guard for Satan, because that's how he works. He is always trying to trick us."

She shrugs, setting her mouth in a grim line. "But that's just how it has to be," she says. "We're engaged in a war."

STANDING AT THE front of the room in a navy sweater, the pastor takes charge of the gathering. He calls for prayers and urges us to make our prayers specific. Karlie is one of the first to speak.

"Oh Lord I just love you so much," she says beseechingly, and then continues in this rhapsodic vein for quite some time. "For you who so loved the world that you gave your only begotten son, oh Lord, without you our lives have no purpose. Oh Lord, please help us to help change the hearts of others so that they can see the truth, oh God, so that they can see that you are the one true God and feel your power, if it pleases you. For you are an awesome God. We praise you! Let our prayers be a pleasant aroma unto you."

Other workers take their turn, asking God to "Raise up a State Director in Tennessee"; "Help our CEF director who is battling cancer"; "Help the coordinator funnel the boys and girls to Good News Clubs in our state."

"Please help us to reach the boys and girls who need to hear the gospel," murmurs a woman in a prairie-style dress that reaches to her ankles. I have noticed a few similarly dressed women in the group; I take them to be members of the Independent Fundamental Baptist movement rather than a style subculture.

"Too many boys and girls think they are OK without Jesus," says a man of around forty who is kneeling against a chair at the back of the room, facing the wall with the forlorn air of a little boy accepting his punishment for having broken the rules. "They think that because they are living in a Christian nation, they are Christian. Lord, they are lost. Help them to see the truth."

A bespectacled woman in an orange T-shirt awaits her turn. "Pray for our CEF worker who has been accused of inappropriate behavior with the children," she finally says in an agitated voice. "If these accusations are allowed to continue, Lord, it could devastate the man, and his family, and the ministry. We can all see that these accusations are nothing more than fabrications. Lord, we pray that the truth shall be revealed."

And with that, the prayer service is over, and it's time for breakfast.

THE TRIENNIAL CEF conference has been an occasion to celebrate the stunning successes of the group. As I sit through a day of speeches and presentations, one number keeps coming up: 728 percent. That's the percentage growth of Good News Clubs in public schools in the past nine years.

After our prayer session and breakfast, we gather in the main chapel for our first full day of the CEF convention. The emcee for the event, Nathan, gambols excitedly on the dais of the large church, where the whole group has convened, riling the audience with cutesy quips and gossipy asides.

Nathan introduces Julie Spiegel, a thirty-year CEF veteran. With her short black hair and neutral attire she has a stolid, no-nonsense appearance. She begins by showering us with statistics of success. In 2001, there were 16,805 children in Good News Clubs around the country. In 2009, there were 139,221 children. "That's 728 percent!" she says.

Seventy-four percent of kids who attend a Good News Club do so in a public school, she tells us, and the average enrollment for each class is forty children. After-school Good News Clubs have a higher attendance than the Child Evangelism Fellowship's "5-Day Clubs," religious clubs for kids that are often held in private homes or public parks. The approximately 3,500 public schools in which the CEF operates represent about 6 percent of all public primary and middle schools in the country. If current growth trends continue, the CEF is just a decade short of achieving its declared goal—to "force open the doors of all 65,000 public schools in America." (In 2010, according to the US Department of Education, the total number of public schools in the country was approximately 98,000, but many of those are high schools, which generally do not have Good News Clubs.)

"The best mission field for children is in the public schools!" another speaker, Joyce, exults. In her Texas district there are now 106 Good News Clubs in public schools. Five thousand kids are enrolled, she tells us, "and last year we had 816 professions of faith." "Take the clubs to where the children are—the public schools," she urges the audience. "It's legal, it's possible, and it's very productive."

"I led one little girl to the Lord, but I didn't really know if she got it," Spiegel tells us. "On the last day of the club, she came in all dressed up in a red velvet dress. I said to her, 'I love your dress.'" Spiegel pauses to gather up her tears. "She said to me, 'It's red like the blood of Jesus, who took away my sin.'" The audience breaks out in approving murmurs.

Then Julie delivers the statistical bottom line: in 2009, Good News Clubs yielded 24,506 professions of faith, an average of seven kids per club. The salvation business, it would seem, is posting good numbers.

FOR CEF LEADERS like Julie, the conversion of schoolchildren is a matter to be managed on an industrial scale. It's not about one red velvet dress; it's about producing those dresses in volume and at low cost. As I listen to her and her fellow CEF leaders, I can't help but feel that I'm at a conference for a multinational corporation determined to use every managerial tool available to expand its conversion operations and maximize efficiency.

Consider this internal summary of one such marketing event:

CEF Across America: Little Rock

Phase one of Little Rock '09 is complete, and the Lord certainly answered our prayers that "He would do exceeding abundantly beyond anything we asked or thought!" It's difficult to know where to begin to recount the blessings of the project, but in every aspect God was good!

- *The Lord sent 109 CEF workers from 26 states to serve 30 partnering churches. That's an increase of 13 workers over Chicagoland '08. We praise the Lord for sending just the right number for the partnering churches He gave us.*
- *1,874 children heard the Gospel during just one week of ministry.*
- *252 were counseled for salvation*
- *60 received assurance of salvation*
- *Over 1,000 people attended the rallies on Friday night, and now the churches are continuing to build relationships with those families and children.*
- *Over 400 volunteers from partnering churches helped with outreach!*
- *567 children enrolled in the CEF Mailbox Club™*

The Lord of the CEF would appear to be one who moonlights as a management consultant. Whether or not He has a Plan for us, the CEF certainly does. It's called *THE PLAN* and it comes down to us in a three-ring binder with more than four hundred pages of carefully tabbed material and an accompanying CD-ROM. *THE PLAN* is a how-to manual for those who intend to start up Good News Clubs in their area.

Much of *THE PLAN* consists of material that addresses the fundamental challenge of marketing to children. "Companies spend billions of dollars to get us to remember what they want us to remember," explains one presenter, shouting out a few advertising jingles to prove his point. "How do we help our kids to remember the word of God?"

Presenting the CEF's latest CD, called *Call Out*, he plays a few of the peppy tunes. The call-and-response format is presented as an effective means of communicating the Good News Club's gospel—belief alone saves, good works don't—to young children, who are told that sin is anything they think, say, and do that doesn't please God:

> *And God cannot let sin come in and be with Him*
> *But he saved us*
> *not because of righteous things we have done*
> *but because of His mercy He washed away our sin!*

"Our new music will be available via iTunes!" he announces. "This will be a huge benefit. You can purchase one song at a time. There will also be new visualized songs available on the web store."

Every year, I gather, the CEF rolls out a new collection of visual materials, incorporating updated graphics and ideas, adapting to the times and trends. From a video presentation, I see that this year's updated materials contained some sophisticated artwork, detailed and visually arresting.

The CEF also relies on a number of partnerships to supply certain key services and products. One group, for example, produces literature for kids' ministries. Another produces videos. Yet another offers high-quality web development services. Their most important partnership, of course, is with Liberty Counsel, which provides legal documents and services for free and ensures that no parent group, uncooperative principal, or set of school- or district-wide rules prohibiting discriminatory practices by outside groups is able to stand in the way of a

Good News Club being established in their community. A good portion of *THE PLAN*'s section on "Securing Permission" to enter the school is devoted to legal matters, with copy-and-send legal documents from Liberty Counsel founder and president Mathew Staver, to be deployed in a variety of troublesome situations.

As I FLIP through the hundreds of pages of *THE PLAN* and its supporting materials, it becomes clear to me just what kind of corporation the CEF is most like: it's a nonprofit, religious version of a multilevel marketing corporation. The CEF provides its affiliated Good News Clubs with tool kits, services, and ideas, or what marketers might call "product." The local Clubs in turn provide the manpower and the money.

As with every other national marketing organization, it takes money to make the CEF go round. At a presentation titled "The Root of All Evil" I catch a glimpse of the financial dynamics of the CEF. In what may be an indication of the importance that the group attaches to the financial end of its operations, the two presenters occupy very influential positions in the organization. Buzz, a tall, avuncular man with gray hair and glasses, is the longtime personal assistant to the president of the CEF, Reese Kauffman. Nerus, an attractive woman with almond-shaped eyes expertly highlighted with green shadow, is Kauffman's sister.

The key to CEF economics, I learn, is that, as in any multilevel marketing corporation, the money rises up the organization instead of flowing down. That is, the organization does not pay its foot soldiers any kind of compensation for distributing its product; rather, the foot soldiers pay the company for the right to represent their product. Each worker who leads a Good News Club is required to "raise support," or give a financial donation of approximately $20,000 a year.

Workers typically raise the money from their church or from a coalition of several churches. Those churches view CEF as being in tune with their evangelical mission, part of the "Great Commission" to spread their form of faith. Perhaps just as important, they also see it as a way of attracting local families to their congregations. Supporting the CEF is a means of evangelical outreach and a clever form of advertising. Sometimes the churches themselves make the decision to partner with the CEF, soliciting congregants who might be willing to lead the clubs.

Ten percent of the money from each worker's "support" goes to the state office, paying for salaries, administrative costs, and other expenses. Another portion, typically 10 percent, flows from the state office up the chain of command to the national office. The rest pays for materials, supplies, snacks for the kids, balloons, and other expenses. The CEF also raises money through its multiple training programs, which create the corps of CEF workers. The main campus of the Children's Ministry Institute is at the Missouri headquarters, but training is also available online, in local ministry areas in the US, and at each of the CEF's nineteen training institutes around the world. Classes are also available for credit at numerous religious schools throughout the country. According to Reese Kauffman, the CEF president, more than a quarter million adults have been trained through CEF programs.

Buzz and Nerus devote much of their presentation to offering tips in the art of fund-raising. I get the impression that they could hold their own against the top experts in the nonprofit subspecialty of raising capital. Their advice: Don't start off a relationship with a potential donor with an "ask." Make a personal connection first, and thank the person for his or her friendship and faithfulness in the ministry. Next, send something in the mail, a note or a small gift. Take the potential donor out for coffee, as a friend. On the fourth approach, ask the person to pray for you. And only on the fifth time you make contact, ask for the donation.

Nerus and Buzz instruct us to write down a list of possible donors for our CEF ministries. "Consider people in your office, people at your church, friends and family," Nerus says. "Try to focus on the top hundred. Then narrow it down to the top twenty-five, and contact each one at least four or five times this coming year."

"If a donor has an urgent need, such as an illness or family members who are not saved," Nerus adds, "volunteer to organize prayer teams for them. Fund-raising is a joyful ministry!"

ASIDE FROM ITS fund-raising, the CEF enjoys the economic benefit of large supplies of volunteer labor. "I want to share with you how we are able to do this work for free!" says a presenter named John Luck, project manager for an initiative called Good News Across America. With these words Luck introduces us to a twenty-six-year-old CEF worker named Johnny Moore. More in turn praises the dozens of young volunteer workers at the CEF convention, extolling their dedication and tireless energy. Such young people, he opines, are the key to the future of the CEF ministries, heading up projects such as the Millennial Generation project at Liberty University. Tim Hickman, a district director, enthuses about the "young people who go out, like an army, spreading the Gospel to every village, every town, every city in America."

I have spotted groups of these young people in the cafeteria a few times since my arrival. This year, the CEF convention attracted more than eighty members in their teens and twenties. With seminars just for them on the third floor of the convention center, they seem to be having their own separate confab, joining the older folks for some of the prayer and plenary sessions but otherwise enjoying unique workshops and activities. A chatty, ponytailed brunette who appears to be in her mid-teens has been assisting at one of the CEF's 5-day Clubs through a group called Christian Youth in Action. Soon, she tells me, she will be ready for the big time: a Good News Club at a public elementary school. "A lot of my friends are doing missionary work in other countries," she says. "But you don't have to go overseas to find unreached people groups. You can, you know, do the harvest work in public schools right here." She, I learn, is homeschooled—and as far as I can tell, so are most of her buddies at the convention.

Through Christian Youth in Action, teenagers get involved in various CEF programs. Some participate in summer missions, and others assist during the year at Good News Clubs. Each year, a one-week convention helps to motivate and coordinate teens from around the country, organizing them into groups. The name given to such groups illustrates their confrontational stance: Student Thunder.

As the CEF has grown, so has its leadership and staff, whose members occupy multiple tiers in its organization. Each collection of several Clubs reports to an area coordinator. The area coordinators in turn answer to regional directors. At this convention, the CEF is introducing another layer of leaders in the organization, "administration coordinators," also known as "great shepherds."

Like any other successful multinational, the CEF focuses relentlessly on future growth, going for the numbers. It identifies attractive market opportunities and then mobilizes the organization for action. "Looking for growth opportunities in our ministry, we focus on a target city where there is significant spiritual need," explains Luck. "We pick places with regional population centers, where we can reach two thousand children a week, and where there is a significant number of churches to partner with."

Clearly, they are not afraid of controversy. Their target city for 2011 is Salt Lake City, the historically Mormon stronghold, and in 2012 they will focus on Washington, D.C. "We are taking Good News Clubs to Pennsylvania Avenue!" he proclaims, and the crowd roars in response. The CEF clearly believes in what former GE CEO and management guru Jack Welch calls "stretch" targets—difficult goals that effect profound changes.

The target city for the fall of 2010 hits very close to home for me. "Boston," Luck warns, "is a hard place for evangelical churches and Christians!" As the crowd turns somber, my mind drifts over the cultural topography of my birthplace—the historic churches, the patriotic monuments, the long-standing tolerance of lesbian and gay relationships, or "Boston marriages," the lowest divorce rate in the nation.

"Boston is a very dark place," Luck continues. "But we've gotten twenty-nine of thirty prayed-for church partnerships already. Boston Baptist College will be our base of operations. I'm going there and have meetings set up with seven more pastors, and we'll have our final partnerships in place very soon!"

As the audience claps, Luck exults, "People, pray that God will show up in Boston!" He asks the group to volunteer for the Boston effort by signing up for the two weeks in July when Good News Club missionaries will descend on partnering churches and teach them how to lead Good News Clubs. The goal, of course, is to debut dozens of Good News Clubs in Boston-area public schools in the fall: "We have 125 people signed up already, and there's only room for 40 or 50 more!"

The birthplace of the American Revolution is just one in a long list of targets for the CEF. In fact, the group is looking well beyond the borders of the United States. The Child Evangelism Fellowship claims to be active in 170 nations around the world. A new program called CEF of Nations, or CEFON, has been launched to expand the roster of countries and deepen ties with existing nations. The top targets at present are Anguilla, Samoa, Cyprus, Lebanon, Gabon, and Lesotho. The CEF's goal is to have a presence in "all 208 nations of the world by our 80th anniversary, in 2017."[1]

As the day of presentations and seminars winds down, I meet up again with Joan, the friendly blonde CEF worker from the L.A. area whom I met at the start of the conference. She is a very satisfied user of the CEF system. There are forty-seven Good News Clubs in her area, she explains. On Thursdays, all the adult workers gather together and view a demo DVD of the coming week's training. A new CD with music and other support materials, produced by volunteers, is made available every Sunday. Joan, like the other CEF workers in her group, reviews it several times in preparation for the coming week's Good News Club. Like other CEF teachers, Joan also has a team of five adults, most of them members of her church, who regularly pray on her behalf, which serves to sustain her emotionally as well as hold her accountable for continuing her work with CEF.

But I sense that Joan has private troubles, and after a few more minutes of conversation I think I get the explanation. "One of my sons is homosexual," she confides. Her voice carries more than exasperation; she feels shame. As she reveals that her son lives with a partner, her mouth forms an expression of disgust. "It almost put me in the grave!"

Her anguish is real, and I can't help but feel a measure of sympathy; she's another mother, worried about her baby boy. "You just want to know that your kids are going to be happy," I start to say. But she finishes my sentence differently. "You just want to know that your kids are going to get into heaven!" she wails. "That they're not going to hell!"

I think back to a curious fact I'd gleaned from the presentation on "The Root of All Evil." The CEF sells a number of books to its members, and the number-one requested book, according to Buzz, is titled *Prayer for Prodigals*. The "prodigal," in this group, is a wayward offspring who fails to conform to the type of religion and values to which the parent subscribes.

"I have a prodigal son," Nerus had told us during the presentation, shooting an anguished look across the room. "Sometimes you hardly know what to pray. . . . Help!"

"It's sad how many prodigals are out there," Buzz chimed in. "Remember that as you pray for your donors. A lot of donors are giving because they have bad kids."

THE CEF'S FUNDAMENTALISM follows the pattern established by other Christian Nationalist groups, such as Coral Ridge Ministries (now Truth in Action Ministries), Focus on the Family, and Concerned Women for America. A central feature of this fundamentalism, for the CEF just as for the others, is a narrative involving the loss of national and moral "purity" and an anxious drive to recover or reclaim that purity. For many groups, this purity was often historically imagined, either explicitly or implicitly, as a "white purity." Indeed, in a passage exhorting members to occupy themselves with "Him and not with ourselves or our experiences," the CEF's Statement of Faith could be interpreted as taking a swipe at Pentecostalism, a form of fundamentalist Christianity that is growing in popularity among African American and Latin American communities. The CEF Worker's Compliance Agreement similarly prohibits "speaking in tongues" and other "controversial doctrines, methods and practices" performed at some Pentecostal and Charismatic churches.

However, the leaders of the CEF and other Christian Nationalist groups are aware that the future is not as white as the past. About 10 percent of the attendees at the CEF convention are nonwhite—of these, perhaps two-thirds are African American or Latino, and a smaller number are Asian—but the CEF leadership has made an effort to feature members of ethnic minorities prominently. Dr. A. Charles Ware, president of Crossroads Bible College in Indianapolis, Indiana, and an African American, is one of the keynote speakers. As I learn from Dr. Ware's presence at the convention, the new inclusiveness really just means a shift in the lines of demarcation between inside and outside, between "pure" and "impure"—lines that are patrolled with as much fury as ever.

"The homosexual agenda is extending its tentacles throughout the United States culture via media, entertainment, education, and the political system," Ware wrote in his book, *Darwin's Plantation: Evolution's Racist Roots*,[2] which is selling briskly in the lobby of the cathedral-like main chapel. Ware blames "Darwinian thinking" for the rise in acceptance of gay men and lesbians, and compares lesbian and gay relationships to pedophilia, necrophilia, and bestiality.

"Society can no longer stand idly by and watch a small segment of the population attempt to normalize homosexual behavior—behavior that is not only morally but also medically and fiscally detrimental to all of its members," he rants.[3]

Ware claims that lesbians and gay men, and those who support them in their bid for equality, are the oppressors. Indeed, "the gay agenda" has oppressed all Americans, who would naturally share such hatreds openly if not for "media pressure and political correctness," he writes. "What a tragedy it would be if we allowed the same fallen spirit of Darwinian evolution and racism to steer us into hateful relationships with the homosexual community!"

Ware categorically rejects the fact that animal species evolved over time. The last page of the book is an advertisement for the Creation Museum in Petersburg, Kentucky. "Prepare to believe," it says.

Ware, who is married to a white woman, is just as preoccupied with notions of "purity" as any white racist. But in his mind, the "purity" in question is defined by religion, not color. Ware seeks to redefine the term "interracial marriage," saying that it should pertain to unions between Christians and non-Christians. When "a Christian marries one who is an unconverted child of the first Adam (one who is dead in trespasses and sin—a non-Christian)," he writes, negative consequences are inevitable. Such "interracial" unions, he tells his audience, are to be condemned.

EACH DAY OF the convention is packed with seminars on every conceivable aspect of running and maintaining a Good News Club. A half dozen focus on the unique challenges involved in working with children of ethnic groups—Asian American, African American, "Urban" (which I gather is code for random nonwhites), and Hispanic or Latino.

I head for a seminar called "Understanding and Reaching Out to the Hispanic Child," led by Claudia Calderon, a Guatemala-born teacher based in the Los Angeles area and director of the CEF Spanish Ministry there. A fiftysomething woman with long reddish hair, she speaks in lightly accented English.

"One thing in the Hispanic community is it is really hard for them to understand the concept of time," she says at the seminar's start, standing in front of a group of about thirty-five conventioneers, nearly all of them white. "They do not understand what it means to be on time. It is not a part of their culture."

"In my country, they call it 'the Guatemalan hour,'" she continues. "If you call a class at four, some people don't even bother to come at four. They come at five."

Hispanic parents, she says, work four jobs, "in order to keep up with all the materialistic things that they want. They really need to keep up with the new culture. They have to blend in!" This is the reason, she said, that CEF has been "forced to use all this fast-paced media."

After delivering a few more pronouncements about the Hispanic character, Calderon devotes the bulk of the seminar to addressing the problem of how to subvert Catholic teachings and practices so subtly that the Catholic-born students won't alert their parents to the fact that the religion of the Good News Club is at odds with their families' religion.

"Hispanics grow up with a big Catholic belief," says Calderon. "It's not that they go to every Mass. It's not that. It's something their parents instill in them since before they are born. That's all their heritage. Because they are very poor. It is very rare in the Hispanic country that they own a home. Or have money in the bank. So the inheritance they give their children is their belief in being Catholics."

"They call themselves Christians," she continues. "The priests told them, 'You know, you're Christians in this church.' It's a very fine line when the children tell me that they are Christians. They say they are Christians because they are born in a Catholic family."

How, Calderon asks us, can we make children understand that being devout Catholics doesn't mean they are the *right* kind of Christians? According to Calderon, like everyone else I've met at the CEF, being Christian and being Catholic are totally different—unless, of course, the Catholic person has been "born again" and attends an evangelical, Bible-believing church.

"One thing to remember whenever you are talking to them is to never, don't discredit the Catholic church," Calderon warns. "At least, not at the beginning. You don't say, 'Catholic church is bad. Catholic religion is bad.' You don't say that to the Catholic people. Because the children go back to their parents and tell them everything that was said, so they will go back and tell them everything. And what is going to happen? The parent is going to say, 'You don't go there anymore, because they are going against our beliefs.'"

"You need to remember that you don't discredit the Virgin Mary and the saints that they believe in," adds Calderon, a tinge of disparagement in her voice. "You just want them to know the love of Jesus."

Of course, at some point, the CEF manages to get its message across to these young children from Catholic families. One audience member, a woman in her late forties, relates an instructive anecdote on the subject. One of her students, a little boy, was grieving the death of an older brother. "The boy said, 'My brother is an angel in heaven,'" she says, pushing her glasses up her nose. "I had to tell him that no, his brother was not an angel in heaven." I gather that the woman knows that the brother can't be in heaven—he went to hell instead—because he wasn't "saved." "I could see the look in this boy's eyes. He was just devastated," she concludes, blinking. Calderon nods, and the two women shrug their shoulders helplessly.

Calderon's advice for dealing with Catholic parents follows the same lines. "Don't tell them right away, 'We're not a Catholic club.' If you say that, they're not going to come! You need to say that fundamentally it's about the kids, it's a Bible club, they can come and see what we do. So there's nothing hidden in their eyes."

She tells us proudly of her success in penetrating a particularly resistant community. "We were going to a building in L.A.," she tells us, "and we were inviting them in for a club. People started putting on their door, 'Don't knock. We're Catholics!'"

"And we knock and we say, 'We are not taking away your religion. We're just having fun with the kids! We are teaching them a Bible lesson, and you are welcome to come!'" It started with one family allowing their child to attend, Calderon tells us, and the numbers grew from there. "Eventually we got almost every kid in that building. And the parents were fine."

I gather that Calderon was able to succeed because she encouraged misperceptions of the nature of her activities—converting children away from the faith of their parents and into a different form of Christianity. "We told them, 'We just want to teach kids about the Bible.' You have to, you know, you have to tell them, 'We're not taking away your religion,' because they are very careful of protecting that security."

"We say in our class that we're not a religion," she continues, "Because we're not! We're just sharing the gospel. And the Holy Spirit will work on their hearts."

Calderon recognizes that Catholic children are a lot easier to convert than children of other religions. "They know Jesus, who he is. The thing they don't actually know is that Jesus actually died for them, and they can have a 'finished' relationship with him! That's the difference."

A man in the audience comments, "It's unfinished work."

"Yes. That's what it is," Calderon concurs. "That *they* can have a relationship with *that* Christ. That's the thing that is lacking. That little thing."

The term "finished" or "completed," I have learned, does not apply only to Catholics. I have been told that, as a Jew, I, too, am "uncompleted." I apparently do have the opportunity to become a "completed" Jew—by being "born again" and converting to Christianity.

As she winds up her presentation, Calderon insists that the Hispanic community offers a tremendous growth opportunity for the CEF.

The relative poverty of Hispanic families, she explains, is good news for the Good News Club. "After-school Bible clubs are an asset for us to use in that their parents are too busy working and they are left alone," she says.

The top management of the CEF has recognized its success in the Hispanic demographic and has therefore begun to translate many of the Fellowship's materials into Spanish. It now offers dual-language CDs of its music, too, so that teachers can teach in either language.

"Some of those kids don't have any adult to talk to," Calderon assures us with a smile, as we prepare to leave. "So we can be a great impact."

IF THERE'S A star of the CEF convention, it's Mathew Staver, who, along with his wife, fellow lawyer Anita L. Staver, founded the Liberty Counsel, an organization that supplies legal support to the CEF. In addition to its work with the CEF, Liberty Counsel has represented the Christian Educators Association, Campus Crusade for Christ (recently renamed "Cru"), Focus on the Family, and other Christian Nationalist organizations. Staver is a key player in the legal strategy that has propelled the astonishing growth of the Good News industry. His group also offers a "Religious Freedom in Public Schools Workshop" at interested churches around the country. At this conference, he is to be a keynote speaker, but is also scheduled to lead a seminar.

For his seminar, he has been assigned one of the larger classrooms. When I arrive, the room is already filled with about fifty attendees; I take a seat in the back.

Staver shows up in patriotic colors: a red tie and a blue button-down shirt with white cuffs. A tall man in his early fifties, he speaks in a sober, matter-of-fact tone. Many of the attendees furiously scratch every word he says into their notebooks. The theme of the seminar is access—specifically how to force public schools to allow the Good News Club on their premises.

After reviewing some of the legal issues, Staver invites participants to describe problems they face in getting access. It soon becomes clear that most of them have encountered stiff resistance
from the school communities in which they operate.

A young woman with fluffy blond hair raises her hand. "The
school in our area said they could let us use the building but all the
rooms are full."

"Did they really not have room?" Staver responds quickly, his
voice exuding disbelief. "If so, ask them to let you see what rooms
you do have here. I have never encountered that as a legitimate
excuse. It's probably not the reality. Find out who is where. They
can't just say they don't have space. If you need help, you can always call us and we will walk you through it. Our phone number is
800-671-1776."

A portly man in a checked shirt raises his hand. "What if the
county says it has to be a school-sponsored club?"

"If it looks like a duck and talks like a duck and walks like a duck,
it's a duck!" Staver responds. "If it looks like they are trying to deny
you entry, then that's what they are doing. They can't, by virtue of
their terminology, keep you out. You can call the Liberty Counsel
and request the Child Evangelism Fellowship letter. We have it and
will send it to you. That usually opens up the doors."

Another man says: "One county told us there has to be a teacher
in the room at every after-school class. And they can't find a teacher
who wants to volunteer."

Staver replies: "First of all, do they require that, a teacher in the
room, of everybody? Schools will say a lot of things. But in most
cases if you dig you will find out that they don't have what they say.
Tell them they need to give you information, showing who is assigned to what room."

"Ask for attendance sheets, and see if they are checked off every
week," he continues. "If the teachers are not checking off the sheets,
they can't prove the teachers were there every time. And if they

can't find a volunteer, they need to assign you someone. And possibly pay for it!"

Staver calls on a woman who complains that her efforts to get into several schools in a well-to-do district have met with resistance. "The doors are shut," she says exasperatedly. They say, 'There are no clubs in our schools.'"

"That is very unusual," Staver replies. "It is possible, but very rare, that they don't have any groups at all. Someone is trying to put you off and put you out of their hair. Check periodically to see if they have changed the policy. Are they doing something without leaving a paper trail?

"Some folks who have been denied access have gone to the school superintendent," he continues. "We found that if we wrote a letter, and sat down with him and explained the situation, he would send it to all his principals. We have an opinion letter and can send it to you. [E-mail] *liberty@lc.org* or call our 800 number. Sometimes the superintendent is the problem. If they deny access they are liable under the First Amendment lawsuit."

In a variety of instances, Staver recommends a public records request, and he now pauses to give step-by-step instructions. "You can send a note," he explains. "We would say, 'Under the state public records law, I want you to produce copies [of documents proving that the school is unoccupied by other groups after hours] for me for my inspection.'" He explains how it is possible to get the service performed for free. "They can charge you a copy fee," he says, "but they can't charge you if you come by and look at them."

Another participant brings up the matter of fees. In general, the CEF pays only minimal fees to schools for the use of facilities. Staver insists that the CEF pay not a penny more than it has to.

"They have to give equal treatment," he says. "If they charge everyone $15, they can charge you $15. But if they have a different schedule of fees, they charge one rate for church groups and another rate for other groups, you should ask for a list. Why are you on schedule B? Highlight the groups that may be similar to yours. And if any of the groups are primarily for kids, the fees have to be the same for you as well."

The attendees also want to know about flyers and promotional material. Schools often try to avoid having CEF literature sent home in student backpacks.

"To promote your club, parents can go to the sidewalk around the school and give information to parents and kids. Kids from your church can give information to their classmates during noninstructional time, between classes, and before and after school. They can't stop the students from talking to each other! Students are compelled to be there, and have a right to free speech. Give your kids gospel tracts that they can give to other kids during noninstructional time."

An older woman speaks up. "I tried to get into this one school but they don't allow anybody to meet."

"They can do that," concedes Staver. "But they can't allow one group in and not the others. Find out if there are any groups meeting, maybe even informally, after school. If they have only one group on campus, even if it's somewhere like in the cafeteria, they have opened the forum, and have to provide other groups with the same opportunity. They can't have a ruse to deny equal access."

Staver reviews the legal thinking that has allowed the CEF to teach religious doctrines in public schools—thinking that construes religious speech as nothing more than speech on a particular viewpoint, like any other. "Thinking of the subjects of other clubs makes it easy to talk about," says Staver.

The easy one is Boy Scouts. Do Good News Clubs address any of those subjects, but from a Christian standpoint? Subjects such as character development, patriotism, morality, or community involvement? The Boy Scouts is a no-brainer.

If you think about it, everything we do is the same as any other group. We just do it from a Christian perspective. Do they have a group that does art? We do art, just from a Christian perspective. Music? We do music too. From a Christian perspective. When you think about it, there is nothing we don't address from a Christian viewpoint. We address all of life from a biblical perspective. Equal access means equal access.

As I glance around the room, I notice many looks of concern and uncertainty. Staver's legal theory is a model of order, but the voices from the audience speak to the messy and often unpleasant experience of attempting to realize that theory in practice. The unending string of questions offers a backward glimpse of communities in conflict—of ruptured friendships, of dormant bigotries revived, of children targeted, of stereotypes hurled like grenades from one neighbor to another. Each of these stories describes an injury or shock to a community, an outrage felt by parents and teachers and administrators on one side or another, of unanticipated strife.

Staver himself seems immune to these concerns. As the seminar winds down, he offers the participants a pep talk. "We have never lost a Good News Club case," he boasts. "There are people who spend up to two years trying to get into a school. Do not be intimidated or think it is un-Christian to go to the mat. Paul was not afraid. I would say try to do it in a nice way, but come prepared, too. To resist a delay, when you approach a school you can say, 'Here's a letter, by the way. What we're doing is legal.'"

As I review Staver's responses to the long list of questions, I can't help but think that his fundamental policy is to stick it to the public schools again and again. In his entire presentation I have not heard one word of concern for the issues raised by the schools and communities disturbed by the problem of allowing one religious sect to operate in a diverse school environment, not a single tip about creating or maintaining neighborly goodwill.

I come to understand Staver better at his keynote address later that same evening. He takes to the podium in another patriotically themed outfit: blue jacket and tie, red-and-white-striped shirt. The assembled convention greets him with a standing ovation.

Staver speaks with the ease and gravitas of a born leader: "If you're in a situation where times are good now, we are twenty-four years away from potential disaster. And if we're in times where we are in disastrous moments, we are twenty-four or less years away from exactly the opposite. And the difference is that transition group of leaders, two generations of K through 12. That's all it takes. . . . If you want to change the direction of where we're going, you focus on the youth.

"As someone who studies humanity, studies warfare, you look at what focus you're going to put your time and energy in. If you want to ultimately take over the world, how are you going to do it when you have limited time and limited resources? . . . The best way to do it, and anyone who studies warfare [knows] you focus on the most strategic part of the human chain link, if you're trying to direct the largest cruise ship in the world. You focus on the one tiny thing in the cabin there that will ultimately change that rudder to change that entire cruise ship's direction. . . . You focus on the youth.

"We're fighting against spiritual powers," Staver says. "Behold there is a battle between two nations. . . . Satan is a strategist of war. He hates Jesus Christ . . . and especially someone who wants to introduce someone else to Jesus Christ, specifically the most strategic link that we have among us, children age five through twelve. . . . If that's the truth, why would we be unaware that that would be the most strategic face of Satan?

"If you want to change the face of the planet," he continues, "you want to focus on those children ages five through twelve; it is the most strategic age group that we have."

"Often we drive by public schools, and the tanks are there on the playground. Bullets are being hurled over their heads as they are in the classrooms. The mushroom clouds are billowing over the tops of those elementary schools. . . . We don't understand the warfare and the battle that is going on for these children. . . . Not only do we ignore the spiritual battle, but we ignore the physical manifestation of the battle that we see in our very neighborhoods. . . . A war zone for the hearts and minds and souls of these young children."

Staver veers into the kind of homophobic territory familiar to me by now. "We are living in times I have never experienced before," he says. "This week, I heard Ray Boltz, the Christian singer. A couple years ago he 'came out' and said he's a homosexual. This week he announced he is coming back. He is going to make songs that are political. Glorifying homosexuality." Staver's voice exudes contempt. "He lives with his male lover while his ex-wife is still managing his website." The crowd murmurs its disapproval.

Staver sees Boltz's same-sex relationship as an "all out attack on children aged five to twelve," and he places the blame squarely on public education.

> That's why, in the 1960s, when the Supreme Court removed prayer and Bible reading from the school, to remove the Ten Commandments from the classroom in 1983, was so fundamentally consequential to the public school. It turned public education on its head! When you take education and you remove the only firm foundation, the knowledge of Jesus Christ, you've ultimately de-educated everybody.
>
> When you remove Christ as the foundation of education, that which was intended for good ultimately becomes a consequence of evil. We are seeing that in our public schools today. An attack on our children. An attack on our values. That's why I am so focused and committed to the Child Evangelism Fellowship. Because of all the things that we battle, controversies in the public school, marriage and the definition of marriage, abortion, all the evils in our society, the real battle is for the hearts and minds of these young boys and girls. And that's what the Child Evangelism Fellowship is all about.

With his view of education as a fervent struggle with demonic forces for possession of children, Staver reiterates his conviction that any opposition to a Good News Club is the work of Satan. "In the context of spiritual warfare, there's a target on your back," he tells the CEF leaders. "If he [Satan] stops you . . . if he delays you in a public school because some bureaucrat says, 'I can't meet with you this week,' or 'I'm not going to meet with you now, you can't come on campus' . . . he has stopped you in your tracks and he has prevented the gospel of Jesus Christ from going to those children.

"There will be parent adversity that will come against you. In more of a raging torrent than ever before. . . . You are on that front battle. The battlefield is right in front of us. It is those children aged five through twelve."

Staver's voice drops to a lower, more matter-of-fact level. "When I encounter opposition, I get energized. Like a boxer who takes a hit in the ring and comes back with redoubled intensity, I like to get in the face of the opposition. It excites me!"

Winding up the plenary speech, Staver raises his voice and shouts encouragement.

"Knock down all of the doors, all of the barriers, to all of the 65,000-plus elementary schools in the country and take the gospel to this open mission field now! Not later, Now!" he rallies his troops with messianic zeal. "Let's march forward, let's ratchet up the heat to another level!"

3

A WALL OF SEPARATION

FROM MATHEW STAVER and others, over and over again, I heard that America's public schools need to be "reclaimed" for Christ. The underlying premise—an article of faith among Christian Nationalists—is that the nation's public schools were all about Jesus until one day the forces of secularism kicked God out of the classroom. "The Supreme Court of the supposedly Christian United States guaranteed the moral collapse of this nation when it forbade children in the public schools to pray to the God of Jacob, to learn of His moral law or even view in their classrooms the heart of the law, the Ten Commandments," said televangelist Pat Robertson in 1991.[1] Unfortunately, many Americans don't know enough about the history of schooling in the United States to recognize that the Christian Nationalist version of the past involves distortions so great as to render it largely a work of fiction.

Pseudo-historian David Barton—a Texas-based darling of the Religious Right and founder of the Christian Nationalist organizations WallBuilders and the Black Robe Regiment—seems to have no problem fictionalizing the history. Years ago, Barton explained everything worth knowing about America's system of public education with a couple of graphs. SAT scores, he showed, were on a steady climb until around 1962 or 1963, when they suddenly began to plummet. Other educational markers, such as literacy and mathematical achievement, followed the same ominous track: up until the early 1960s, then collapse. How to explain this mysterious and unfortunate development in our nation's children? What else happened in 1962 and 1963? Barton had a ready answer: the Supreme Court banned school prayer in a pair of decisions in 1962 and 1963, thereby separating forever the schooling of children from the religion of their forefathers. There, he claimed, was the explanation for the collapse of public education in America!

No credible researcher into public education has yet taken seriously Barton's analysis. After all, one could take the evidence he cites and blame it all on the Beach Boys, who also happened to make it big in 1962. One would also have to ignore, as Barton does, the many other dramatic changes in the school systems and the country in general that were taking place at the same time. And yet the underlying story he tells about the trajectory of religion in public education has long been accepted as an article of faith among the rank and file of the Religious Right.

According to that hallowed narrative, God was a welcome and vigorous presence in America's public schools until the day that a cabal of activist justices, in cahoots with liberal interest groups, contradicted the will of the majority and decided to kick Him out of the classroom. "The framers of our government did not believe that encouraging religion in schools was unconstitutional; rather, they believed just the opposite; only in recent decades have courts ruled otherwise," said Barton in 2010.[2] In the absence of God, according to this version of events, the schools became temples of secular humanism, indoctrinating children in a warped philosophy of moral relativism. Rising divorce rates, child abuse, drug addiction, gangs, nose rings, teen suicides, out-of-wedlock births, and, of course, falling SAT scores—all of this and more was the inevitable consequence.

Yet this story is false. In fact, it is not just false, but an inversion of what actually happened. America's public schools lost most of their religion well before the Supreme Court decisions of the 1960s. Dating from 1827, when a Massachusetts law prohibited the use or purchase of school books "which are calculated to favour any particular religious sect or tenet," schools gradually became secularized not through the capricious orders of a few activist justices but through countless well-reasoned acts of parents, educators, and public officials who collectively and over the course of nearly two centuries came to understand that in a pluralistic society the injection of religion into public schools is divisive, inherently unfair, and unsustainable.[3] In the past three decades, paradoxically, the level of religious activity in public schools has risen—and along with it, the level of religion-related conflict. Most surprising of all, this increase has been due in no small measure to a genuinely activist Supreme Court, which, in a series of narrow decisions, has effectively legislated religion back into the schools, often against the will of school administrators and the communities they serve.

The Christian Right has been so effective in spreading myths about the evolution of religion's role in the public schools that even secular liberals often believe they are true. Liberals tend to take for granted the part of the right-wing narrative that suggests that religious activity in the public schools arises from a grassroots demand for it. They assume that the courts, insofar as they are active, use their power to limit (or not) these expressions of the popular will according to the relevant civil rights and First Amendment law.

But in fact the new form of religious activity in public schools is far from a spontaneous emanation from the heartland. Rather, it is the handiwork of well-funded and very well connected conservative Christian legal groups, and is imposed upon rather than demanded by communities. And the First Amendment—at least as it is now construed by the majority on the Supreme Court—won't defend anybody from this kind of judicial activism. On the contrary, Christian

Nationalist legal groups, in cooperation with a sympathetic court, have learned to manipulate the rhetoric of equal rights, civil rights law, and the Free Speech Clause of the First Amendment as a way to tear down the wall between church and school through judicial rulings.

THE LIE BEGINS with an origin myth. In the beginning, we have been told, America's schools blended religion and education in a harmonious whole. Except that it didn't exactly happen that way. Certainly during the Colonial era, when schools were private or church-run, the question of religion's role was determined by the communities that the schools were intended to serve and was resolved outside the public sphere. However, as soon as the schools became a public service using public funds, religion became a source of intense controversy.

In Massachusetts in the early nineteenth century, as soon as the state began to establish publicly funded schools, the dominant Congregationalist faith quickly set about attempting to gain control of these new schools. The less numerous Unitarians and Episcopalians just as quickly cried foul. It wasn't long before Lutherans, German Reformed, Friends, Mennonites, and Presbyterians expressed their displeasure with the situation by attempting to establish their own parochial school systems. The situation became so fraught that when Horace Mann—often hailed as "the father of American public education"—became the first secretary of the newly created Massachusetts Board of Education in 1837, he declared that public schools should be nonsectarian—meaning that the schools should restrict religious teachings to commonly shared Protestant values, which he, a Unitarian, regarded as universal and believed could be taught without offending any sectarian sensibilities. According to Mann, such values were closely tied to the principles of the active civic ethics that were necessary for participation in the republic. Representatives of a number of sects immediately and vigorously attacked him, but large majorities agreed with this policy, and it soon became the norm in the "common school," or public school, movement.

To be clear, the consensus Mann achieved was pan-sectarianism within the Protestant faith, as opposed to genuinely nonsectarian. As long as the overwhelming majority of Americans were Protestant, as was the case in the first decades of the republic, this approach proved workable. But when large numbers of Catholics began to immigrate to America, that consensus was shattered—in shockingly violent ways.

Common school textbooks at the time were filled with racist characterizations of the Irish, and the Pope and his clergy were described as "libertine, debauched, corrupt, wicked, immoral, profligate, indolent, slothful, bigoted, parasitical, greedy, illiterate, hypocritical, and pagan," according to former Professor of History at the City University of New York, David Nasaw in his 1979 book, *Schooled to Order: a Social History of Public Schooling in America*,[4] Catholics, naturally reluctant to educate their children in such undermining stereotypes, asked for a share of tax money in order to establish their own school systems but were roundly refused. Even the Methodists and the Baptists, who had asked for the same type of division of tax money that the Catholics now requested, switched sides on the matter quickly and stated that tax money should be used for common schools alone.

In the early 1840s, leaders of the growing Irish Catholic immigrant community of Philadelphia began to pressure school officials to allow their children to read from the Catholic version of the Bible, the Douay-Rheims translation, rather than the King James Bible then in use in the schools. Nativist Protestant groups detected a "Romanist" plot to breed a nation of infidels. "We must never forget that this is a Protestant land," thundered Walter Colton, an Episcopal navy chaplain, in an inflammatory tract titled *The Bible in the Public Schools*.[5] He called on every native-born American to "stand by these schools and protect them as he would his heart's blood."

Rumors concerning the public schools began to circulate through Philadelphia, including one that a Catholic public school director had ordered a Protestant school principal not to read from the King James Bible. Nativist groups twisted the facts to fuel anti-Catholic sentiment. Many liberal Protestants supported removing the Bible as a way to resolve the school conflict, but their proposals went unheeded. In the spring and summer of 1844, Protestants and Catholics took to the streets in two separate weeks of rioting. It was one of the deadliest episodes of civil strife in the nation's history. By the time it was over, at least twenty-five residents of the City of Brotherly Love lay dead in the streets. More than one hundred were wounded, and dozens of homes, as well as two churches, had been torched. After the bodies were buried and the dust settled, Catholic leaders decided that the public school system was not ready for them, and so they began to invest heavily in their parochial schools.

In the 1850s, it was Boston's turn to grapple with the same conflict. At the time, Massachusetts law mandated that the Protestant version of the Ten Commandments be recited in every classroom every morning, along with passages from the King James Bible; the Douay-Rheims Bible was forbidden. At St. Mary's Parish Sunday School, a Jesuit priest urged his pupils not to recite Protestant prayers at their public school, lest they fall into "infidelity and heresy." Ten-year-old Thomas Whall, a student at Boston's Eliot School, took his urging to heart, and one day in 1859, he refused to recite the Protestant version of the Ten Commandments when called upon by his teacher. A week later, he refused again.

They beat him for thirty minutes.

Outraged at the treatment of their fellow student, four hundred boys marched out of the school, in what came to be known as the Eliot School Rebellion. The incident led Catholic leaders to conclude that the public schools could not serve their community. In response, they launched a movement to create Catholic parochial schools in Boston and across the nation.

The Civil War eased sectarian tensions for a time, as Catholics showed that they, too, could serve their country in the Union Army. But conflicts similar to that in Boston continued to erupt all over the country. In 1869, for example, the nation watched as the Cincinnati

Bible War raged on the streets and in the courts of Ohio's largest city. In an effort to accommodate Catholic concerns about the sectarian nature of the public schools, Cincinnati's board of education had resolved to ban the reading of the Protestant Bible. Its aim, the board said, was "to allow the children of all parents of all sects and opinions, in matters of faith and worship, to enjoy alike the benefit of the common school fund." Activist Protestants saw this as an attempt to de-Christianize the schools and took to the streets in protest. The leaders of the Catholic community, fearing backlash, withdrew their support from the plan, but the school board went ahead with the proposed ban despite the uproar. Many Protestant leaders, aghast at the decision to ban the Bible, were moved to foretell the impending collapse of American civilization. The case progressed all the way up to the Ohio Supreme Court, which ruled unanimously in favor of the board's decision to take the Bible out of the schools.

During the Reconstruction era, tempers continued to flare over the sectarian orientation of the public schools. Many Catholic leaders continued to insist, as did Bishop McQuaid of Rochester, New York, that "public schools give Catholics a defective, injurious, and poisonous education."[6] Many Protestants, conversely, warned darkly of the "popish" menace to the American way of life and fought to keep as much of their own religion in the schools as possible.

By the latter half of the nineteenth century, Lutherans as well as Catholics had developed extensive systems of parochial education. For many Protestants, however, the loss of students from those denominations was not a welcome development. It was feared that the combined force of the Lutheran and Catholic electorate would endanger the existence of public education altogether. The tensions between those who wanted universal public education and those who wanted their schools to look like their churches continued to grow. In 1874, President Ulysses S. Grant declared that if a new civil war were to erupt, it would be fought not across the Mason-Dixon Line but at the door of the common schoolhouse. In an 1876 speech in

Des Moines, Iowa, he articulated the conclusion many people had already drawn concerning the continuing struggles over religion in the public schools: "Leave the matter of religion to the family altar, the church, and the private school, supported entirely by private contributions," he said. "Keep the church and state forever separate. With these safeguards I believe the battles which created the Army of Tennessee will not have been fought in vain."[7]

LARGE WAVES OF immigration in the late nineteenth and early twentieth centuries made the need for nonsectarian public education still more obvious and pressing. The immigrants included not just additional numbers of Catholics, but also many Jews, Orthodox Christians, Asians of various religious denominations, and an ever growing diversity of Protestant sects. An explosion of home-grown religions such as Mormonism, Pentecostalism, and other Christian denominations added to the diversity of US religious culture.

Also putting pressure on the remaining vestiges of sectarian public education were the growth of science and technology and the process of industrialization. The new industrial economy required graduates with skills that went well beyond the ability to recite biblical commandments, embrace theological doctrines, or even master the basic skills needed to staff the country's factory floors. Education in the sciences, history, and other specialties was more important than ever before in meeting the needs of a modern society.

In 1925 the Scopes Monkey Trial captivated the nation and drew still more attention to the problem of religion in public education. The case arose when a Tennessee high school biology teacher named John Scopes was accused of violating a Tennessee law that prohibited the teaching of evolution. Although the school district won the case, it lost dramatically in the public opinion war. Defense attorney Clarence Darrow, representing the supporters of modern science, made a fool of William Jennings Bryan, the aging former presidential candidate and defender of Tennessee's antievolution statute. "I knew that education was in danger from the source that has always hampered it—religious fanaticism," Darrow said.[8]

Press coverage portrayed the fundamentalist groups backing the anti-Darwin forces as anti-intellectual and chauvinistic—"the sharpshooters of bigotry," in Darrow's words. A 1955 play and 1960 film about the event, *Inherit the Wind,* reinforced what was by now a widely accepted view: that those who supported the teaching of creationism in public education were motivated by fear, superstition, and prejudice. The fallout was so toxic that Christian fundamentalism retreated as a political force for decades.

Although debates about religion in the public schools continued to create sensational headlines throughout the twentieth century, the reality on the ground was shifting slowly but irreversibly in one direction. Beneath the radar of the national media, communities all across America were working things out quietly, responding in their own ways to the needs and populations of their communities. Local control of school districts allowed for a certain amount of regional diversity. In some areas, sectarian religious rituals such as scripture readings remained an entrenched part of the life and culture of the schools. In thousands of school districts, however, teachers, principals, and school boards made decisions that shaped the system of public education in a different direction. Taken together, their tendency was to promote harmony among diverse religious communities and protect the rights of religious minorities by removing the public education system as much as possible from matters having to do with religion.

By the time the Supreme Court took up its landmark cases on the subject, official, school-sponsored prayers at the start of the school day were really the last vestige of the once substantial presence of religion in public schools. Many schools and indeed many states had in fact abandoned the practice on their own. Less than half the schools in the country had prayer, and prayer was in the vast majority of cases limited to five minutes at the beginning of the school day. Contrary to the right-wing myth, the Supreme Court cases on school prayer in 1962 and 1963 were easily decided, receiving the support of eight of the nine justices, including three of the four conservatives.

The cases were easy to decide because, for a period of four decades or so that began with a pair of landmark decisions in 1947 and 1948, the US judicial system had arrived at a straightforward and consistent philosophy on matters having to do with religion in public schools. This approach drew principally upon the Establishment Clause of the First Amendment, which, according to Thomas Jefferson's interpretation, erects "a wall of separation between church and state."

According to Steven K. Green, director of the Center for Religion, Law, and Democracy at Willamette University and former general counsel for Americans United for the Separation of Church and State, the Supreme Court's view about the importance of keeping religion and public education separate had three central features. First, the Court believed that the proper way to respect the Establishment Clause in public education was for the schools to remain secular, which is to say, neutral about all religion, neither advancing nor opposing it in any manner. Second, the Court took particular note of the coercive forces of peer pressure and the desire to conform to officially approved views that affect children in a school environment. And third, the Court presumed that organized religious activity taking place *in* the schools necessarily amounted to religious activity *by* the schools and thus could not be dissociated in perception or in practice from school policy.

The first feature, pertaining to religious neutrality, received its most robust statement in Hugo Black's majority opinion in the 1947 case *Everson v. Board of Education*, in which the Court disallowed payment by the local school board for the costs of transportation to and from private schools, the large majority of which were Catholic. Black wrote:

> The "establishment of religion" clause of the First Amendment means at least this: Neither a state nor the Federal Government can set up a church.

Neither can pass laws which aid one religion, aid all religions or prefer one religion over another. Neither can force nor influence a person to go to or to remain away from church against his will or force him to profess a belief or disbelief in any religion. No person can be punished for entertaining or professing religious beliefs or disbeliefs, for church attendance or non-attendance. No tax in any amount, large or small, can be levied to support any religious activities or institutions, whatever they may be called, or whatever form they may adopt to teach or practice religion. Neither a state nor the Federal Government can, openly or secretly, participate in the affairs of any religious organizations or groups and vice versa. In the words of Jefferson, the clause against establishment of religion by law was intended to erect "a wall of separation between Church and State."

The second feature of the Justices' thinking, which recognized the effects of peer pressure on young children, received particular attention in the 1962 school prayer case *Engel v. Vitale*, which noted the "indirect coercive pressure upon religious minorities to conform to the prevailing officially approved religion." In decisions throughout the postwar period, the Court paid attention to the susceptibility of children to peer pressure. "Nonconformity is not an outstanding characteristic of children," Justice Felix Frankfurter drily noted in *McCollum v. Board of Education*.

The third presumption, the idea that what happens in the school affects the school community as a whole, also figured prominently in the McCollum case. Here, the Court took notice of the "invaluable aid" that the "use of the state's compulsory public school machinery" provided to religious activities involving students in the schools. In a variety of other cases, the Court regularly acknowledged the "great authority and coercive power" of schools, whether through "mandatory attendance requirements" or "because of the students' emulation of teachers as role models."

Though this was construed by many later conservatives as an attack on religion, the reigning judicial philosophy of the postwar period was not in fact hostile to religion. In his majority opinion on

McCollum, Hugo Black explained that "to hold that a state cannot consistently with the First and Fourteenth Amendments utilize its public school system to aid any or all religious faiths or sects in the dissemination of their doctrines and ideals does not . . . manifest a governmental hostility to religion or religious teachings . . . for the First Amendment rests upon the premise that both religion and government can best work to achieve their lofty aims if each is left free from the other within its respective sphere."

The judicial philosophy of the postwar period, though undoubtedly imperfect in many details, largely reflected America's hard-won consensus on questions of religion in public education. Indeed, the courts had assimilated the lesson taught on the ground in the long history of sectarian conflict over religion in the schools. As Justice Frankfurter explained, any activity that "sharpens the consciousness of religious differences" among children in public schools "causes precisely the consequences against which the constitution was directed when it prohibited the government common to all from becoming embroiled, however innocently, in the destructive religious conflicts of which the history of even this country records some dark pages."

IN THE 1960s and 1970s, a new set of voices began to be heard in the public square. Fundamentalist Christians, who had been chastened by the Scopes trial and its aftermath, had for several decades assumed a lower profile, often separating themselves from politics. Now, alarmed by the massive social transformation taking place in America—in particular the new diversity of religions and ethnicities, the shifting of gender roles, a loosening of sexual mores, and some seemingly relativistic ideas about morality and truth—they were preparing to assume a more public presence and reengage with political life.

This newly awakened movement construed itself as a silent, underrepresented religious majority in modern society. It was overwhelmingly white, Christian, and Protestant at the beginning, although it soon formed a common front with conservative Catholics and other religious and ethnic groups. Because it could not conceive that a majority would of its own accord remove the Bible from public education, the new movement blamed a liberal elite, and "activist judges" in particular, for having separated church and school. This new group believed that it represented the authentic will of the people, and sought to gain political power.

In 1979, Reverend Jerry Falwell founded the "Moral Majority" to represent that movement. "Modern US Supreme Courts," he later explained, "have raped the Constitution and raped the Christian faith and raped the churches by misinterpreting what the founders had in mind. . . . We must fight against those radical minorities who are trying to remove God from our textbooks, Christ from our nation. We must never allow our children to forget that this is a Christian nation."[9] Beverly LaHaye, the leader of Concerned Women for America, likewise claimed that Americans had been "forbidden . . . to teach Judeo-Christian values in our public schools . . . because of an imaginary 'wall of separation' conjured by non-believers."[10]

The new movement played a significant role in the conservative revival that began with the election of Ronald Reagan in 1980. Yet, despite its influence on the Republican Party, it never quite achieved the ambitious policy goals it set for itself through its electoral strategy. The politicians whom it helped to elect balked at actually banning abortion, enforcing moral and sexual codes through legislation, reinserting prayer into public schools, or, in general, governing the country on the "biblical principles" in which they claimed to believe. Though the explanations for the failure are many and complex, they mostly boil down to a simple paradox about the so-called Moral Majority: namely, that it was never in fact the majority it claimed to be. The anxieties to which it appealed, to be sure, may have afflicted a majority of the population; but the prescriptions it offered were far from the actual consensus.

As a minority, the new movement should have expected to find an ally in the courts. But the demonization of the judicial system, with which the movement first began, made an appeal to the courts seem anathema to its leaders. Courts are traditionally perceived as defenders of minorities against the imposition of the majority, and since the Religious Right conceived of itself as a moral majority, it had low expectations for the courts. Furthermore, the leaders of the movement had long criticized the judicial system, accusing it of being dominated by liberals and elites. It took a while for them to grasp that they could advance their cause by adopting the tactics of the minority that they were (and are), while continuing with the rhetoric of the majority that they pretended to be.

In the 1990s the Christian Right began to invest serious money in its legal teams. Even then, a judicial strategy must have seemed far-fetched. The aim of the new Christian Right, after all, was in essence to tear down the same wall of separation between church and state that the courts were charged to defend, at least according to Hugo Black and Thomas Jefferson's interpretation of the Constitution. Also, the courts were traditionally thought to be the protectors of minority rights—whereas the Christian Right always maintained that it spoke for the silent majority of Americans. But the Right had come to understand that the courts could be a vehicle to achieve its ends.

The movement quickly developed a legal strategy, and from that strategy a new judicial philosophy took power on the American bench. The new judicial philosophy would ultimately destroy the postwar consensus that kept religion and schools separate. It would lay the legal foundations for an unparalleled assault on families and communities, forcing religion in through the back door of US schools against the wishes of the majority. And as we shall soon see, the courts became a more effective tool of Christian Nationalism than anyone—right or left—could have possibly imagined.

4

THE ORIGINALISTS' NEW THEORY

THE NEW JUDICIAL strategy of the Christian Right called for moving beyond traditional ways of thinking. It required creativity, imagination, and a willingness to take risks. It would not have come to fruition if not for the efforts of some remarkable and energetic people, including Jay Sekulow.

Sekulow started out in life with little money, no grand plans, and an overabundance of unfocused energy. He also started as a Jew. As a teenager, he moved with his family from Brooklyn via Long Island to Atlanta, where he drifted into the Atlanta Baptist College (now Mercer University), mainly because it happened to be five minutes from home. His father, delighted that his son had at last opted for college after all, didn't mind—"Baptist, schmaptist," he supposedly said. At college, Jay befriended a student—a "Jesus freak," he recalls—who suggested that he read Isaiah 53. Jay read the Old Testament passage, which describes the coming Messiah, and had a flash of inspiration. The passage, he was sure, referred to Jesus, and so his destiny was set. He became a "Jew for Jesus."

After picking up his law degree, Sekulow decided to try his hand at the real estate business. The venture went bankrupt, and he was sued by a dozen angry investors.[1] But Sekulow meanwhile had discovered a better place to invest his energies. He volunteered his legal services to the Jews for Jesus organization, which was founded in 1973 by Moishe Rosen, and eventually rose to become its general counsel. It was in that capacity that, while still in his early thirties, he began to argue cases before the Supreme Court and to help overturn the central tenets of the reigning judicial consensus on religion in public schools.

In 1990, television evangelist Pat Robertson brought Sekulow together with a handful of other lawyers to form the American Center for Law and Justice—the ACLJ, so named to suggest that it would become a kind of anti-ACLU. The new outfit lined up alongside the Liberty Counsel, which was founded in 1989 by Mathew and Anita Staver and became affiliated with Jerry Falwell's Liberty University in 2004. In 1994, the Alliance Defense Fund, or ADF, added its name to the growing roster of Christian legal defense organizations with the backing of a group that reads like a Who's Who of the new Christian Right: Bill Bright, founder of Campus Crusade for Christ; D. James Kennedy, founder of Coral Ridge Ministries; Larry Burkett, founder of Christian Financial Concepts; James Dobson, founder of Focus on the Family; Marlin Maddoux, President of International Christian Media; Donald Wildmon, founder of American Family Association; and more than two dozen other prominent Christian ministries and organizations.

Together with several other legal advocacy groups including the Christian Legal Society, which was founded in 1961, and the Rutherford Institute, another influential conservative legal entity, they rapidly coalesced to become a key driving force in support of the Christian Right's judiciary agenda for America. Although each group has its own strengths and areas of concern, many are deeply interconnected through interlocking board memberships, shared sources of funds, shared cases, and a common strategy. Similarly oriented legal groups, such as the Pacific Justice Institute, are now also playing forceful roles in promoting Christian activity in public schools. The organizations are staffed by graduates from Jerry Falwell's Liberty University School of Law, Pat Robertson's Regents University School of Law, and other institutions that are producing tens of thousands of lawyers schooled in a "biblical" take on jurisprudence and eager to do pro bono work on behalf of the cause of Christian Nationalism.

The new legal juggernaut of the Christian Right threatens much more than public school classrooms. One of its principal declared aims, for example, is to defeat what it calls "the homosexual agenda." Alan Sears, head of the Alliance Defense Fund since its inception, explains it all in his book *The Homosexual Agenda: Exposing the Principal Threat to Religious Freedom Today*,[2] and Mathew Staver weighs in with his own book, *Same-Sex Marriage: Putting Every Household at Risk*.[3] The ADF and Liberty Counsel also encourage spiritual leaders to endorse political candidates from the pulpit, rail against a perceived "war on Christmas," and strongly oppose reproductive freedoms. The ADF was a major factor in the 2005 "pro-life" spectacle surrounding the Terri Schiavo case, a conflict between the husband of a woman who had been in a vegetative state for nearly fifteen years, who wished to disconnect her from life-support machinery, and her parents, who wished to keep her connected to that machinery.

Yet much of the energy this new legal movement has invested—and its greatest successes—has to do with public education. Even the effort to cleanse America of the alleged evils of same-sex attraction focuses on the schools. With its "True Tolerance" initiative and an annual "Day of Truth"—recently renamed "Day of Dialogue"—the ADF and its allies invest considerable effort in seeking to overturn antibullying school guidelines, on the grounds that such policies persecute the "Christian perspective" on such matters and serve as a front for promoting "homosexual lifestyle choices" and "homosexual values" among public school children.

The numbers tell much of the story of the growth of legal activism from the Christian Right. The ADF's budget rose from $9 million in 1999 to $16 million in 2003, $21 million in 2007, and $32 million in 2009. It now boasts a network of more than 1,800 lawyers across the nation, trained and funded to pursue cases that answer to its national goals. Sekulow's ACLJ has kept pace with the pack. In 1999 its budget had reached $9 million per year, and by 2010 it was over $30 million. Liberty Counsel has grown to comparable size and was recently absorbed within Falwell's Liberty University, which runs an annual budget of over $300 million.

By way of comparison, the American Civil Liberties Union (ACLU)—the only legal group of comparable dimensions that might oppose the efforts of the Christian Right—has an annual budget of about $110 million. But this money is spread over a much wider range of issues than religion, and in religious cases the ACLU often takes the side of those who wish to expand the right to exercise it, such as street preachers and teens who wear T-shirts to school bearing controversial religious messages. Americans United for the Separation of Church and State has an annual budget of approximately $6 million. The Secular Coalition for America, an umbrella organization representing ten groups with an interest in church-state separation, has a yearly operating budget of under $1 million.

Behind the Christian Right's new legal establishment stands an awesome fund-raising machine that pulls in hundreds of millions of dollars per year through media ministries and other activities. Major donors to the legal groups include entities such as the Covenant Foundation, which is financed by the "Granddaddy" of the Religious Right in Texas, businessman James Leininger; the Milwaukee-based Bradley Foundation, which supports various conservative causes; the Bolthouse Foundation, whose money derives from the Bolthouse Family Farms; members of the Amway-Prince Automotive empire, including the Edgar and Elsa Prince Foundation, whose son, Erik Prince, founded Blackwater USA; and the Richard and Helen DeVos Foundation.

Now, at the age of fifty-six, Sekulow sits astride a network of nonprofit and for-profit enterprises whose principal business is to supply the Christian Right with legal advocacy services. He also runs a Christian radio talk show and appears regularly on Fox News as a legal commentator. He pulls down millions of dollars in income, owns multiple homes, and is known to hop into his private jet for spur-of-the-moment golf trips. Business has been good for the family, too. Sekulow's wife, brother, sister-in-law, and sons have all drawn salaries, contracting fees, or other luxury perks from his network of enterprises. Sekulow is also generous with his jet, which he has used to ferry around important public officials. One such passenger has been Supreme Court Justice Antonin Scalia.

WHEN ANTONIN SCALIA joined the Supreme Court in 1986, he brought with him a set of convictions concerning constitutional law matched in their firmness only by his equally immovable faith in the Catholic religion. The original intent of the country's founders, he said, was the only basis from which to draw clear and certain rules for today's world, and Scalia wanted nothing to do with anything that was not clear and certain.

The long history of church involvement in state matters beginning in the eighteenth century—the Thanksgiving Day proclamations from early presidents, the prayers delivered in victory celebrations, and so on—provided Scalia with plenty of evidence to support his conviction that the founders had never intended to separate church and state. Indeed, according to Jeffrey Toobin, author of *The Nine: Inside the Secret World of the Supreme Court*, Scalia maintains that the Constitution not only permits entanglement between church and state, but encourages it. The Establishment Clause, Scalia has said, "applies only to the words and acts of government. It was never meant and has never been read by the court to serve as an impediment to purely private religious speech."[4] At the time of his appointment, Scalia's judicial philosophy put him well outside the mainstream of the court and of scholarly opinion, and he spent his first years on the bench in relative isolation. That did not bother him in the least. On the contrary, resisting intellectual fads and peer pressure from fellow judges seemed to satisfy a need in him to demonstrate the strength and purity of his convictions. Scalia's religion, just like his legal philosophy, was all about standing firm in the face of persecution. Scalia positively welcomed the hatred of liberal elites. "Be fools for Christ," he implored his fellow believers. "Have the courage to suffer the contempt of the sophisticated world."[5]

Scalia's theories about the Constitution would ultimately prove much more malleable than he let on—for, as many critics noted, he, like other originalists, tended to emphasize the founders' intentions chiefly when they coincided with his own convictions. Far more consequential were his ideas about religion. According to Scalia, the secularism of today's liberals is really just another religion—and an unattractive one at that, suitable for the weak of mind and character. It is a creed of relativism, which says that no belief is better than any other, and no value is better than any other. This philosophy of religion is the genuinely immovable part of Scalia's judicial philosophy in cases involving religion, and it has proven to be the real source of his disdain for the Establishment Clause. For, if secularism is a religion, it is no more deserving of establishment than any other religion; or, conversely, if religion is everywhere in everything, then it can be neither established nor disestablished, but merely treated in such a way as to avoid discrimination among its many forms.

In 1991, Scalia got his first reliable partner on the Court with the confirmation of Clarence Thomas. Thomas, too, called himself an originalist, and he also took pride in his strongly held religious faith. Justice Thomas and his wife, Virginia, attend the 3,000-member Truro Church, in Fairfax, Virginia. The Truro Church is known for its support of the antiabortion movement (through its activities with Anglicans for Life at Truro); for its split with the US Episcopal Church over the election of openly gay clergy; and for its participation in the Charismatic movement, whose adherents speak in tongues and offer divine prophecies. According to Toobin's The Nine, Truro is also part of the "shepherding" movement, which places emphasis on lines of authority. In shepherding, churches are split into cells, with each cell overseen by a pastor/shepherd who is under the authority of the church's senior pastor. Participants are encouraged to submit to the authority of their cell's shepherd, and rely on his or her judgment to help make critical decisions in their personal lives.

Thomas's beliefs on the role of religion in public education were on record well before his ascension to the Supreme Court. As a participant in a forum sponsored by the conservative Heritage Foundation in 1985, says Toobin, Judge Thomas was asked about his thoughts on school prayer. He replied, "As for prayer, my mother says that when they took God out of the schools the schools went to hell. She may be right. Religion," he added, "is certainly a source of positive values, and we need as many positive values in the schools as we can get."[6]

An incident in 2009 revealed that his years on the Court had done little to change Thomas's views about the proper role of religion in public education. In a Washington ballroom, responding to questions from the winners of a high school essay contest, he spoke candidly about his view that we were all much better off when the schools made sure that all children were raised to be good Christians as well as patriotic Americans. "How can you not reminisce about a childhood where you began each day with the Pledge of Allegiance as little kids lined up in the schoolyard and then marched in two by two with a flag and a crucifix in each classroom?" he asked.[7]

Thomas's deep-seated conviction that religious people like him are victims of discrimination is something that he has in common with Scalia, Sekulow, and the other leaders of the Christian Right's judicial strategy. All came of age in the civil rights era, and all absorbed its lessons and its rhetoric well. The difference, of course, is that the discrimination with which they are concerned is that which, in their view, has been directed against religious people and in particular Christians of a certain stripe. The operative words in the preponderance of their legal arguments are "discrimination" and "persecution." When Christian children are reprimanded for telling their classmates that homosexuality is an abomination, for example, this represents discrimination against their religious point of view. In conversations with Christian Nationalists, the sense of persecution comes out even more baldly. When school officials put on a "holiday concert" rather than a "Christmas concert" or break for "winter vacation" rather than "Christmas vacation," they are allegedly "stamping on Christians"—a phrase that seems to crop up frequently. When schools attempt to exclude groups that aim to proselytize the children of non-Christians and practice religious discrimination in their staffing, this, too, is persecution. Whatever can be suspected of failing to affirm them in their views is condemned as intolerant.

The judicial strategy of the Christian Right advanced by people like Sekulow and validated by judges like Scalia and Thomas, considered in most general terms, amounts to an effort to turn civil rights law on its head. It is an attempt to use the principle of tolerance to secure a place for intolerance, discrimination, and religious bigotry in the public schools and elsewhere. It is an attempt to protect the right of one group within society to take away the rights of others. So far, it has been working very well.

THE FIRST SIGNIFICANT crack in the postwar consensus that had governed the Supreme Court's judicial philosophy on matters of religion in public schools appeared before either Scalia or Thomas had joined the Court, in the 1981 case of *Widmar v. Vincent*. In that case, a state university had excluded a religious group from meeting on campus facilities out of concern that accepting the group would involve the university in a violation of the Establishment Clause of the First Amendment, which prohibits the government and its representatives from endorsing religion. But the Court decided that the facts did not support a significant cause for Establishment Clause concerns. It ruled instead that the exclusion of the religious group amounted to an impermissible violation of that group's free speech rights. The case was noteworthy because it suggested that matters involving religion and education could be judged on free speech grounds.

In *Widmar*, there was only one dissent, and yet it proved prescient. The opinion of the majority, Justice Byron White argued, "is founded on the proposition that because religious worship uses speech, it is protected by the Free Speech Clause of the First Amendment." White concluded: "I believe this proposition is plainly wrong. . . . Were it right, the Religion Clauses would be emptied of any independent meaning in circumstances in which religious practice took the form of speech." In other words, reducing religion to a form of speech protected by the Free Speech Clause leaves us with two additional clauses in the First Amendment that have no use or meaning: the Free Exercise Clause, which prohibits restrictions on the free exercise of religion, and the Establishment Clause, which prohibits the government from establishing religion.

Among the first to see the opening created by the *Widmar* decision was Jay Sekulow. In 1984, the airport police at Los Angeles International Airport, in accordance with an airport policy intended to minimize nuisance to passengers, evicted a representative of Jews for Jesus who had been distributing leaflets. According to traditional constitutional theory, the issue at hand was one that had to do with the clause of the First Amendment that guarantees the freedom to exercise religion—that is, the Free Exercise Clause. But Sekulow saw things differently. The leafleteer, he reasoned, was simply expressing his views on a particular subject (the divinity or not of Jesus) from a certain viewpoint—one that happened to be religious—and should be afforded the same protections accorded to those who express themselves from any other viewpoint. The whole case, he said, was about the Free Speech Clause of the First Amendment, not the Establishment Clause or the Free Exercise Clause.

The case wended its way up the judicial hierarchy until one day in 1987, when, as Sekulow later described it, "Me, a short Jewish guy from Brooklyn, New York, went before the justices of the Supreme Court of the United States to defend the constitutional right to stand in an airport and hand out tracts about Jesus!" It was a big moment for Sekulow, but he was ready. "I had walked into the courtroom thinking about Jesus and how he overturned the moneychangers' tables at the Temple. Jesus was an activist; he stood up for what he knew was right. I drew strength from his example."[8]

Board of Airport Commissioners v. Jews for Jesus was in a sense a small case, easily decided (no one thought that leaflets in an airport were a big deal one way or the other), and yet it served as a vital beachhead for a new theory of constitutional law that would soon prove decisive in changing the role of religion in public schools. Having found a crack in the postwar consensus on matters involving religion and the First Amendment, Sekulow drove a locomotive of change through it.

Henceforth, Sekulow would appear repeatedly before the Supreme Court, playing a song with just one note: religious activity is really just speech from a religious viewpoint; therefore, any attempt to exclude religious activity is an infringement on the freedom of speech. What to some legal observers might have looked like a dubious inference in the Supreme Court's reasoning concerning the separation of church and state, looked to Sekulow like a heaven-sent loophole. "Our purpose must be to spread the gospel on the new mission field that the Lord has opened—public high schools," he told the supporters of his newly formed ACLJ in 1990. "Yes, the so-called 'wall of separation' between church and state has begun to crumble."[9]

The case of *Lamb's Chapel v. Center Moriches School District* advanced this effort to redescribe religion as merely speech from a religious viewpoint. In that case, the school district, citing a policy preventing use of school facilities by any religious group, repeatedly refused requests by Lamb's Chapel to use its facilities for a religious film series on so-called family values by Focus on the Family leader James Dobson. When the chapel, represented by Sekulow, brought suit against the school in federal court, the court ruled unanimously in favor of Lamb's Chapel, justifying the decision on the grounds that the film series offered a religious viewpoint on a topic otherwise admissible in the forum that the school had created, and argued that the school's restrictions to access of their premises must be "viewpoint neutral."

In *Lamb's Chapel* and subsequent decisions, the Court relied increasingly on a distinction between "viewpoint" and "content" to analyze religion cases. "Content" refers to the nature of the activity in question—art, science, and the nature of family life, for example, refer to the content of school activities. A "viewpoint," on the other hand, is any set of claims or beliefs that offer a particular perspective on a content. "Life was created 6,000 years ago" and "homosexuality is evil," for example, may be viewpoints on the topics of life science or family life.

Throughout history, to stick with this somewhat slippery distinction, people have tended to view religion as a content, that is, something in the same category as, but different from, art, science, and politics. Most people, for example, are fairly certain that they can identify a practice as religious worship without necessarily knowing anything about the viewpoints involved in that worship. But the Court now appeared to be advocating a novel theory, according to which religion is in essence a viewpoint—something that floats free of any particular content, but rather expresses an attitude or judgment about any and all contents. And a viewpoint, of course, is precisely the kind of speech that is protected by the Free Speech Clause of the First Amendment.

The case of *Rosenberger v. University of Virginia* pushed the argument still further. In this instance, Ronald W. Rosenberger, a University of Virginia student, asked the university for several thousand dollars from a student activities fund to subsidize the cost of *Wide Awake*, a Christian magazine. The university refused, but a 5-4 decision by the Supreme Court ruled that the university's denial of funding to the student, based on the religious message, amounted to viewpoint discrimination. In his dissent, Justice Souter observed that the University of Virginia was directly subsidizing religion by paying for a magazine that exhorts its readers to convert to Christianity. But the *Rosenberger* case now made it clear that for the Court's conservative majority, such obvious concerns with respect to the Establishment Clause were rapidly fading in light of their newfound allegiance to the Free Speech Clause of the First Amendment.

Is religion just a form of speech from a religious point of view? One could expend quite of bit of energy looking for a definitive metaphysical answer. And yet in this instance, as Justice White pointed out in the *Widmar* case, one does not have to look very far at all to see how strange the Court's reasoning is, since the Constitution itself only makes sense on the supposition that religion is, in an essential and fundamental way, something other than just speech from a particular viewpoint. For, insofar as religion is just a viewpoint, the Free Exercise Clause and Establishment Clause are either redundant or meaningless. The prohibition against "establishment" of a viewpoint, after all, would be just a prohibition against restrictions on speech; and the prohibition on interfering with the "exercise" of a viewpoint would also be just the prohibition against restrictions on free speech. Was it the intention of the country's founders to include redundant or meaningless clauses in the Constitution? The "originalists" on the Court did not seem particularly bothered with that question.

The real aim in categorizing religion as a form of speech with a viewpoint was to undermine the first principle of the postwar consensus on religion in public schools—that the proper way for schools to respect the Establishment Clause is to remain secular, that is, to exclude religion from the objects of their concern, neither advancing nor attacking it. In the language of the Court's emerging view, the earlier consensus supposed that religion is a content that may be included or excluded from the school in the same way that science or art might be, without incurring any violation of free speech rights. But if religion is speech from a particular viewpoint on any of an unlimited number of contents, then it cannot be excluded without infringing on freedom of speech. There is, according to this odd chain of inferences, a religious viewpoint on science, art, family life, and everything else, and to exclude it while allowing for the secular view-point is discrimination and represents the "establishment" of the religion of secularity. Consequently, the proper way for the state and its schools to remain neutral about religion is not, as the postwar consensus maintained, to exclude religion altogether, but rather to include religion in any and all forms on a par with secular viewpoints on all subjects.

The next aim of the Christian Right's judicial strategy was to undermine the second plank of the postwar consensus—the idea that every organized activity taking place in a school is in some sense an activity by the school. In the 1990 case of *Board of Education v. Mergens*, Sekulow represented a Christian group that had been denied after-school privileges that it claimed were available to other clubs in the same secondary school, Westside High School. At stake in the case was the constitutionality of the Equal Access Act of 1984, which ordered that secondary schools receiving federal funding must grant access to student-initiated religious groups if they have any other noncurricular programs. The school believed that the law was forcing it to compromise on the separation between school and church required by the Establishment Clause. The Court disagreed, finding in favor of Sekulow's client and upholding the constitutionality of the Equal Access Act.

In her majority opinion, Sandra Day O'Connor proposed that there is a "crucial difference between government speech endorsing religion . . . and private speech endorsing religion." Once again, the presumption was that religion is principally a form of speech, but the crucial further inference was that any such speech that did not obviously originate from school authorities would amount to private speech, thus falling under the protection of the Free Speech Clause.

While the distinction seemed obvious and anodyne at first, its effect was to extend a form of speech protection to religion that does not exist for other categories of speech in general and specifically in schools. The Free Speech Clause, after all, famously does not protect the right to shout "Fire!" in a crowded theater, nor the right to commit libel or slander. Schools routinely apply far greater speech restrictions than those that apply to the population at large. Children are not allowed to engaging in bullying or even impolite behavior, such as insults and snide remarks; otherwise they risk being reprimanded or punished. They are often told to lower their voices or speak in turn, to foster a positive learning environment. Demeaning other children on account of their ethnic origin or skin color is generally prohibited. And yet O'Connor now appeared to suggest that whenever a child expresses religious convictions of any type on his or her own initiative, whether on a homework assignment, in a classroom, or in a crowded theater, such expressions are necessarily protected forms of speech.

By 2001, the pieces were in place for a dramatic reversal of the judicial consensus that had defined the place of religion in the public schools for half a century. The Court was as conservative as it had ever been in recent history; the legal teams serving the Religious Right were as strong as they had ever been. The redefinition of religion as a form of speech replaced much of the focus on the Establishment Clause with an opposing focus on the Free Speech Clause of the First Amendment, paving the way for a rejection of the very idea that schools needed to remain secular. The distinction between public and private speech undermined the central idea that everything taking place within a school was part of the school. All that was needed was some pushback on the coercion thesis—the understanding that students are particularly susceptible to pressure from authorities and peers—and a case to put all of these new ideas together in front of the Justices in the right order. In *Good News Club v. Milford Central School*, the legal strategists of the Christian Right found just what they needed.

In 1996, the Child Evangelism Fellowship applied to establish a Good News Club at the Milford Central School, a K–12 school in upstate New York, which had previously adopted a policy restricting use of the school property by individuals and organizations for reli-

gious purposes. On the grounds of that existing policy, the school rejected the application and cited concerns about violation of the Establishment Clause. The ADF pushed the case through Federal and
Second Circuit courts, which both upheld the school district policy
and dismissed free speech claims, until it arrived at the Supreme
Court. In 2001, the Court ruled 6-3 in favor of the Club. (Justice
Breyer joined the conservative majority with a concurring opinion
that sought to limit the applicability of the ruling, though with little
real impact.)

In his majority opinion, Justice Thomas laid out a philosophy that
essentially destroyed the postwar consensus on the separation of
church and school. The first step, following the path blazed by Sekulow, was to redefine religion as nothing more than speech from a religious viewpoint. While the lower courts that had upheld the Milford
school's decision to exclude the Club all pointed to the religious
nature of its activities, Thomas replied, "We disagree that something
that is 'quintessentially religious' or 'decidedly religious in nature'
cannot also be characterized properly as the teaching of morals and
character development from a particular viewpoint." Indeed, Thomas
went further and rejected even the possibility of characterizing religion as anything other than speech from a religious viewpoint: "It is
quixotic to attempt a distinction between religious viewpoints and
religious subject matter." In his concurring opinion, Justice Scalia
backed up Thomas's reasoning, saying that religion is such a complicated thing that the court should refrain from attempting to define it.

Ironically, in defiance of their own claims that religion could not
be defined, Thomas and Scalia had supplied an implicit definition
of the purpose of religious activity—the teaching of morals and
character—and their definition did not describe the religion of the
Good News Club. In its statement of its creed, the CEF makes quite
clear its commitment to the evangelical doctrine that no amount of
ethical and moral behavior or good works can spare a person from the
fate of an eternity in hell. Only a genuine conversion to the belief in

Jesus as our savior can save us, it declares, and indeed the entire purpose of its Good News Clubs is to inculcate that belief in children. Justices Stevens and Souter, in their scathing dissents, noted that the majority's attempt to rebrand the Club simply ignored the facts. Souter observed that the group teaches purported facts (or doctrines), such as that "If you have accepted the Lord Jesus as your Saviour from sin, then you belong to God's special group," and that "the Bible is important—and true—because God said it."

Having redefined the Club according to their own philosophy of religion, in any case, Thomas and Scalia put themselves in a position to construe the exclusion of the Club on the grounds that it is a religious activity as a form of discrimination against its religious viewpoint. Thomas wrote that he could "see no logical difference in kind between the invocation of Christianity by the Club and the invocation of teamwork, loyalty, or patriotism by other associations to provide a foundation for their lessons." Thus, the Club sought "to address a subject otherwise permitted under the rule, the teaching of morals and character, from a religious standpoint," said Thomas. Scalia agreed, going so far as to suggest that the Club was no different from a soccer team, which also seeks to instill values such as teamwork in its players.

Scalia also took time to wave aside the coercion thesis. "So-called peer pressure, if it could be even considered coercion," was immaterial to the case, he said. He mocked "Justice Stevens's fears [that the Clubs'] actions may prove (shudder!) divisive." Indeed, Scalia sought to reverse the force of the coercion thesis, arguing that people have a right to attempt to coerce children into adopting their beliefs by proselytizing. Religious peer pressure, "when it arises from private activities," is "one of the attendant consequences of freedom of association," he argued. "The compulsion of ideas—and the private right to exert and receive that compulsion (or to have one's children receive it) is protected by the Free Speech and Free Exercise Clauses." In other words, the only people who do not have a right to coerce children as they wish are school officials; for everyone else, the children are fair game.

Thomas, with similar bravado, echoed this reversal of the coercion thesis. When considering the argument that children might incorrectly perceive that their school endorses the Good News Club's religion, Thomas was entirely unmoved. No reasonable observer would conclude that the school is in the business of endorsing the views of its after-school groups, he said, and this is especially true of the parents, who are in any case the relevant audience. And therefore, no reasonable person would feel pressure or coercion to conform to the Club's viewpoint. Thomas next argued, however, that if the school were to reject the Club, the wider community might (just as incorrectly) perceive that the school is thereby expressing disapproval of its religion. This wider community, paradoxically, would naturally feel coercive pressure to conform to the school's allegedly antireligious viewpoint. So, according to Thomas, the coercive effects of concern are not those at work on the children, but those at work on unspecified groups of adults who might feel slighted by the school's policies.

In the eyes of Thomas and his allies on the Court, the thrust of the Good News Club decision was to place religious programs on a par with nonreligious programs in the competition for after-school resources. In reality, and as a direct result of the illogical structure of their thinking, the effect of the decision has been to elevate religious groups to a supercategory that enjoys a substantially greater degree of access than any other kind of group.

In their eagerness to characterize religion as speech from a religious viewpoint, no different in kind than speech from a soccer coach about teamwork, the Court majority overlooked the fact that all those other activities are always defined in an essential way as something more than just speech. A soccer team, after all, may involve speech about moral values, but it is also, as a matter of fact, a soccer team. A partisan political group certainly involves speech from a viewpoint, but it is also a partisan political group. All such groups may conceivably be—and in the case of partisan political groups, almost always are—excluded from a school on account of the *nature* of the activity without making a judgment about the *viewpoint* they represent. But not religious groups, according to the reasoning supplied by Thomas. Since religion is in essence nothing but a viewpoint, to exclude a religious activity is necessarily to discriminate against its viewpoint.

The incoherence of this reasoning is neatly illustrated by a glance at the concluding section of Thomas's majority opinion. "When Milford denied the Good News Club access to the school's limited public forum on the ground that the Club was religious in nature, it discriminated against the Club because of its religious viewpoint in violation of the Free Speech Clause of the First Amendment," wrote Thomas. Substitute the words "artistic," "political," or "pornographic" for "religious" in the above sentence and the absurdity becomes clear. Only in the case of religion is it possible to say that to exclude a program on account of its nature is to exclude it on account of its viewpoint. Here, of course, was the big payoff for the Christian Right: religion, as a supercategory of pure viewpoint, is now implicitly the default program for every school—the one activity which, because it can never be excluded, will ultimately always be included by force of law.

In his dissenting opinion, Justice Souter warned that, if the majority opinion were understood in anything more than generic terms, then "this case would stand for the remarkable proposition that any public school opened for civic meetings must be opened for use as a church, synagogue, or mosque." On the ground, that is precisely how the decision has been interpreted. Any school open for any activity must let in any religious group that applies. It may find reasons to exclude other groups, but never religious groups. And the consequence of such favoritism for religion has indeed been to turn schools into churches around the country, as the next chapter of this book will detail.

The only thing Souter got wrong in his prediction was the reference to the mosque and the synagogue. As it plays out on the ground, freedom of "religious viewpoints" really means the freedom of the majority religious viewpoint. (In the wake of the furor over plans for building a mosque in lower Manhattan, what mosque would dare to install itself in a public school?)

The Supreme Court may have excluded the coercive effects of peer pressure and majority pressure from its reasoning in the Good News Club case, but those effects haven't gone away. Children still feel the pressure to conform or "blend in" with their Christianity-promoting peers, and frequently suffer social ostracism when they resist. In the rare instances that minority religions seek to flex their muscles in public schools as conservative Christians do, it becomes clear that our society has a two-tier system of religious freedom—the top tier for Christians, and a lower tier for just about everyone else. Minority faiths, as it turns out, are often blocked by the majority from exercising the very freedoms that the majority claims to be defending.

The privilege of the majority is particularly evident with respect to the distribution of religious literature in public schools. Thanks in part to Court decisions related to the Good News Club case, many public schools today are awash in religious literature. But that literature is overwhelmingly of a single flavor. The Gideons International, the Bible-distributing ministry, passes out tens of thousands of Bibles each year at public schools and, through its Life Book Movement initiative, has distributed more than half a million evangelical Christian religious tracts, written with teenagers in mind, on public school campuses. LivingWaters, a California-based ministry, targets public high school students with a special edition of Darwin's classic book, *On the Origin of Species*, that includes a creationist introduction. In Montgomery County, Maryland, a Christian group was allowed to distribute flyers touting "ex-gay conversion therapy" to students in the county's schools in 2010. And flyers advertising Good News Clubs go home in children's backpacks all over the country.

But when non-Christian groups seek to exercise their speech rights in the same way, they are regularly shut down—if not by the law, then by prejudice. A family in Miami, Oklahoma, inspired by

The Gideons International Bible distribution in their public schools, tried to do the same with Korans. The school prohibited them from doing so, and the family received so much hate mail that they feared for their lives. In Albemarle County, Virginia, humanist activists Mary Ellen Sikes and Amanda Metskas, inspired by the Good News Club flyer program, sought to distribute a flyer publicizing a humanist summer camp, Camp Quest, which Metskas directs. The school approved in accordance with the law, but teachers refused to distribute them, calling them "offensive," "disgusting," and "outrageous," and the school received so much e-mail from "Christian activists" that its server crashed. The ensuing fracas prompted the school to cancel the backpack flyer program altogether.

The strange but central proposition of the new judicial philosophy—that religion is just speech from a religious viewpoint—has now made its way into actual legislation, such as the 2007 Texas Religious Viewpoint Anti-Discrimination Act. To ensure that schools do not "discriminate against a student's publicly stated voluntary expression of a religious perspective," the Act mandates that schools permit religious expression in any context in the school within which a student is called to speak or express views. Not just pep rallies and sports events, but homework, artwork, and written and oral assignments are included as suitable venues for religious expression. This line of thinking, pursued to its logical conclusion, means that a school may exclude art projects from a science fair, for example, but can't exclude religious projects from the same science fair. It can fail students who substitute a homework assignment in biology class with an essay on the virtues of vegetarianism, but it can't stop them if the essay offers a religious viewpoint on the creation of life. It can't penalize students who respond to questions on a geology test with the answer "Because God did it."

Many traditional legal observers have expressed dismay over the twisted reasoning at the heart of the Court's new philosophy of religion. Of particular concern has been the way in which it has gutted the long history of jurisprudence associated with the religion clauses of the First Amendment. In her 2005 book *God vs. the Gavel: Religion and the Rule of Law*, Marci A. Hamilton observed, "Compared with other Civil Rights law, it's like living with Alice in Wonderland."[10]

For Jay Sekulow, on the other hand, the judicial strategy of the Christian Right has worked like an American dream. His radio show claims one million listeners. Fox News puts him on the air whenever there is a Democratic judicial nominee to oppose or a Republican one to support. He was listed by *Time* magazine in 2005 as one of the nation's 25 Most Influential Evangelicals. The private jet and chauffeur-driven cars are presumably God's will, too. "We are all so blessed," he says. When the matter of public education comes up, he speaks with the confidence of one who feels that all the cards are turning up aces. "Our public schools began as ministries of the church," he has said. "Now it is time to return them to the Lord."[11]

5

LITTLE RED CHURCH-HOUSE

From our apartment you can see the front door of our school. It's a bright red double door made of solid wood and framed in red-brown brick. I've spent quite a bit of time over the past month looking at that door with anticipation. We moved from Santa Barbara to New York City in August, and we chose this neighborhood on Manhattan's Upper East Side for its well-regarded public school.

The second Sunday after classes began, happy and hectic, I glanced out my window and saw a group of people gathered in front of the schoolhouse door. They had a table, brochures, a four-foot-tall sign, and a large tray of lollipops they were handing out to passersby. It turns out that they are members of an evangelical ministry, and that our school is their church.

I decide to visit the "church" and see what they are all about.

This is my first chance to wander inside the building unimpeded. On school days, parents may accompany children into the school yard, but not through the doors of the school. I'm not sure if this is for security reasons or just to keep the helicopter parents out of the airspace. Outside school hours, the school remains locked—unless, of course, you happen to be participating in one of the events held here by the various outside groups such as sports clubs and a children's theater program.

The silent walls of the auditorium are festooned with the handwritten names of children on colored poster paper: Abigail. Amadou. Luke. Chen. Jose. Next to their names the kids have drawn distinctive swirls, pirate swords, and small happy faces. In the empty hallways, the names come with photos and charming, identifying details. "Hi!" reads the caption over the photo of a perky seven-year-old named Tamar. "I am a girl. I have brown eyes. Brown hair. I like art. I have a little sister. I was born 2003. My birthday is June 4." Clustered around Tamar are dozens of other photos of children, each advertising likes, dislikes, birthdates, and pet names. In the lunchroom, the names of all the children in the school appear on pieces of paper that have been taped to the wall in bold, colored letters, organized by class, so that every time a child sits down for lunch, he or she feels a sense of belonging.

Outside room 206, my daughter's new classroom, I find the poster I helped her make to tell her new classmates about herself. There are the photos of her and her brother playing on the beach and a cut-out magazine picture of a bathing suit to let the kids know how much fun she had in our old neighborhood in California. Glancing around at other children's posters, I can see that the families of our new public elementary school are a cosmopolitan group. They are from Norway, Pakistan, Guatemala, Germany, Iran, and China, and they spend their summers in some enviably interesting places.

In the library, I find Pastor George Gregory, a middle-aged African American man with an oval face and a dark blue suit, addressing a half-dozen congregants who have assembled for an early prayer service. "When we go into the auditorium in one hour," he intones, holding a well-worn copy of the Bible, "notice the names of children on pieces of paper. These are the children of the school. Pray for each of them! Pray for their families! Pray for any unsaved family members! Pray that they will come to know you, Lord Father, that they will be enlightened by the words and love of Jesus!"

A solidly built woman has planted herself atop one of the library's low bookshelves, which bends under her bulk. She murmurs softly to herself, her eyelids half closed and fluttering. A man named Ralph paces back and forth, gazing in the direction of the artwork on the far wall as he utters long strings of flowery pleas to "Father God." A slim young woman, her hair pulled back in a messy bun, sits on the floor grasping her Bible, hands shaking.

"Reveal yourself to those who don't seek you," Gregory continues, in quietly beseeching tones. "Pray for this moment on the East Side, Father God! Pray that entire families of this school will come to know Jesus and say, 'This is a house of God!'"

Technically, he is correct: this is a house of God. On weekdays, this building is P.S. 6 (the abbreviation stands for Public School), also known as the Lillie Devereaux Blake School, a highly regarded K–5 public elementary school. On Sundays, thanks to a kind of transfiguration ordered by the United States judicial system, it becomes a place of worship for Morning Star New York, an evangelical ministry associated with Every Nation, an organization that claims to operate churches in fifty-two countries.

On the way to the auditorium, I chat with Jennifer, Pastor Gregory's daughter, an adorable eight-year-old in jeans and pigtails. Jennifer has not the slightest doubt about the nature of the space we now share. "This is my dad's church!" she tells me proudly, the sweep of her hand taking in the hallway outside the administrators' office and a glass display case stuffed with photos of teaching staff. "My friends and me like to play all around this church," she continues. "We go all the way around the church and come back." She pauses. "I also like to tease my brother."

I learn that she attends the Geneva School, a private Christian day school affiliated with the Calvary Baptist Church in midtown Manhattan, where the tuition runs about $20,000 per year. From my brief exchanges with more than a dozen members of the congregation, I have found none who actually live in the school zone or send their children to P.S. 6.

A half hour later in the auditorium, the intimate scene of the library prayer service has given way to high-pitched drama. "Ask Jesus to come into your life and into your heart in your own words!" Pastor Gregory's words boom through the speaker system. The worshippers, now numbering over one hundred, begin to emit cries and other sounds. A middle-aged woman beside me holds her hands aloft and speaks in tongues. A young, slender man clasps his hands together facing skyward. A heavyset woman hops up and down, tears streaming down her cheeks. A tall man in khaki pants kneels facing a wall of poster paper on which the children of P.S. 6 have written their names. I hear him muttering something to himself. I glance at the names in front of him: Max, Jesslyn, Halima, Tyler, Rachel.

When it comes time for the pitch for financial contributions, the assistant pastor who takes the stage is direct and forceful. "When you are thinking about how much money to give to the church," he says, "think about Abraham, who was willing to sacrifice his only son!" From the literature in my hands, I gather that tithing (ideally calculated at 10 percent of one's gross income), rather than human sacrifice, is the norm.

Leaving the auditorium, I find Jennifer again, this time in classroom K-104, sitting on a chair that has the name "Madison" neatly written on a piece of cardboard taped to the back. She is there with about twenty children of varying ages, and several adult "children's ministry" instructors are leading the activities. On my way into the classroom, I notice a handwritten message taped to the door, presumably by a P.S. 6 teacher: "If you use this room *DO NOT MOVE THE FURNITURE* and do not use the school supplies. And please clean up after yourselves."

The furniture has obviously been moved. Desks have been cleared from the front of the room, and the chairs on which Jennifer and friends sit have been formed into a circle. School supplies have been pushed to the side to make room for boxes of religious instruction materials. While I am watching, one of the instructors dispenses about a dozen animal cookies each to seven of the younger children. The preschoolers are sprawled across a large, colorful rubber floor mat that is clearly used for story time and other teaching activities. The preschoolers tuck into their cookies, leaving behind a feast of crumbs. When the Sunday school teacher finishes doling out the treats, she brushes off her hands over the mat, adding her crumbs to the pile.

I return to the auditorium as the prayer service winds down, and I ask Pastor Gregory how the school has reacted to the presence of his ministry.

"They love it!" he says, his face lighting up. By "they," I soon realize, he means the custodians. "The head custodian really wants us here," he explains. "We pay a fee to the custodian's union. The more money we give them, the more custodians they can hire. So now that we rent the space all day on Sundays, plus on some Wednesday and Friday nights, they're really happy!"

I ask him about the rent—how much is it? How was it negotiated?

"Oh no," he clarifies. "We don't pay rent. Real estate in New York is way too expensive! We just pay the custodians' fee."

I establish that Morning Star New York does not pay for the cost of heating, electricity, air conditioning, or maintenance on the school facility. They didn't renovate the bathrooms, which cost the PTA $100,000 last year, nor have they contributed to the $33,850 the PTA has designated for repairs and renovations of furniture and equipment in the 2010–2011 budget. They do not pay for wear and tear on the floors, nor the cushy library chairs, nor the low-slung bookshelves of the library—shelving built to withstand children's books, not the bulk of supersize adults. They won't repair the ripped screen in the auditorium or replace the scuffed and frayed auditorium chairs.

I do the math in my head. For something in the hundreds of dollars per week, Morning Star New York gets use of a facility that can house a congregation of a thousand and would surely cost them millions of dollars to acquire and operate were it on the open market. This must be the best real estate bargain in New York! For a price per member that must work out to less than the cost of a latte at the nearby Starbucks, the church gets a large auditorium, spacious foyer, multiple classrooms to use, heating and air conditioning, full cleaning and maintenance services, ample furniture, and more than enough children's names and faces to pray upon.

Back at home, I look up the Every Nation group, of which Morning Star New York is a member. I find out that Every Nation is part of a movement called the New Apostolic Reformation, which believes in something called "spiritual warfare" and exhorts its followers to put their faith into action in all areas of life, including the public sphere, in order to establish a "biblical" government. One of their leaders, a man named Jim Laffoon, said at Every Nation's 2004 convention: "God wants to do something, where we not only begin to reach nations, we literally begin to possess them. . . . We believe that we are called to not only reach but to rule. We believe that we are called to change history. We believe that we are called to produce a generation that will rule. I believe that one day we will leave to our children NATIONS and REGIONS and CONTINENTS!"[1]

While the organization often couches its aims in soft language in order to appeal to a broad spectrum of congregants, its radical roots are clear to anyone with the patience for a short investigation. Even contributors to the ultraconservative American Family Association's Agape Press, I find, are not impressed. Every Nation, they write, is "a cult movement that covertly believes its leaders are the collective reincarnation of Jesus Christ."[2] Indeed, Pastor Gregory told me that the group has "prophetic leaders." Some of the leaders of Every Nation, it turns out, previously operated a group called Maranatha, which concentrated on converting college students. Maranatha imploded in the late 1980s when it was accused of using psychologically abusive tactics in recruiting and retaining members.[3] Every Nation continues to focus heavily on campus recruiting through Every Nation Campus Ministries and Victory Campus Ministries, and an annual convention, Campus Harvest. Campus recruiting, they say, is one of the "three pillars" of the Every Nation movement.

Every Nation appears to draw heavily on Dominionism—the idea that Christians should seek to dominate all aspects of secular politics and society until the return of Christ, no matter when they think that will occur. C. Peter Wagner, a leader of the NAR, titled his latest book *Dominion! How Kingdom Action Can Change the World*.[4] While Dominionism comes in a variety of flavors—some more agreeable to modern sensibilities than others—Every Nation seems to get some of its guidance from the most austere and intellectually rigorous form of Dominionism, the theology of Christian Reconstructionism. Conceived in the mid-twentieth century by Rousas John Rushdoony, Christian Reconstructionism seeks to replace modern democracy with a theocracy overseen by a cadre of Christian males. Public education was a favored target of Rushdoony. In his 1963 screed *The Messianic Character of American Education*,[5] Rushdoony wrote that the goal of "statist" education is "chaos," "primitivism," and "a vast integration into the void." Gary North, another leader of the movement, has made the endgame for the schools clear: "Until the vast majority of Christians pull their children out of the public schools, there will be no possibility of creating a theocratic republic."[6] Every Nation's own think tank and pastoral development group, the Victory Leadership Institute, works with, among others, George Grant, a theologian who has argued forcefully that public schools are "dens of iniquity" submerged in a "tidal wave of debauchery and corruption" and "a very real threat to the survival of Christianity in America."[7]

Back at home, I glance out the window at the bright red door across the street. Henceforth, I realize, I will have to accept that on Sundays my daughter's public school, the furniture that my PTA contributions help to buy, and my daughter's smiling photograph will be turned over to a group that is dedicated at its core to destroying public education in America. I remind myself that the school will be ours again on Monday. But the truth is, I don't really believe in that door anymore.

THE FIRST CONVERSION of a New York City public school into a house of worship took place in 2002, as an immediate consequence of judicial decisions directly related to the Supreme Court's 2001 ruling in the case *Good News Club v. Milford Central School*. By 2004, there were twenty such school-based churches in the city. In 2006, the last year the New York City Department of Education conducted a count, the number had climbed to sixty. As of 2011, there was no accurate count—the city does not keep track—but an informal survey found churches in about one in five public schools in New York City, putting the likely number north of two hundred. In the tonier areas of Manhattan, where real estate is most precious and expensive, a majority of public schools turned into churches on Sundays.

In all but one or two cases, the religious groups in question were evangelical Christian, and in a large proportion of these, the churches were the work of "church-planting" organizations. "Planted" churches operate independently, yet typically maintain ties to an existing religious organization or network. Most often, the church planter (a pastor or group of pastors) is selected from within the sponsoring organization and already agrees with its values, vision, and mission.

Leaders of the church-planting movement have declared their ambition to turn all 1,200 of New York City's schools into churches. In many cities across the nation, similar developments are unfolding at high speed. In Los Angeles, Boston, Chicago, and innumerable urban and suburban communities in the United States, public schools are increasingly hosting worship services on weekends for conservative evangelical congregations.

The church-planting industry is a worldwide business, operating on something like a franchise system. Every Nation, for instance, claims to have established sixty new church plants between 2007 and 2008. Morning Star New York was developed specifically for New York City, and it captured P.S. 6 after first absorbing Park West High School on Manhattan's West Side, another public school. Go2 Church Planting Ministries, Sojourn Community Church, the Church Planting Network, and Mosaic are among the other national and large-scale organizations that successfully planted churches in multiple numbers of

New York City's public schools. Redeemer Presbyterian Church—a ministry that seeks "to spread the gospel, first through ourselves and then through the city" and is part of the same breakaway movement as the ultraconservative Coral Ridge Ministries—planted churches in at least seven public schools in New York City, Brooklyn, Queens, and New Jersey.

Christian evangelicals of a generally conservative type overwhelmingly dominate this new field of state-subsidized church facilities, in part because they are more ambitious and better organized. It is also the case that other religions and denominations do not see this as an appealing or viable option. A crucial factor favoring Christianity over other religions, however, is that the schools are usually available only on Sundays. On Saturdays, most schools in New York City host sports, tutoring, and other activities connected with school programming, leaving them unavailable at that time. Jews and Muslims, among other groups, therefore have a much more limited set of opportunities.

In all cases in New York, just as in P.S. 6, the arrangement represents a substantial financial boon to the churches involved. On the free market of New York real estate, a congregation with several hundred members might expect to pay several hundred thousand dollars or even millions for a suitable facility. By comparison, the public schools, setting aside trivial use-fees, are practically free. For example, the Bronx Household of Faith, a congregation with about one hundred active members, reckoned that it would need about $900,000 just to complete construction of a suitable facility—to say nothing of furniture, staffing, and other operating costs. When a nearby primary school, P.S. 15, became available for them, that number dropped to $381 per week. That terrific savings has helped keep the church in business.

The church planters have clearly done the math: why bother to pay for your own church facilities when you can get taxpayers to do it for you? Pastor John Hall of the Bronx Household of Faith wrote in a 2002 newsletter, "We have been enjoying meeting in the school these past two months. It is certainly a much easier venue for new-comers. Attendance has been up. There is room to grow. . . . We have a nicer place to have our coffee time together. Afterwards, it is a nice new auditorium, a new school that was built in 1995." In the next paragraph, he continues, "Most important, however, is what we have been saying all along. This is a much larger issue than just this church—it has to do with church planting and evangelism in New York City and State." Hall has also said, "Let there be a church renting in every school." Hall's colleague, Pastor Jack Roberts, echoes that wish in his sermons. "God in his sovereignty picked us to be the ones through whom this would happen. . . . Praise the Lord for that!" he said. "May there be a church in every city—a church in every school in New York City, and grow to a large size for the Glory of God if that's what he wants."[8]

It's not just that the real estate is free, it also comes with added benefits. Public school buildings convey an aura of respectability and state approval. They have traditionally functioned as commu-nity centers. Ours, at P.S. 6, also operates as a polling site and has been identified as a secure facility in the instance of earthquake, hurricane, or terrorist attack. As Mike Harris, a Michigan pastor who sought to plant his church in a local public school wrote on the website XPastor.org: "People equate a secure, pleasant facility with credibility."

The attraction, however, is more than money and a credible venue. The churches want to be in the schools precisely because they are schools, and therefore provide the churches with an implied as-sociation with public school children and families. Many churches correctly perceive that by establishing services in the local public school, they have an entry point into the community.

Much of the church-planting movement is driven by the new vi-sion that sees the public schools as missionary Christianity's "harvest fields"—places where evangelicals can identify and pursue potential converts. Ryan Abernathy of the Journey Fellowship Church, a planted church in Oklahoma City, commenting on a speech given by Dr. Ronnie Floyd of the Southern Baptist Convention, wrote:

> *Instead of abandoning public schools as some have advocated at the Southern Baptist Convention the past several years, we should be infiltrating them. . . . What can be accomplished by committed Christians in a public school setting is nothing short of miraculous. We need to focus on grounding our believing young people in the faith so they can serve as front line missionaries in the hallways AND challenging our adults to serve as tutors, room mothers, teacher assistants, volunteers, and donors to help the schools with the goal being teachers and administrators won to the faith through the service actions of the church. My prayer is more churches will buy into this type of missions strategy and flee screaming from the "abandon the schools" philosophy.[9]*

The legal theory supporting the installation of churches in tax-payer-financed school facilities involves the claim that their presence outside the school day makes it clear enough that they represent "private speech" from a "religious viewpoint" that is not part of or endorsed by the school. When I looked into particular cases, however, it became quite obvious that this is not how many of the churches saw it, nor is it how many in the school communities saw it. Indeed, beginning in 2002 the New York City Board of Education invested a considerable amount of time and money in a legal struggle to persuade the federal courts to accept its earlier policy of excluding religious worship, along with partisan political groups, from schools precisely because it saw the inclusion of such groups as a substantial harm to its educational mission.

In M.S. (Middle School) 51, for example, a popular gifted-and-talented middle school in the picturesque, brownstone-filled Park Slope section of Brooklyn, the Sovereign Grace City Church operated a church, pursuant to a court order, from 2004. (Several years ago, Sovereign Grace moved to occupy a different public school in Park Slope, P.S. 282.) At first the church seemed to limit its activities to the day of the week for which the permit was issued—Sunday. Then, one Wednesday in March, on the first warm day of the year, a team of congregants from Sovereign Grace wearing green shirts announcing their affiliation set up a tent in the park across from the school building and started serving hot cocoa and candy to the kids.

Although the park is public, the school has traditionally made use of it as the school playground. Children play in the park during their lunch hour, and students and teachers alike call it "the school yard." Not surprisingly, on that day the children were thrilled to discover that sugary treats were being served in a large tent that had been set up in their "school yard," and they lined up in front of it to receive the sweet beverage in identical cups, as well as free candy.

Assistant principal Gail Rosenberg, however, was less than thrilled. M.S. 51 had been recently conducting drug and alcohol awareness programs for students, and one of the first and most strongly emphasized lessons to students was that they should not accept food or drink in open containers from people they do not know.

"From my observation," she commented, "hundreds of students accepted the hot chocolate." Rosenberg observed church members telling students they were from the church that meets in their school on Sunday. Each student who received hot cocoa or candy from Sovereign Grace members was also given a postcard inviting the children to attend church services at M.S. 51, says Rosenberg.

The following day, members of the Sovereign Grace Church returned to the park during lunchtime with more hot chocolate.

"Middle school students are very impressionable," says Rosenberg. "From my observation, the children at my school were excited about the free hot chocolate. It also appeared to me that some children believed it must be all right to take it because the church members said they met in the school."

Both Rosenberg and the school's head principal, Xavier Castelli, felt keenly uncomfortable with the situation. Distributing treats to the children, informing kids that the church meets at the school, implying that there was a connection with the school and the church— it all seemed inappropriate. Castelli eventually told church members not to approach students during the day. He also made an announcement to the students over the PA system reiterating that they should not accept free food or drink from anyone they do not know.

But word of the event got out, and a number of parents were furious that church members had essentially been using their association with the school to try to recruit their kids. In response, Rosenberg told them that the school was merely complying with a court order. There was nothing more she could say.

In 2003, Tom Goodkind and his six-year-old daughter, Olivia, walked the four blocks from his Tribeca apartment to Pier 26, locally known as "Bob's Pier," where his daughters' public school, P.S. 89, was holding its annual Welcome to the School Year party. Jutting out over the Hudson River, and with expansive views of New Jersey, the pier was a popular spot for school events, and this annual gathering was an important social milestone for the kids. An involved dad who had clocked plenty of hours at PTA events and in the classroom, Goodkind had helped organize the party, and Olivia was excited to meet new friends and have her face painted. But then a group of people whom Goodkind had never seen before greeted the kids with balloons, he says, and gave the kids pamphlets that said, "Without letting Jesus into your heart, you'll be doomed to hell."

"I looked around and saw kids grabbing the pamphlets," says the tall, brown-haired father of two whose craggy demeanor speaks to his youth as a musician with the rock band the Washington Squares. "I turned to my friend and said, 'What's going on here?' He shrugged and said, 'It's just this new religious group that moved here after 9/11.' I said, 'Why did they move here?' and he said, 'I think they think we are all sinners and want us to repent.'"

Like many of his peers, Goodkind had believed the religious wars that had once plagued schools and communities in his parents' generation had faded away. His mother, who is Jewish, had been forced as a child to recite Christian prayers at her own public school in Long Island. Having lost relatives to the Holocaust, she worked hard to instill in her children pride in their religious heritage and a sense of belonging as Americans. In Goodkind's view, the presence of a religious group in a public school setting undermined those hard-won accomplishments.

Goodkind fired off a letter to the chancellor of the New York City Department of Education, Joel Klein, asking what right the church group had to be at a back-to-school event. Klein responded immediately, agreeing that it was inappropriate. But then Goodkind made a discovery that worried him even more: the Mosaic Church had adopted the school facility as its home, and was occupying space there on a weekly basis.

"The pastor was always hanging around the school, and you know how kids are, he's a grownup and they thought they had to be nice to him to do well in school," he says.

Goodkind recalls a day when he saw Mosaic members outside the school handing out candy and inviting kids to services. "My daughter said, 'I'll take your candy, but I'm not going to go to church,'" he says. "Later, she asked me, 'Daddy, is the church a part of our school?'"

The legal theory behind the judicially sponsored planting of churches in schools also tends to involve the assumption that the churches in question arise from the community and serve some need expressed by its members. In the cases I investigated in New York, many churches had few if any ties with the school communities, other than those that they created after their arrival.

At P.S. 6's Morning Star New York Church, for example, the pastor hails from North Carolina. The church's parent group, Every Nations Ministries, is part of an "International ministry team" with central offices in Nashville, London, and Manila. (The organization was founded in the Philippines by a group of Baptist missionaries.) When I asked Pastor Gregory why he decided to plant a church in New York rather than his home in North Carolina, he said, "After the horrific tragedy of September 11, we decided we had to reach out to this city . . . which is full of darkness, broken families, and unconventional lifestyles."

I asked whether there was divorce and poverty back home in North Carolina, and he shook his head and smiled. "New York is . . . it's worse here," he said.

In fact, the state of North Carolina has the seventeenth-highest divorce rate in the country, while New York State ranks at number thirty-three. Residents of New York City have some of the lowest divorce rates in the nation, according to the *New York Post* (though, to be fair, New York City may also have some of the nation's lowest rates of marriage). The North Carolina poverty level too exceeds that of New York. The P.S. 6 school district, which Pastor Gregory is presumably seeking to "reach," is hardly known for poverty; the school is located a block away from Central Park and the Metropolitan Museum of Art.

Over at P.S. 15, which on Sundays becomes the Bronx Household of Faith, many of the congregants do in fact live in the district—but they refuse to send their own children to the public school, preferring to homeschool them instead. Susan Swift, an active church member and mother of three who lives just across the street from P.S. 15, explains her reasoning: "In the public school, they teach the kids about evolution and God knows what!"

The Mosaic church in Goodkind's P.S. 89 did not originate with any people already living in that Lower Manhattan school community. Even after several years of operation, most of its members came from outside of the P.S. 89 zone. Recently, the Mosaic church that had been planted in P.S. 89 gave itself a new name, the Lower Manhattan Community Church, perhaps in order to dissociate itself on the surface from what once was, in fact, their parent church: Mosaic, a multisite church based in Southern California. Until recently, Mosaic Manhattan and the Southern California Mosaic shared the same logo on their websites.

Mosaic was founded by a charismatic and controversial preacher who was born in El Salvador, changed his name to Erwin McManus, and founded a church in the Los Angeles area.[10] Today, Mosaic actively plants churches all across American and indeed the world. *Church Report,* a Scottsdale, Arizona-based publication, named it one of the fifty most influential churches in America in January 2007.[11] Though its doctrines are similar to those of Southern Baptism, Mosaic, like many such churches, prefers the "nondenominational" label, as it proves an effective and nonthreatening marketing tool. Mosaic incorporates music and the arts into its worship services and hosts concerts and performances to appeal to young people. Its outreach is carefully focused on the youth. In keeping with that mission, Mosaic has held weekly services at what is probably the best-known public building in L.A. and the most famous high school in the country: Beverly Hills High School, 90210.

Pastor Gregory's claim that the events of September 11, 2001, prompted Every Nation to plant churches in New York City, including the Morning Star New York church in P.S. 6, is not all that surprising. After the terrorist attack on the World Trade Center's twin towers and other targets, numerous outside groups traveled to the city to relieve New Yorkers of their godlessness, which some thought had caused the terrorist attacks. Perhaps they agreed with Jerry Falwell, who in his telecast on the 700 Club on September 13, 2001, said: "The pagans and the abortionists and the feminists and the gays and the lesbians that are actively trying to make that an alternative lifestyle, the ACLU, People for the American Way—all of them who have tried to secularize America—I point the finger in their face and say, 'You helped this happen.'"

THE NATIONAL CHURCH-PLANTING organizations have mastered the rhetoric of the management world in their effort to advance their national goals for church planting in Gotham and other urban hubs. New Hope New York, for instance, is part of a nationwide program called Strategic Focus Cities Initiative, which seeks to change the complexion of America's largest metropolitan centers by planting conservative evangelical churches there. According to their promotional materials, Strategic City Focus forms church-planting teams, identifies places for new churches, then follows various steps to ensure those churches will succeed.

On its website, which read like an ambitious business plan, NHNY detailed how it set New York City in its sights:

> The initial phase of NHNY began in 2002 with the establishment of a Grand Strategy Team comprised of more than 30 local ministry leaders joined by state and national leaders representing the Metro New York Baptist Association, Baptist Convention of NY, NAMB, and LifeWay Christian Resources. The Grand Strategy Team set forth the vision, focus areas, core values, and theme for the NHNY process as it continues to the end of 2005. This team developed a new name, theme, etc. The next phase of the process was to establish a Metro Strategy Team comprised of more than 50 individuals who served on sub-teams representing each of the focus areas. . . . Town Hall meetings further promote and involve grassroots ownership and participation.[12]

While the churches effectively market themselves under the "nondenominational" label, they tend to fall on the conservative end of the evangelical spectrum, and the leadership of some of the groups planting churches is Christian Nationalist. C. Peter Wagner, leader of the New Apostolic Reformation, the movement of which the Every Nations church in P.S. 6 is a part, subscribes to the Seven Mountains Mandate—a directive that Christian evangelicals shall gain control of the "seven moulders" of culture: religion, family, education, government, media, arts and entertainment, and business. In part of a letter Wagner sent to Global Harvest, he wrote, "The 9 components of Global Apostolic Network are grouped under four headings: Government, Wealth, Warfare, and Teaching. The '7-M Coalition' is a new organization being birthed to implement the 7-M Mandate in a practical and effective way for transforming our society. Isn't this exciting? We have reorganized in obedience to the word that the Lord gave us through Chuck last December."[13]

Indeed, at a December 2010 service at the Every Nations church at P.S. 6, my daughter's public school, we congregants were urged to pray for those seven areas every day for seven days: one day for the government, one day for media, one day for education, and so on. The prayers were to accompany a seven-day fast, and by focusing our prayers in this way each day, we were told that we would hasten the glorious day when America would be brought under Christian control.

The church in Tom Goodkind's Tribeca neighborhood was similarly founded by a coalition of religious groups with ambitious aims for the city. Text on the website of the Orchard Group, an organization dedicated to planting churches in New York and the Northeast, reads: "2002 brought the first foray back into Manhattan, as an intern was placed in a new congregation started at 'Ground Zero' called Mosaic Manhattan. The joint venture with Saddleback Valley Church and others, proved a great proving ground for the new churches to be planted in New York City during the first decade of the new millennium."[14]

Also attractive to the church-planting movement was one of Manhattan's most liberal and gay-friendly neighborhoods—the West Village, home to P.S. 3. Squarely situated on a picturesque block between Bedford and Hudson streets, a hundred feet away from Christopher Street, P.S. 3 is widely regarded as one of the best public schools in Manhattan. The neighborhood is known for its progressive politics and for its large gay and lesbian community, whose children make up a part of the student body at the school.

Since 2003, P.S. 3 has also been home to the Village Church, which meets in the school's auditorium and classrooms on Sundays. One of the Village Church's ongoing ministries is called GAME

(Gender Affirming Ministry Endeavor). GAME, a member of the "ex-gay" Exodus International Church, is part of a movement dedicated to "curing" lesbians and gay men through conservative evangelical faith.

The Village Church's website has a link to GAME's "Statement on Homosexuality," which cleverly frames the issue of same-sex attraction as one of "freedom" and "choice":[15]

> *The Village Church is committed to celebrating gender, the deeply Biblical reality of our identities. We believe that it is dehumanizing to compel anyone to found his or her identity on sexual desires. So we resist efforts to coerce people into labeling themselves as "gay" or "lesbian" just because they have same-sex attractions. We harm people when we make the nature of their sexual attraction their identifying characteristic. Rather, all of us can find healing and direction through more deeply understanding and affirming our genders as women and men. . . .*
>
> *Finally, the Village Church vehemently resists the denial of choice to those seeking change. The process of change takes different forms for different people, but we pledge to walk beside those with unwanted same-sex desires, who wish to take the Scriptures, and the sanctifying power of the Holy Spirit, seriously.*

The Village Church is an offshoot of the Redeemer Presbyterian Church. Like its parent group, the Village Church claims to be in the Presbyterian tradition. However, some of its rites have little in common with those found in traditional Presbyterian congregations. At a Sunday morning service in 2011, a man wearing a clerical collar stood behind a low table bearing a mixed assortment of religious paraphernalia including a menorah, a Kiddush cup, a rosary, and an Eastern Orthodox cross. "This table doesn't belong to Jews or Catholics or Orthodox or even Christians," he said before administering a communion-like "Lord's Supper" of grape juice and crackers. "It belongs to our Lord, Jesus Christ."

During the service, the pastor and his wife, a friendly young couple from Texas, passed out copies of the church's annual budget in advance of soliciting donations from that Sunday's attendees. The budget was notably short on the details, but operating costs for the church were put at over $270,000 per year. Considering that the main facility is paid for by the state, and many renovations and equipment covered by P.S. 3 families and the PTA, the number was mystifying; where, I wondered, does all that money go?

After the service, a slight, fortysomething congregant explained over bagels and coffee that she used to attend Redeemer services uptown in the auditorium of another public school, Hunter College. Those services attract more than one thousand attendees to its religious ceremonies every week, with a live jazz band and the dynamic pastor, Timothy J. Keller, who cowrote the *Redeemer Church Planting Manual* along with J. Alan Thompson.[16] However, the congregant said, "I was told to come to this one instead because they wanted to start a church here at this school. Basically it's so cheap, even cheaper than renting space at a regular church. And it's just been repainted. See? They really keep it up nice."

From a logistical perspective, planting a church can be a major project—for school administrators as well as church officials. In Brooklyn's diverse, working-class Bushwick neighborhood, for example, the Bushwick High School comes close to megachurch status. The Christ Tabernacle, which takes over the school on Sundays, occupies eleven classrooms, the cafeteria, a dance studio, and an auditorium that seats nearly eight hundred.

In September 2004, church staffers made the kind of request that any large corporation might make to a landlord. They asked to install a T1 high-speed internet connection within the school to improve their church operations. Sean Walsh, assistant principal for organization at Bushwick High, pointed out that installing a T1 line could create a problem if the line were to interfere with existing school lines. In particular, he was concerned about possible breaches of confidentiality of student data on the school's computer system. "I explained that any electrical work would need to be done by a DOE contractor, to minimize risk of interference with or damage to the school's existing electrical system," he said.[17]

Sometime after the 2004 meeting, according to Walsh, a representative from Verizon came to the school to begin the process of installing a T1 line. "I told the Verizon rep that the installation had not been authorized," Walsh says. "I contacted Reverend Castillo about the incident, and he acknowledged that the church had arranged for Verizon to begin the installation. I reminded him that the T1 line request had not been approved." But the message, apparently, failed to transmit. Even after this conversation, Walsh says, Verizon came out two or three more times to install the line; each time, Walsh had to tell the Verizon worker to leave.

Also in September 2004, Walsh was surprised to discover that the church had installed a satellite dish on the school roof. "The church never sought or obtained approval to install the satellite dish from myself, principal Ana Santiago, or any other school official," he says. "The installation involved tapping into the school's electrical system and running wires through an air duct from the roof to the auditorium." For Walsh, the issue raised a host of serious concerns—about security, integrity of the building, and respect for school authority and procedure. "Also, I learned that someone from the church had offered money to the custodial staff member who gave the church access to the school roof," he says. "This situation was very uncomfortable for the school because we were required to investigate the actions of a church whose members are part of the school community."

Christ Tabernacle, however, had little to worry about. After all, it did not have a contract with the school, nor a lease, nor a deposit to cover possible damages. It does not pay rent. All it had was a court order that says that the school must allow the church to make use of its property on Sundays.

THE EXPLOSION OF school-based church-planting in New York and across the nation that began in 2002 did not reflect a spontaneous

eruption of religious enthusiasm. It was simply the direct consequence of the Supreme Court's decision in the case of *Good News
Club v. Milford Central School* in 2001. An alien visitor to Planet
First Amendment could be forgiven for summarizing the entire story
thus: Clarence Thomas and Antonin Scalia, together with a few fellow travelers on the Supreme Court and their friends in the ADF
and ACLJ, got together and ordered that the United States should
establish a nationwide network of evangelical churches housed in
taxpayer-financed school facilities.

In the years before the Good News Club decision, many schools
regularly denied access to groups that wished to turn the schools into
churches, and the courts supported them. In 1994, for example, the
New York City Board of Education rejected an application from the
Bronx Household of Faith Church to rent a public school building
for Sunday services.

The church persisted in its efforts, and in 1995 Alliance Defense
Fund senior counsel Jordan Lorence filed a lawsuit on behalf of the
church in federal district court. The ADF provided funding for the
case. After the church lost again in 1996, in federal district court, it
then appealed to the US Court of Appeals for the Second Circuit.
The church lost a third time, and Lorence filed a request for review to
the US Supreme Court, which declined to review the case in 1998.

The 2001 Supreme Court decision in *Good News Club vs. Milford
Central School* changed everything for the Bronx Household of Faith.
In a surprising footnote to his majority opinion, Justice Thomas com-
mented that the Bronx case may have been "wrongly decided." Jor-
dan Lorence at the ADF wasted no time in pursuing the suggestion.
On behalf of the Bronx Household of Faith, he filed suit once again.

This time, the complaint filed on behalf of the Bronx Household
of Faith used the language and logic enshrined in Thomas's opinion
on Milford. The Bronx church, it argued, wasn't really a church; it
was a group that engaged in "singing, teaching, social interaction,
and other expressive activities," all of which simply happened to be

expressed from a religious viewpoint. The school accepted other groups involved in singing and so on, such as the Girl Scouts. Therefore, its exclusion of the Bronx church amounted to discrimination against the "religious viewpoint" of the church in violation of the Free Speech Clause of the First Amendment. There could be no Establishment Clause issue, moreover, because the Bronx church wasn't really religion anyway, just private speech from a religious viewpoint, which no reasonable person could ever imagine was in any way supported or endorsed by the school.

Unwilling to buck the manifest will of the Supreme Court, the same judge who denied the Bronx Household access in the first place reversed herself. On appeal, the Second Circuit Court backed up the reversal in a 2-1 vote. In his dissent, Judge Roger Miner, United States Court of Appeals, Second Circuit, wrote: "Today the majority commits a public school building in the Bronx to be Middle School 206B and the Bronx Household of Faith." But he acknowledged that it was all really the work of the Supreme Court. "Considering the present direction of Supreme Court decisions in the area of Church/State separation," he added tartly, "we may once again see church services be conducted in the Supreme Court courtroom."

As the members and staff of the New York Board of Education watched the consequences of the new judicial policy unfold, they decided to take action. Alarmed by the complaints from parents and administrators and concerned about violation of the intent of the Establishment Clause, the Board of Education vigorously pursued legal action to attempt to reverse the decisions in the Bronx cases. Its aim was to support a policy of excluding religious groups from using schools as houses of worship.

In 2011, the school board's legal response finally bore fruit. On June 2, the United States Court of Appeals for the Second Circuit ruled that the city could restrict religious congregations from conducting worship services in schools. To exclude an activity from a school because it is religious in nature, Judge Pierre N. Leval wrote, is not to discriminate against it on account of its religious viewpoint. But the case is far from settled. The decision has been appealed, and some legal experts predict it will make its way to the Supreme Court. If the Court follows the strange logic of the Milford case, it cannot be expected to look favorably on the Second Circuit's decision.

Robert Hall of the Bronx Household of Faith understands what is at stake. No doubt repeating what he has been given to understand by his legal team at the ADF, Hall realizes that the point of the judicial strategy of the Christian Right is to erect a system of state-subsidized churches in the schools. "This is a much larger issue than just this church. It has to do with church planting in this city and New York State," he says. "They established a beachhead on D-day. We've established a beachhead here."

6

Thy Neighbor's Children

The 4/14 Window

WHY WERE THEY so focused on the children? And why were they so intent on reaching children through public schools? In my travels through the world of the Religious Right, these questions haunted me. I had generally thought of missionary work as something that happens in faraway lands or in houses of worship, and I imagined that missionaries aimed at people of all ages, though tilting toward young adults of college age, in their years of seeking. Yet in Seattle, in New York, in Alabama, and in Santa Barbara, the missionaries I encountered were aiming at little kids, and they all seemed to agree that the public schools were where the action was. In many cases, these activists seemed really excited about the focus of their work, as if the idea of concentrating on schoolchildren was something that had just occurred to them spontaneously. I wondered: how could so many people from so many different places and organizations have hit upon the same idea at the same time?

It wasn't coincidence, of course. The Religious Right is not a single organization, and yet it is surprisingly well organized in a certain way. It is a "grassroots movement" by definition, not answering in any formal way to a command-and-control hierarchy. And yet the grass often seems to grow in surprisingly tidy rows. The coherence of the movement, such as it is, is of the mind. It rests on a set of ideas, and an avalanche of resources pours down upon whoever happens to share those ideas. If there is anyone in charge, it is the big-picture strategists who, through a number of well-coordinated events and organizations, are able to mobilize the movement around a few simple messages.

Luis Bush is one such thinker, and it was he as much as anyone who directed the movement toward children. It came into focus in Switzerland, home to some of the most influential evangelical retreats, study centers, and think tanks in the world. The first of such centers was L'Abri (The Shelter), founded in Huemoz-sur-Ollon in 1955 by American theologian Francis Schaeffer and his wife, Edith. Arguing that Christianity is a "whole system of truth," Schaeffer devised a multi-faceted Christian critique of US culture and helped revive a politicized form of evangelical faith, eventually collaborating with Rev. Jerry Falwell, who then went on to form the Moral Majority.

In 1974, Billy Graham joined with an all-star cast including Samuel Escobar, Francis Schaeffer, John Stott, and Carl Henry to form the Lausanne Movement, a committee dedicated to "unite all evangelicals in the common task of the total evangelization of the world." It was in Lausanne that Ralph Winter introduced the term "unreached people groups," to great applause in the missionary world. And it was amidst the group of people who frequent Lausanne that Luis Bush first articulated a new strategy that would energize the world of mission as perhaps never before.

A missionary strategist who trained in Intercultural Studies at the Fuller School of World Mission in Pasadena, California, Bush built the first half of his career around the concept of the "10/40 Window." His thesis then was that Christian missionaries needed to target their efforts on the area of the globe between ten degrees and forty degrees north latitude. Subsequently, missionaries were dispatched to swaths of North Africa, South Asia, and the Middle East in order to convert "unreached people groups" in the designated latitudes.

Then at a Transform World Connections conference in September 2009, a gathering of high-level mission strategists, Bush announced a new unifying vision for missionaries around the globe. He called it the "4/14 Window." The largest and most strategic group of people in the world, he said, are children between the ages of four and fourteen. Kids are the key to the "Great Commission," or the theological tenet, popular in the evangelical world, that there is a mandate to convert all of humanity to evangelical Christianity.

The idea of targeting children had been kicking around in some corners of the mission world for some time. The term "4/14 window" made its first appearance in Dan Brewster's essay in the 1996 book *Children in Crisis: A New Commitment.*[1] Under the title "The 4/14 Window: Child Ministries and Mission Strategy," Brewster claimed that children are often overlooked in mission literature, and urged his comissionaries to focus on them as "the world's most fruitful field." While Brewster may have devised the term, Bush was the first to articulate it as a coherent strategy, and to be listened to by a wider group of the people who matter.

Bush's argument was simple and blindingly effective. He pointed out that 85 percent of conversion experiences occur to people between the ages of four and fourteen. He also said that when you get them young, you have a better chance of keeping them for life. "It is imperative that we see children and young people as a strategic force that can transform a generation and change the world," he wrote. "Our vision and hope is to maximize their transformational impact while they are young, and to mobilize them for continuing impact for the rest of their lives."[2]

Bush's ideas lit up the skies of the missionary community like a bright flare in the night, illuminating the path for evangelicals worldwide and missionaries in particular. "Political movements (like Nazism and Communism) trained legions of children with the goal of carrying their agenda beyond the lifetimes of their founders. . . . Even the Taliban places great emphasis on recruiting children," wrote Dr. Wes Stafford, president of Compassion International, one of the largest worldwide missionary groups, in an introduction to Bush's 2009 book, *The 4–14 Window: Raising Up a New Generation to Transform the World*. "May God inspire you to join us in His battle for the little ones!"[3]

Bush also provided the theoretical rationale for the charge on public schools. In a nutshell: it's a matter of taking the battle to the enemy.

"While universal primary and secondary education may be considered a worthy goal, its ultimate effect can sometimes be negative," wrote Bush. "Unless the teachers and administrators are Christ followers, the world view that is taught will not transform the minds of the 4/14ers." Bush continued, "Secular education does not enlighten, rather it dims one's grasp of the 'real reality' rooted in the truth of scripture."[4]

In order to get the message from Switzerland to the American heartland, the "ideas people" need to come down to earth. One very important vehicle is the conference circuit, a combination of face-to-face meetings, seminar-style discussions, book sales, and missionary "festivals." All serve to help put the missionary world on the same page.

IN ORDER TO learn about the process, I register for Missions Fest Seattle 2009—a sprawling, "nondenominational," three-day conference for thousands of evangelical Christians involved in missionary work around the world. The gathering is taking place just two months after Bush's announcement of the mission world's great philosophical shift. I want to learn more about how the ideas of the philosophers are communicated down to these foot soldiers. I also want to understand how one joins them. Mission "expos" or "fests" take place every few months in various parts of the United States and around the world. The Missions Fest in Seattle has been an annual event since 2005. The venue this year is Westminster Chapel, a stone-and-glass megachurch in Bellevue, just across the river from downtown Seattle. The main hall accommodates 1,100 people, and the rest of the structure can hold thousands more.

On a gray fall day, the fest is bustling. Outside, buses drop off large cohorts of missionaries and would-be missionaries. Most are dressed for comfort—pants and sensible shoes for the women, warm sweaters for the men. The interior of the cavernous entrance hall is partitioned into prefab booths featuring a colorful variety of groups. One organization promises to build homes for the poor in Uganda; another is titled "Reaching Muslims En Masse for Christ" via radio networks in the Middle East; another aims to convert Native Americans; yet another promises to minister to women suffering postabortion regrets. A substantial number of the exhibitors are targeting the producers rather than the consumers of missionary service. There are technology support services, security services, transportation specialists, musical production companies, and psychological and "spiritual" advisers, all promising to help missionaries stay productive and on-message.

The first thing that one notices about the convention, in fact, is that it has a familiar, business-to-business feel. On the surface, it isn't very different from a convention for spa product specialists or outdoor equipment manufacturers. It's about making new contacts, refreshing old ones over a cup of coffee, getting up to speed on the latest developments in the field, and clinching deals. In the snatches of overheard conversations, there is a palpable feeling of in-the-trenches camaraderie. One hears in-jokes, shared lingo, and the buzz of breezy exhilaration that arises when people with a common passion encounter one another.

For many of the participants, the fest functions as a job fair. A number of college-age adults roam the booths seeking overseas missionary adventures, gap year jobs, or volunteer opportunities. In the chapel, the honored speakers intersperse the hosannas and citations from the Bible with talk about "effectiveness" of outreach programs, "market penetration," "conversion rates," "community relations," "strategic partnerships," and even "God's strategic plan."

The other thing one notices is the children. There are pictures of them everywhere. And there are real, live children here, too—although just now some of them are heading out on a guided field trip to Seattle's Discovery Institute, an organization that promotes the theory of intelligent design. But if this were a business convention, it would seem that the chief business is children. Many of the advertised missions either aim directly at children or involve children in some central way. The Young Life ministry, for example, brings the Good News about Jesus to adolescents. World Vision is dedicated to feeding, educating, and spreading the gospel to impoverished kids overseas. Antioch Adoptions seeks to channel the children of unplanned pregnancies into adoptive Christian households. Youth Missions International trains young people for missionary work. Global Mission Prison Ministry works with the children of the incarcerated. The convention program exclaims: "Our purpose is to get kids involved in the harvest"—meaning involve them in converting people to evangelical Christianity.

For the younger children present, there is an ongoing program in the church's brightly lit basement area. There are games, lessons, speakers, and even field trips. The Creation Association of Puget Sound, for example, offers to take kids ages six to twelve on an excursion that will study "God's Amazing Creatures" and present them with proof that God created the earth in just six days between six and ten thousand years ago. A second chapel holds hundreds of teens. Youthful pastors sporting faded jeans and T-shirts lead them in prayer and worship sessions. On stage, good-looking young musicians play contemporary-sounding soft rock, all on Christian themes.

"If you walk around the Missions Fest now, you will see images of children everywhere," Sylvia Foth tells me. "This is very different from ten to fifteen years ago." Foth is the president and founder of Kidzana Ministries, an organization that focuses on equipping people around the world to convert children to Christianity. She is a tall, charismatic woman with short blonde hair, glasses, and a wide, friendly smile. Motherly and energetic, she transmits an infectious enthusiasm for her work. She urges me to attend her seminar the next day, and I promise to do so.

Front and center in this festival is the Child Evangelism Fellowship. The CEF is Missions Fest's "featured mission" this year—an honor that comes with a monetary prize. Its main booth is positioned directly opposite the entrance, right next to the convention's welcome booth. The CEF also has a second presence, an informational booth farther inside.

Prominently displayed in one CEF booth, in blown up letters, are the words of the renowned nineteenth-century English preacher Charles Spurgeon: "A child of 5, if properly instructed, can as readily believe and be as regenerated as anyone." The informational booth also presents a number of pictures and graphs.

A picture is worth a thousand words, but a graph can sometimes count for even more. In the CEF booth stands a graph that I have seen before, on page 17 of Luis Bush's book *The 4/14 Window* and, even before that, in Brewster's essay for *Children in Crisis.*[5] The graph appears to have first been presented at an Evangelical Fellowship of Mission Agencies (EFMA) executive retreat in 1992 by Bryant L. Myers, who delivered a talk titled "The State of the World's Children: A Critical Challenge to Christian Mission in the 1990s." (See the graph on the next page.) Myers currently holds a high-level position with the international missionary organization World Vision International. He joined Bush's alma mater, Fuller Theological Seminary, as professor of transformational development in 2006. He has also served in various leadership roles within the Lausanne Committee on World Evangelization for the past twenty years.

My first experience with training to become a CEF missionary in the public schools begins with about two dozen fellow attendees in a large side room, at a seminar called "Teach N Transform—Transform Your Counseling Skills." Our seminar leader is Jan Akam, a solid woman with a heart-shaped face and ruddy cheeks who appears to be in her sixties. She is the director of the CEF chapter in Snohomish County in the northern part of Washington State.

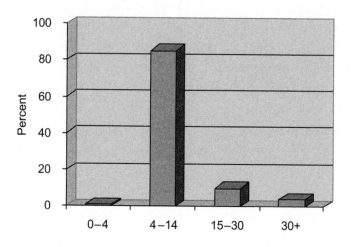

FIGURE 6.1 Age at Which People Convert to Christianity

Akam starts with a brief introduction to the CEF. "We have shared the gospel with over nine million kids worldwide," she says. The CEF has more than twenty-seven different programs, she tells us, but she quickly focuses on the Good News Club program and its setting, the public schools. "I used to teach Sunday school. But when I heard that you can go to a public school and share the gospel with kids who have never heard about God, I got really excited!"

"My parents led me to the Lord," she continues. "But there are so many kids out there who don't have peace in their homes. They may be in the class because they just have a desire for attention or fellowship." She shakes her head sadly.

Then she gets down to business. Her aim is to teach us how to lead children to salvation. "What happens when a child says to you, 'I want you to lead me to Christ?'" she asks. "A lot of people get panicky. This class will walk you through the steps of counseling a child."

She begins by offering a set of simple tips:

"These are very young children we're talking about—you want to speak childrenese.
"Find a quiet place and speak with a gentle voice.

"Make it really personal. It really helps to use their name.

"Don't assume the child is saved just because he or she is responding to the invitation."

The best way to promote spiritual growth, she tells us, is to ask thought-provoking questions:

"Ask the child, 'What did you want to come to speak to me about?' Then refer him back to the message of salvation.

"Ask him, 'What is sin?' Go over what sin is. I always say, 'God really loves people who do bad things.' The kids, can't believe it! They say, 'Really? Really?'

"I say to the kids, 'Can you guys tell me something that is a sin?' Something easy, like fighting with your brother or sister."

Akam instructs us what to say to children who don't believe they have sinned.

"Show him Romans 3:23 ['for all have sinned and fall short of the glory of God'] if the child seems resistant to the idea of sin.

"Ask them, 'What is God's punishment for sin?' Tell them that the punishment for sin is being separated from God forever.

"Ask a child, 'Can you think of anything you can do to get rid of your sin?' Guide them toward salvation by asking questions like, 'Who is the Lord Jesus? Why did God send his son into the world?'

"Ask questions to see if the child understands how to receive God's salvation. Explain God's condition for salvation: You have to admit that you sinned, and you have to believe in the Lord Jesus if you want to be saved."

Once the child has the basics, Akam continues, you need to convey the practical side of the message, which comes down to four simple points:

"God wants you to go to church. You need to go to a *Bible-believing church*," she draws out her words for emphasis. The term "Bible-believing" is a self-descriptive term widely used by conservative Christians to mean that they take a literalist interpretation of the Old and New Testaments.

"The second step is that you need to read the Bible. We give the kids free Bibles.

"The third step is to obey the word of God.

"The fourth step is witnessing and telling others about Jesus."

Her voice goes up a notch with excitement on the last point. "Children can reach other kids with the gospel message so easily," she exclaims. Then she holds up the CEF's Tel-a-Story cards, credit card–size and printed on thick paper stock decorated with colorful pictures of pumpkins or pastoral scenes. These cards invite children to call a toll-free number to speak to a CEF representative who will talk to them about salvation. "Tell the kids," Akam instructs, "when you trick-or-treat, pass these cards out to your friends!"

Stacks of these cards are being distributed throughout the conference, destined for little children's hands across the state. Later, when I call the 800 number on the card, an adult woman on the other end of the line tells me I have to choose whether to go to heaven or "be separated from God forever." She tells me I'm only the second adult to call her; usually she "counsels" children. The youngest, she says, was six years old.

"Teach them how to count on their fingers," Akam says, winding up the first part of the seminar. She holds up her right hand, and says in a loud, childrenese voice: "I. Will. Never. Leave. Jan." As she says each word, she closes one of her fingers, until her hand forms a fist. By the time she pulls in her thumb, to the sound of her own name, her voice has an explosively gleeful edge.

"The joy of doing that [leading children to Christ] is unbelievable," she exclaims. "You're hooked!"

For the next part of our seminar, Akam requests that we pair up with a partner in order to practice "counseling for salvation." I turn to the person sitting to my left, a woman in her sixties with puffy blonde curls and a placid smile. She is a grandmother who lives in the Seattle area.

As we go through the motions of converting one another, I discern her reason for being here: her grandkids. She is afraid of losing them to liberal churches and damnation.

"My daughter goes to a liberal church," she says despairingly. "Congregational," she sniffs, with a combination of disdain and embarrassment.

"Their father told the kids that there is no hell! And my daughter says she wants to move away from our 'fundamentalism.' So I guess it's up to me." Her voice is almost ragged with exasperation.

When I ask her how their counseling is going, she indicates with her body language that she's doing her best, but she's not altogether sure. "My grandkids say, 'Our daddy says there is no hell. But Grandma, you make it sound so real!'"

Upon breaking with Grandma, I meet Ray Paulson, a CEF worker since 1980. A short, stout man in a crimson T-shirt with a meticulously styled goatee, Paulson describes himself as an expert in the art of "ballooning." He transforms long blow-up balloons into animals and other objects, and then uses them to spread the word about Jesus to children.

"With ballooning, I was able to get into a New Age church," he says. "I was able to get in there and share the gospel three times!" The church in question, I learn, is a United Methodist Church.

"Afterward the pastor said to me, 'That was a great program!' She didn't know what I was talking about!" he concludes derisively. He continues boasting about how effective he has been in sneaking into enemy territory with his balloons. "With ballooning, I got into a *Catholic* church, an *Episcopal* church," he says with a roll of the eyes and a knowing wink.

Recently, he adds, he has been making real headway in the public schools. "You have to be sneaky about it," he cautions. "You can't say to a kid, 'If you come to the group I'll give you a balloon,' because that's considered a bribe and can get you in trouble. But you can stand outside the school doing balloons, or have kids tell other kids about it.

"I've been in trouble in just about every kind of every which way!" he gloats, puffing out his chest. "But you have to be very careful," he adds with a dark, knowing look. "We have an enemy. And he is real. And he is effective."

A woman with curly brown hair joins the conversation, stressing the importance of the local Good News Clubs. "Washington is the most heathen state in the US," she pronounces. "Only 2 percent of people in this state claim allegiance to any church. And less than 1 percent belong to a Bible-believing church."

How can that be? I ask. I'm from out of state, I tell her, and Seattle appears to be full of church buildings.

"But only 29 percent of people who claim to be Christians have a biblical worldview," she replies, shaking her head disapprovingly. "They are either secular, or belong to some other kind of religion. You know," she confides, "they get into mysticism out here."

Jan Akam calls us back to order for the conclusion of our seminar, which consists mainly of rousing talk. "There are only a few thousand CEF workers, but what we have been able to achieve with such small numbers is truly amazing," she says. "We are having an effect on school children across the nation."

We end the session by closing our eyes in prayer. Akam leads from the front of the room: "God, it's so exciting that we can teach in the public schools . . . and we pray that if we could cultivate enough teachers to teach in every public school in the nation . . . we could transform this country in one generation!"

As the energized group files out the door, I pause to chat with Jan about community relations. I ask her if she worries that her message and methods might upend harmonious relationships within families or communities.

Her response is fast, short, and unequivocal: "The Bible tells us we don't have to worry about anything!"

To SEE THE training in action, I head downstairs to observe a typical Good News Club program with live children.

With red, gold, and green carpeting covering steps and ledges, the underground auditorium is the perfect place for kids—relaxing and yet invigorating. At the CEF table, I meet Karin Fleegal. She isn't leading the seminar today, but I realize that I am familiar with her work. She is the author of the article that I read on "Rice Bowl Communication" in a November/December 2000 publication of CEF. In that article she makes the claim that Asian children find it "difficult . . . to recognize lying as a sin for they do not have moral absolutes." It is one of the pieces of literature that incensed parents at the Loyal Heights Elementary School (see Chapter 2).

The kids troop into the auditorium behind me. There are twenty-six in all, most in the five-to-twelve age bracket. The Good News leader today is Deborah Rowe, the CEF chapter head for King County, Washington. Rowe is a pretty, thirtysomething woman from Orange County with a freckled complexion and dark auburn hair. Her five-week-old daughter, Annika, is strapped to her chest in a cute fuchsia-colored baby sling. With her baby accessory and her colorful shirt printed with hearts, she could not have a more child-friendly appearance.

Rowe has been working with the CEF since age twelve. She is from a religious family. Her dad had an audiovisual business in Orange County, and she and her sister were homeschooled. Her mother had an after-school club in her neighborhood that attracted some of the local school kids.

"At three and a half, I was saved," she tells me. "My mom doubted it and asked God to see a change in my behavior. The next day I woke up and told my two-year-old sister that she was going to hell!" Her mother saw this as a sign of Deborah's future. "My mom said, 'Huh! I guess evangelism is her gift!'"

Rowe opens the meeting with a song for the kids, "Be a Missionary Every Day."

"Be a missionary every day," the children sing. "Tell the world that Jesus is the way."

On the podium, Deborah's demeanor is bold, clear, fun—all primary colors and cheer.

"The Lord is soon returning. There is no time to lose," the song continues.

Deborah holds up the "flipper-flapper." This is a version of the "wordless book," intended to guide children through the stages of religious conversion.

"The dark heart reminds us of sin," Rowe intones, lowering her voice. "Anything you can think or say or do that separates you from God is a sin. We have all sinned. We are born in sin."

Rowe gestures to the child strapped to her chest. "Do you see my baby? Her name is Annika. She's only five weeks old. But guess what? The first thing she did after she was born was *sin*.

"Do you want to know how she sinned? Do you know what's the first thing she did after she was born?" Rowe scrunches up her face in an ugly expression. "*Waah waah waah!* She wanted her own way! Do you know that that's *sin*? She wanted her own way! We are born wanting things our own way, not God's way. And," she looks at the children for emphasis, "*that's a sin*."

As Rowe continues to speak, her voice begins to take on the stylized, hiccupy cadence of an old-school Southern preacher.

"The Bible says we've all sinned. Can you think of another example of sin?"

The kids excitedly raise hands and offer examples of all the bad things their brothers and sisters did. Some confess to having been naughty themselves.

"And what is the punishment for sin?" Rowe asks sharply.

The children make various conjectures.

"The Bible says the punishment for sin is death," Rowe announces firmly, pausing for effect.

"But God made a way so that you don't have to suffer. You can be saved from punishment for your sin. God loves you so much that he sent his son Jesus.

"To be saved from your sins is as easy as ABC," she tells the kids. "A. Admit to God your sins. B. Believe Jesus died on the cross for your sins.

"He's the *only* way to go to heaven," Rowe says, insistent that the kids understand this crucial point. "Did you know that? You can't get to heaven just by doing good things. The way to get to heaven, the only way, is by believing in Jesus. C. Confess that Jesus is the Lord, and you shall be saved from the punishment that your sin deserves. You'll get to go to heaven!"

"Another way to grow to be more like God is to tell your friends about Jesus. Another way is by going to church." But Rowe wants the children to understand that not just any church will do.

"You want to make sure you go to a church that talks about Jesus!"

She wraps up with a question to the kids: "If you go to public school, can you talk about God?"

She answers her own question: "You can! Praying during school is a good way of telling your friends about Jesus!"

After class, Rowe tells me that she is "thrilled" that she can operate now in the public schools. However, she does not intend to send her own kids to public school—she'll homeschool them, or send them to Christian schools.

She adds, in a tone of wonderment, "A lot of the parents don't understand what we do. And yet they allow their children to attend. An atheist mom came to me and said, 'I don't believe in God but I want my child to decide for herself. So here, she can go.' Great! Another guy said, 'My son asked me about God and I don't know anything about God so he can go.' Great!"

Rowe takes evident delight in taking advantage of the parents' ignorance.

I ask her if she ever worries that putting Good News Clubs in public schools might sow disharmony in the communities where they operate.

Rowe sighs. "Yes, there will inevitably be conflict. But that is the price of sharing the gospel. Some people say to me, 'It offends me when you speak about sin.' But I share the gospel in every class. And I show them the place in the Bible where it talks about sin.'"

Rowe and I discuss the fact that there are no other religious groups operating in public schools on anything remotely approaching the scale of the CEF initiatives.

"Mormons can't do it because you need a million-dollar insurance policy to run an after-school program," Rowe says. "And they don't have that."

She shrugs and says with a smile as she walks away, "Thank God they haven't identified children as a mission field!"

IN SYLVIA FOTH'S classroom, I get a summary of Luis Bush's idea that missionaries should pursue the "low-hanging fruit"—the kids, who are young and easy to convert and even easier to keep. As the founder of Kidzana Ministries, Foth has dedicated her life to equipping people around the world to evangelize and disciple children. She is excited by the creation of this radical new vision in the field of missionary work. The title of her seminar comes directly from Luis Bush: "The 4/14 Window: A New Age of Opportunity."

Several dozen attendants sit in the sixty-odd metal folding chairs that have been arranged in rows facing the podium. A group of eight or nine college-age girls wearing jeans, sweatshirts, and thumb rings listen solemnly and take notes. Most of the attendees, however, are somewhat older—women and men in late-middle age. With her wire-rimmed glasses, round face, and a large, easy smile, Foth radiates friendliness and enthusiasm for her cause.

She opens her talk with a history lesson. "From 1980 to 2000 there was a huge church-planting mission thrust," she explains. "It was a huge effort, and hundreds of thousands of churches were planted. Today, there are 3.8 million congregations in the world!"

Summarizing the previous strategy of the "10/40 Window," Foth transitions quickly to the 4/14 Window and explains the thinking behind it.

"People began to realize," says Foth, "that we have so many children at risk. Two-thirds of the world's kids are unreached. They need urgent rescue from Satan."

Children will be "agents of transformation" that God will use in the various spheres of society, Foth says.

"Now," she asserts, "we are watching an explosion of focus on children around the world. There is an absolute growing awareness that if you don't reach children for Christ early, they are set in their beliefs for life."

As her talk progresses, it becomes clear that Foth is mindful of the efficiency of missionary processes. One excellent reason to concentrate on "the harvest field of children ages four to fourteen," as she calls it, is that converting young people requires so much less expenditure than converting older people. "Why not put your efforts there," she asks, "rather than later, at the repair stage?"

Another excellent argument for the 4/14 window is leverage. "When we reach children, it changes their families and communities," Foth explains. "It filters in and starts to challenge the parents.

"Sometimes we don't think about how strategic it is to raise kids who help others to love him," she elaborates, clearly alluding to the effectiveness of child-to-child evangelism. "When we focus on the 4/14 and focus on Jesus-ship, there is the potential for transformation of the entire world."

For Foth, the change in mission focus has been a long time in coming. "I've been watching for mainstream leaders to understand this view of kids and ministry. I've been waiting for them to understand why it's so strategic as part of the obedience plan to reach our world for Jesus." Now that they have come around to her point of view, she says, she is exultant. "The 4/14 Window has taken on new meaning this year in a huge, huge way. It's what mission is about in the next ten to twenty years."

As the seminar winds down, I ask Foth whether targeting children without passing through their parents first could be construed as undermining the integrity of the family.

"You have to believe Jesus is the answer," she says firmly. "If there's any wavering on that, and if you think that maybe Buddhism is okay, you will have problems."

I press her again, asking if she worries about whether parental authority ought to be undermined in spiritual matters.

Foth becomes visibly flustered. Clasping her Bible to her chest, she reiterates a common refrain in this group: "The Bible tells us *we* don't have to worry about anything!"

MY FINAL DAY at Missions Fest brings a video program from the CEF and a meeting with the organization's top man in Washington State, Jeff Kiser. Jan Akam and a number of the other CEF activists with whom I have become acquainted join several dozen other participants.

Kiser is a tall, blue-eyed father of seven, perhaps in his early fifties, who speaks in a somewhat stilted fashion.

In his seminar, "Open Doors, Open Hearts," Kiser describes walking into his first training class for the CEF.

"I said to God, 'Where are the guys?'" he recalls, relating the conversation as matter-of-factly as if he had been asking a passerby for directions.

"And He said to me, 'You're a guy.'"

Kiser turns the program over to the prepared video on the Good News Club. "One of the most fruitful mission fields—the public schools," intones the voice-over. The face of Liberty Counsel president Mathew Staver appears on-screen, professing the legal right of the CEF to operate in the public school environment. "We are in a spiritual battle," he says. "We need to take this opportunity. Otherwise the enemy will take it from us."

A dark-haired pastor appears on the video. "Good News Clubs provide great opportunity to carry out 'The Great Commission.' It dovetails into the philosophy of our church," he says. A second pastor adds, "If we do not reach children at this age, we will not reach them at all."

Kiser puts on another video, this one featuring a cute little girl named Brenna. Brenna tells us how she managed to recruit every single child in her first-grade class to join the Good News Club. At video's end, a dark screen is illuminated with the words of Isaiah: "And a little child shall lead them."

After the video, Kiser stands up in the front of the room and resumes his talk, focusing on practical issues involved in starting up a Good News Club.

Get to know the secretary and the janitorial staff, he advises. "They are the most important people for you to know at the school."

Jan Akam interjects, "A lot of times they want us! This one school superintendent wanted us in! He called and said, 'When are you coming?'"

"We tell the boys and girls that they are missionaries, and that they can invite their friends," Kiser continues. "We tell the boys and girls that they can give out literature if it doesn't disrupt the school day.

"Try not to have Good News Clubs on Mondays and Fridays because kids might have other family obligations and there are more holidays that fall on those days," he advises. "Tuesdays, Wednesdays, and Thursdays are prime days."

Jan Akam breaks in again. "At our Good News Club, we'd sing songs about Jesus real loud, and the kids in the classroom next door could hear us!" Her expression turns contemptuous. "They were doing Indian things, or who knows what."

"At one school open house," says another audience member, "I got a table at the end of the serving line for ice cream. Every kid came through to get their ice cream, and after they came through the line, they saw our booth!"

The longest part of Kiser's discussion, however, revolves around legal strategy. "When it comes to schools seeking to exclude the GNC or limit its scope," he says, "some doors of the public schools are harder to open than others.

"One thing I hear from school administrators is, 'If we let you in, the Satanists will come in,' et cetera," he says. "But other religious groups are not interested in coming into the public schools," he asserts, confirming what I have found in my own research. "That's because kids don't have money," he theorizes. "Other religions don't think children are worth going after."

"If the Boy Scouts can be there, we can be there too!" Akam chimes in.

When legal problems arise, Kiser continues in his matter-of-fact monotone, "we know how to handle those problems by now. The public schools have to be informed. Usually they run it through their legal department and then it's okayed."

His point is blunt. With the Liberty Counsel and the Alliance Defense Fund on its side, the CEF has a huge and essentially free arsenal of legal weaponry at the ready. Public schools that struggle to pay for teachers' salaries, building renovations, and "extras" like music and art simply do not have the resources to undertake what they know will be an expensive and protracted legal battle with the CEF.

IT IS TRUE that there is no one organization running the show on the Christian Right. In the course of my weekend at Missions Fest Seattle, however, I realize that it would be quite wrong to imagine that the nature and direction of its activities are entirely in the hands of the troops who make up the movement.

To be sure, no one on the ground appears to be taking orders; everyone is acting according to his or her own deep-seated impulses and convictions. Yet their behavior on the whole seems as predictable as the tides. It is not controlled, but it is channeled. And those channels are laid down with some forethought and care. Above all, they are the work of the legal strategists who have made possible the most important field of activity in which the CEF is engaged; the mission strategists who have focused so much of the movement on children; and the managers who have brought to the work an impressive degree of discipline.

While schools like Loyal Heights in Seattle experience the arrival of the Good News Club as an unexpected local event driven by idiosyncratic personalities, in fact the CEF moves with industrial precision over great swaths of the country, like a multinational corporation homing in on a new market opportunity.

"The mainstream liberal approach," says Chip Berlet, a prominent researcher of Christian Nationalism, "is to say, 'These people are crazy, why are we paying attention to them?'" He shakes his head. "We need to be paying attention. This movement has tremendous momentum. It was put into motion three decades ago," he says, referring to Falwell's revival of politicized evangelical Christianity with the creation of the Moral Majority, "and it is snowballing."

He's right. It is easy enough to dismiss these new missionaries on account of their extremely narrow notion of what constitutes Christianity. It is easy to disdain them in the same way that they disdain United Methodists, Roman Catholics, and U.S. Episcopalians. It isn't hard for most observers to detect the authoritarian impulses and undercurrents of hostility and aggression that drive them to seek "spiritual" authority over others and embolden them to pit children against children, children against schools, children against their own parents.

But moral outrage does little to change the facts on the ground. We are witnessing the creation of an industrial-scale evangelical conversion machine. New communications technologies and modern organizational concepts are being combined to manufacture religious purity on a global scale. We may find such a project strange or futile. Yet experience also tells us that even the most irrational human projects—everything up to the project of eliminating entire races—can be organized according to rational economic principles.

Experience also tells us that a movement such as this will never succeed in changing the world in quite the way that it imagines, but that it may very well change the world in ways that we would not wish to imagine.

7

Don't Know
Much About History

The Texas Textbook Wars

It's not just about the little kids. Even as the Religious Right aggressively pursues children in public elementary schools, as articulated in the "4/14 strategy," it has also launched a number of aggressive initiatives to reach middle and high school students through their public schools. As it shifts its target to older students, the movement necessarily expands its scope to cover the contents of children's education. For younger children, a colored "wordless book," as presented in an after-school Good News Club, may suffice. With older kids, it's desirable to get the message into the actual lesson plan. Religious activists have set their sights on embedding their religious and political messages into the nation's textbooks, and with the help of the ultra-conservative Texas State Board of Education, they have found an opportunity to do just that. Because Texas is one of the largest textbook markets in the nation, and because publishers are often unwilling to produce variant editions, what Texas decides about textbooks goes for much of the rest of the country.

In order to investigate the efforts by the Religious Right to shape course curricula according to their views, I traveled to Austin, Texas, to sit in on the hearings of the State Board of Education.

Two blocks north of the state capitol building sits a modern structure of stone and glass that houses the Texas Education Agency. On a pleasant afternoon in March 2010, I'm wandering through a large room among a crowd that includes hundreds of reporters, textbook professionals, teachers, and activists, as well as the fifteen members of the Texas State Board of Education who sit in a semi-circular arrangement of high-backed chairs. With a combination of luck and careful positioning, I get a chance to meet three of the people who, perhaps more than any others in the country, will determine the content of the textbooks used by public school students throughout the nation.

Don McLeroy, the chairman of the Texas State Board of Education, is a dentist from the town of Bryan, in the central part of the state, who delivers bold pronouncements from under a broom-handle moustache. "Evolution is hooey," he tells me forcefully after I strike up a conversation with him. I ask him what he believes is the proper role of religion in public education. "We are a Christian nation founded on Christian principles," he replies, stabbing the air with his finger for emphasis. "And our education system should reflect that."

Garrulous and direct, McLeroy gives me an enthusiastic version of what he told Mariah Blake of the *Washington Monthly*: "The way I evaluate history textbooks is, first I see how they cover Christianity and Israel. Then I see how they treat Ronald Reagan—he needs to get credit for saving the world from communism and for the good economy over the last twenty years because he lowered taxes."

Notwithstanding the fact that he chairs the board for one of the largest systems of public education in US history, McLeroy is deeply ambivalent about the very idea of public education. "One of the first real breaches of limited government was public education," McLeroy said in a debate in February 2010.[1]

Although McLeroy fell one vote short of the two-thirds approval he needed to maintain his position as Senate chair, his vision continues to dominate the activist, right-wing bloc that controls the board. McLeroy's replacement as chairman, Gail Lowe, continues in the ideological path blazed by her predecessor. "Our country was founded on religious principles . . . and our students will know that," she says. "I think [the founders] fully intended that our government not separate church and state."[2]

The rightwing bloc that Lowe and McLeroy represent has forced hundreds of changes to the existing standards in order to give a sharply conservative slant to the material taught in public schools across America—a slant that conforms to Christian Nationalist narratives of history. Owing to vagaries of the textbook market—the fact that Texas is the largest single market; the fact that California won't be revising its standards for another several years; and the reluctance of textbook publishers to produce different textbooks for different states—McLeroy and his followers occupy a position of tremendous power. As *New York Times Magazine* journalist Russell Shorto points out, the Texas School Board represents "a single-handed display of arch-conservative political strong-arming" aimed directly at determining the content of public education throughout America.

Cynthia Noland Dunbar, who remained on the board until December 2010, when she declined to run for a second term in order to take a position as assistant professor of Law at the late Jerry Falwell's conservative Christian educational institution, Liberty University, also plays a prominent role in the debates. When I catch up with her during a break in the proceedings, she is wearing a well-cut blue suit paired with high-heeled boots. She is a blunt yet attractive woman in her forties, with dark hair that hangs just past her shoulders. A graduate of Pat Robertson's Regent University School of Law, she is a practicing attorney and a mother of two.

From her book *One Nation Under God: How the Left Is Trying to Erase What Made Us Great*, I have a pretty clear idea where she stands on education policy. The Founding Fathers, she has written, created "an emphatically Christian government." In support of this claim she offers evidence that purports to be rigorously quantitative: "Roughly ninety-four per cent of all quotes of the Founding Fathers at the time of America's Founding were either directly or indirectly from the Bible." Government should therefore be guided by a "biblical litmus test," she maintains. "Any person desiring to govern," she declares, should possess "a sincere knowledge and appreciation for the Word of God in order to rightly govern."[3]

The Word of God, as Dunbar interprets it, has nothing to do with using the power of government to help the less fortunate in society. "The biblical worldview, or the mindset that is based on a clear application of scripture," she writes, "understands that civil government is to have no involvement or jurisdiction over the realm of benevolence to the poor." The Word of God also has little to say in favor of public education. Indeed, Dunbar describes the system of public education variously as a "subtly deceptive tool of perversion," unconstitutional, and even "tyrannical" inasmuch as it threatens the authority of families, granted by God through Scripture, to direct the instruction of their children. "We are throwing them into the enemy's flames even as the children of Israel threw their children to Moloch," she says, referring to parents who send their children to public middle schools.[4]

True to her convictions, Dunbar does not send her own children to the public schools on whose board she sits. Instead she rears them with a combination of homeschooling and stints at Christian schools.

When I ask her why someone who does not believe in public education would wish to serve on a school board, she shoots Abraham Lincoln back at me. "'The philosophy of the schoolroom in one generation will be the philosophy of government in the next,'" she says with a smile. "Why wouldn't I want to be involved in this process? It should be a concern for everyone. Period."

"Now I homeschooled and sent my kids to private schools," she adds, "because I wanted them to be educated within that framework. It was a personal decision, but it didn't mean that I'm unconcerned with the overall impact of public education. At the end of the day, it boils down to the conflicting viewpoint of ideals. Somebody's going to win. Someone's ideals and principles are going to win out."

Dunbar, McLeroy, and their like-minded bloc may control the board with their votes, yet after several days of observing their meetings I get the impression that they aren't the most important people in the room after all. In the course of the hearings, a short, stocky man with dark brown eyes and a brusque manner blogs during the proceedings, and regularly passes notes to members of the controlling faction. He catches them for brief discussions in between votes and on breaks. When votes are cast on the most contentious motions, he ostentatiously walks in front of the board and snaps a photo of the electronic scoreboard showing how each member has voted, as though to remind the members that they are being monitored. He is the representative of Focus on the Family, and his name is Jonathan Saenz.

He agrees to grant me an early-morning interview in his basement-level offices at the Free Market Institute, a think tank affiliated with Focus on the Family, in the shadow of the state capitol building. There I get the distinct impression that Saenz lives in a state of constant anger at perceived persecution for his religious beliefs, and that this is what motivates his work influencing the Texas State Board of Education on its textbook hearings. Groups like the ACLU, Saenz tells me darkly, are happy to promote the activities of pornographers and NAMBLA—the National Association for Man-Boy Love. But "when it comes to Christianity, they are always looking for opportunities to attack."

He motions to a book titled *The War on Christmas*, which has been set out on the desk in anticipation of my visit.

I think of the ubiquity of Christmas everywhere I've lived in America—the trees and lights on the New York avenues, angels and Santa Clauses decorating California's boutiques, crèches festooning Boston's suburban lawns, familiar Christmas carols pouring forth from every radio station—and I can't stop myself from saying, "Forgive me, but isn't the 'War on Christmas' hyperbole?"

At this, Saenz becomes visibly angry with me. "This year, Lowe's stopped calling their trees 'Christmas trees,'" he says vehemently. "They call it the 'Holiday section.' Why have we gone to a place where we don't call it Christmas anymore? There have been many displays where they banned Christmas trees, a nativity scene. . . . Schools are prevented from calling it a 'Christmas Vacation.' They call it 'Winter Vacation.' . . . At what point do we say that it's enough and that we're allowed to call it a war?"

I try to put myself in the mindset of someone for whom every cheery "Happy Holidays!" counts as a bullet in a religious war.

"Well, it is true that at our school they call our winter musical program a 'Winter Sing . . . '" I begin.

"You see?" Saenz exclaims.

"Because we have kids of different faiths at our school . . . " I continue.

Saenz harrumphs.

"So the kids sing a bunch of Christmas songs and throw in a couple Hanukkah songs and maybe one about Eid or Diwali. . . . "

"It is oppressing!" Saenz exclaims.

"Do you feel personally oppressed?" I ask.

"Are you kidding me?" he fumes.

SEVERAL HOURS LATER, at the State Board of Education hearings, I'm invited to consider the question: Who is more important for understanding the philosophical influences on the revolutions of the early modern period, from 1750 or 1850: Thomas Jefferson (1743–1826) or Thomas Aquinas (1225–1274)?

The question comes courtesy of board member Cynthia Dunbar. Each member of the State Board of Education has a chance to propose changes to the Texas Essential Knowledge and Skills, or TEKS in the local parlance. A committee of teachers and experts of various kinds have labored for a year to revise these standards. Now Dunbar has a couple of days to change them, and she has her list ready. This morning she is unhappy with a prepared textbook standard that reads: "The student is expected to . . . explain the impact of Enlightenment ideas from John Locke, Thomas Hobbes, Voltaire, Charles de Montesquieu, Jean-Jacques Rousseau, and Thomas Jefferson on political revolutions from 1750 to the present."

Dunbar proposes to change this to: "Explain the impact of the writings of John Locke, Thomas Hobbes, Voltaire, Charles de Montesquieu, Jean-Jacques Rousseau, Thomas Aquinas, John Calvin, and Sir William Blackstone."

Even without going very deep into the history, Dunbar's proposal is genuinely odd. Board member Bob Craig—one of the three remaining moderate Republicans on the board—points out that the curriculum writers clearly intended for the students to study Enlightenment ideas and Jefferson in this part of the standard, not a mix of Protestant and Catholic theologians. Stranger still, Dunbar wants to replace the Thomas who led one political revolution and influenced other revolutions in the early modern period with another Thomas, a theologian who lived and died five hundred years before the early modern revolutions ever occurred. "This is the first time I have ever heard of the *Summa Theologica* described as a spur to any revolution," historian Susan Jacoby later remarked.[5]

In fact, Dunbar's proposal is not only absurd; it's a kind of antihistory. The main political concern of St. Thomas's thirteenth-century masterpiece was to legitimize the power and glory of the theocratic feudal order—precisely the kind of system that Jefferson and his fellow revolutionaries of the Enlightenment period were rebelling against.

One does not have to spend much time with the comic-book history supplied by Christian Nationalist propagandists like David Barton, however, to understand why St. Thomas Aquinas's shadow suddenly looms over the Texas schoolbooks. The Christian Right now regularly (and speciously) cites the reference to "the laws of Nature and of Nature's God" in the first sentence of the Declaration of Independence as proof that the United States is founded on a Christian version of the theory of Natural Law; and since St. Thomas was one of the earliest Christian theorists of Natural Law, St. Thomas is thus anointed as an honorary Founding Father and early modern revolutionary.

The other Thomas—the one who actually wrote the Declaration of Independence—drops out of Dunbar's history presumably because he was something of a Deist and a representative of the Enlightenment, which of course disappears in Dunbar's revision of the textbook standard. Ironically, many historians believe that the phrase "Nature's God"—which came from Jefferson's pen and which the Christian Right uses as a flagpole for its theocratic conception of American government—came from the philosophers of the Enlightenment, notably Lord Bolingbroke and Alexander Pope, both of whom were vilified as Deists and infidels by representatives of orthodox Christianity in their own time, even as they were read and admired by, among others, the young Jefferson.

In defense of her proposal to replace Jefferson with Aquinas and Calvin, Dunbar says merely that "Thomas Jefferson's ideas were based on these political philosophers." It seems safe to suppose that she has no idea that Jefferson had only harsh words for medieval theologians like Aquinas; or that, with respect to John Calvin, Jefferson wrote to John Adams in 1823: "If ever a man worshipped a false god, he did. . . . It would be more pardonable to believe in no god at all, than to blaspheme him by the atrocious attributes of Calvin."[6]

The question of the two Thomases, in any case, is clearly one that most people would want to refer to historians and genuine specialists in the subject. There is a discussion to be had about America's religious heritage, but the ill-informed demagogues of the Texas School Board are not the ones to lead it. The Texas School Board has little interest in the opinions of experts. As I watch the board confront a series of questions that touch upon economics, sociology, and the history of ideas, over and over again it passes judgment without even considering bringing in a credible authority on the subjects under discussion.

In her proposal, Dunbar seeks to overrule the standards that have emerged from the board's own appointed committee of "expert reviewers." Yet, even that committee of experts can hardly be said to be comprised entirely of credible authorities. The panel ostensibly consists of academics and others with specialized knowledge. But one of the six reviewers, who submitted input separately from the curriculum committees, is David Barton—the former high school math teacher and largely self-educated historian who founded Wallbuilders, the far-right organization whose chief talking point is that church-state separation is a myth. Vice chairman of the Texas GOP from 1998 to 2006, Barton recently launched the Black Robe Regiment, an association of conservative clergy members and "concerned patriots" whose goal is to "restore the American Church in her capacity as the Body of Christ, ambassador for Christ, moral teacher of America and the world, and overseer of all principalities and governing officials, as was rightfully established long ago."

Another one of the "expert reviewers" is Peter Marshall, the founder of Peter Marshall Ministries, an outfit that seeks to "reclaim America for Christ" and is "dedicated to helping to restore America to its Bible-based foundations through preaching, teaching, and writing on America's Christian heritage and on Christian discipleship and revival." Calling for a third "great awakening," Peter Marshall has said, "Jesus calls us to take the offensive," and counsels, "we must recover the zeal of our evangelical forefathers."[7]

The right-wing bloc on the board has obviously heard the criticisms enough times to develop a sensitivity to them, but its response is merely to build more defenses. "I keep hearing the term, 'experts, experts, experts,'" says board member Terri Leo, who doubles as the chairman of the Instruction Committee, which oversees all curriculum, textbooks, and instructional issues. "They say, 'You're ignoring the experts.' Well there are a lot of experts, so to say the experts disagree with the board is just not true. There are plenty of experts who agree with us."

First elected to the State Board of Education in 2002, Leo has worked as a teacher of special education for the visually impaired. She favors an exuberantly feminine wardrobe: frilly blouses, sky-high heels, and elaborately styled hair. Today she is wearing a silvery purple leather jacket over a lavender satin tank top. Her voice gets more petulant and self-righteous as the hearings wear on and her team's triumphs pile up.

Other board members demonstrate a frankly terrifying combination of ignorance and disdain for genuine research. In grappling with a proposal concerning gender and socialization, for instance, right-wing faction member Barbara Cargill boasts that she bases her analysis on the results of a hasty Google search. "This allows students to go into the world of transvestites, transsexuals, and God knows what else!" Cargill concludes. The faction members in fact take pride in opposing the dictates of the learned. As Don McLeroy said, "Someone has to stand up to the experts!"

The reporters working the meeting, not surprisingly, do not have the inclination or the background, nor the responsibility, to make up for what the board patently lacks. A reporter for a national newspaper pulls me aside and asks who Sir William Blackstone is—the relatively conservative legal theorist from the eighteenth century who, as a Tory, would have opposed the American Revolution in the first place and who Dunbar nevertheless wishes to include in the standards. I glance over at the correspondent for Fox News. As he's writing his section, there's a Wikipedia page for Thomas Aquinas up on his computer.

In a matter of minutes, the debate, such as it is, is over. Dunbar's motion has been raised and passed, and Thomas Jefferson's place in the education of public school children drops down a notch. Dunbar forges ahead.

In an amendment to the US Government course, she moves to insert "John Jay" after James Madison in a list of important figures. "I know we tried to promote brevity," she explains, but asserts that "it would seem appropriate to add John Jay, so I move to insert John Jay after James Madison. . . . Part of the rationale is we have Alexander Hamilton and James Madison listed, and John Jay was the third writer of the Federalist Papers," she explains, adding that he also served as the first chief justice for the US Supreme Court. In fact, Jay wrote only five of the eighty-five Federalist Papers.

Mavis Knight, one of the five board members representing the minority on the board, interjects: "And the rationale again is?"

"It just seems to be a glaring oversight," responds Dunbar.

In fact, her motive is transparent to anyone who is familiar with the David Barton school of history. John Jay was an open and enthusiastic promoter of the Christian religion—in marked contrast to a large number of the other leaders of the revolutionary generation—and so the modern conservatives are determined to carve out as large a role as possible for him in the history. The same impulse is at work in another proposed amendment, in which the board majority makes room for an eclectic array of ancillary figures from the revolutionary period: Charles Carroll (a Catholic from Maryland), John Witherspoon (a minister who signed the Declaration of Independence), and Jonathan Trumbull (a painter). What these three marginal figures in the history of the American Revolution have in common, other than being dusted off from high shelves and promoted by the board, is the fact that they were loud defenders of orthodox Christianity. Meanwhile, major players like Thomas Paine and Benjamin Franklin—by any reckoning far more influential figures in the history of the period— barely make it into the standards at all, I suspect because Paine wrote a blisteringly anti-Christian book and Franklin was widely regarded in his own time as a Deist or an "infidel."

Following the majority's successful efforts to Christianize the textbook standards, Democratic board member Mavis Knight makes a proposal related to the treatment of religion in the Constitution. Elected to the State Board of Education in November 2002 and reelected in 2004 and 2008, Knight has thirty years of volunteer service working with civic and education organizations. She is active in her United Methodist church, where she teaches Sunday school. One of two African Americans on the board, she has a penchant for colorful brimmed hats, and delivers her contributions to the debate with a dry sense of humor.

"I'd like to add to the list of expectations the student understands," she says. "Examine the reasons the Founding Fathers protected religious freedom in America by barring government from promoting or favoring any particular religion over all others."

The motion is seconded by fellow Democrat Mary Helen Berlanga, an attorney and the senior member of the board, having first been elected to serve in 1982.

In support of her proposal, Knight explains, "We know that religion was one of the major influences, but not the only influence in the founding of our country. We need students to understand the importance that the Founding Fathers placed on the wall of separation between church and state." Perhaps seeking to sway the ultrareligious members of the board, she adds diplomatically, "I found it interesting that this concept was often credited in the original form to the English political philosopher John Locke, and the phrase 'separation of Church and State' can be traced . . . to the Danbury Baptists."

Knight here is alluding to the famous letter from Thomas Jefferson to the Baptists of Danbury, Connecticut, a letter subsequently cited in crucial Supreme Court decisions, in which America's third president writes: "I contemplate with sovereign reverence that act of the whole American people which declared that their legislature should 'make no law respecting an establishment of religion, or prohibiting the free exercise thereof,' thus building a wall of separation between Church & State."[8]

Dunbar, of course, has little use for Jefferson. She opposes Knight's proposal with a lengthy and hard-to-follow speech:

We get into a whole constitutional debate when we start addressing these issues that are too complex to even discuss, let alone put a preconceived ideology into the textbooks for these children. To have a concept that the Founding Fathers had, there's no way. This [Knight's amendment] is not an accurate perception. It is certainly not something that the Founding Fathers would have presented as far as barring, it was actually a jurisdictional concept.

Dunbar continues in this vein for some time, though her basic point is the simple one that she shares with the more blunt-spoken fellow board member David Bradley, who told the *New York Times* on March 12, 2010: "I reject the notion by the Left of a constitutional separation of church and state. I have a thousand dollars for the charity of your choice if you can find it in the Constitution."

The conservative bloc's views follow directly from David Barton's *The Myth of Separation*, in which the author strings together enough out-of-context quotes and specious inferences to give the impression that America's founders never intended to separate church and state. As Patrick Burkhart, an associate professor of communication at Texas A&M University notes, Barton's book "looms over the social studies standards." In muscling in Barton's ideas, the board conservatives depend on Dunbar, who has the ability to toss around enough intellectual jargon to convey the impression that she is a learned authority on constitutional law. In fact, most of her arguments are cribbed directly from Barton's books, and her comments border on the unintelligible.

David Barton has spent the last fifteen years bringing his program about America's "Christian heritage" to churches across the country. After critics pointed out that a number of the Bible-thumping quotes he attributed to Founding Fathers turned out to be false, Barton was forced to acknowledge that at least twelve of them were unsourced or outright false. But that hasn't stopped him from spreading his myths and rewriting the history of the early revolutionary period.

Barton is denounced by numerous academics in the field. Professor Mark Lilla, a professor of Ideas at Columbia University, derided Barton's "schlock history" in the *New York Times*, decrying Barton's use of "selective quotations out of context to suggest that the framers were inspired believers who thought they were founding a Christian nation."

Unfortunately, there are only a handful of academic historians at the proceedings. One is Professor Steven K. Green, director of Willamette's Center for Religion, Law, and Democracy, who made the trip to Texas to remind the board that "the Supreme Court has forbidden public schools from 'seeking to impress upon students the importance of particular religious values through the curriculum.'" Like most of the other hundred-plus outsiders who signed up for a chance to offer their opinion on the hearings, he speaks for his allocated three minutes and is duly ignored by the board. When the board had previously sought to chip away at the teaching of evolution, scientists organized a substantial presence in the debates—limiting, though not preventing, damage to the teaching of science. In the field of history, however, the academic community appears to be disorganized or uninterested. Aside from Green and perhaps a couple of others, there is no substantial representation of historians present.

Steven Schafersman, a geologist and president of Texas Citizens for Science, an advocacy group that opposes teaching creationism as science in the public schools, attempts to pinch hit for the missing historians. The United States, he tells the board during his three minutes, was "founded as a secular government by individuals who based their philosophies on European Enlightenment principles. Our country was founded to be a secular, inclusive country . . . we should be teaching our students about the founding documents of our country, not trying to force things that are not true."

Ken Mercer, speaking up for the board majority, makes an effort to rebut Schafersman by referring to the "actual minutes of 1789," notwithstanding that the constitutional convention took place in 1787, and there were no "minutes"—although James Madison, perhaps the greatest early supporter of the separation of church and state, did take a few notes.

"You are believing something you read from David Barton," says Schafersman. Within a matter of minutes, however, the grand debate is over.

Not surprisingly, Knight's motion to teach students about the separation of church and state fails. It is voted down, 10-5, on a party-line vote.

Jonathan Saenz stands up in view of the board, walks to the front of the room, and snaps a few photos of the votes recorded on the electronic scoreboard.

AS THE BOARD of Education meeting progresses, outside the building various political groups take turns holding forth, like acts in a motley circus. Student protesters in school-bus-yellow shirts gather at the building's front steps with bullhorns and hand-painted placards, proclaiming their demands for a "smarter" and depoliticized board. Civil rights organizations demand minority representation in the TEKS; a veterans' group hands out fact sheets about their important historical role; a parade of conservative activists give God-and-country speeches. There is even a spat between state officials and Fox News, which had sent a crew to report on the proceedings.

Mid-morning, at a press conference held by the Free Market Foundation, approximately a dozen politicians, citizens, Tea Party members, and others gather to promote the teaching of "American exceptionalism," to oppose "the war on Christmas," and to celebrate other items on the list of right-wing talking points. Wearing a red sweater, conservative board member Ken Mercer stands with the group, as does Jonathan Saenz. "The worst day in America beats the best day in any other country," says Jason Moore, a tall, bearded Tea Party member from Odessa, Texas. Standing to my right, a member of the Fox News team looks over at me and rolls his eyes.

"American exceptionalism" is a term I keep hearing throughout the proceedings. In most history books, that term is used to mean that America is qualitatively different from other nations owing to its particular history and ideology. But among the Texas School Board majority it means not that we are different but that we are unfailingly superior. We're number one! The conservatives on the board are clearly determined to inculcate high school students with the idea that America is just great, all the time and in every way. My mother always told me that part of being great is knowing when you're wrong. But in their eyes, America can do no wrong, and never has—other than empower America-hating liberals and the undeserving poor, that is. The board's faith in American exceptionalism, it is clear, is less a matter of patriotism than religion. We are great because we started with the right religion; and we will remain great as long as we stay on God's side.

Social studies curricula have been an arena of political dispute since 1994, when Lynne Cheney, wife of former vice president Dick Cheney and then chairperson for the National Endowment for the Humanities, attacked a not-yet-released history standard, written by historians at the University of California, Los Angeles, for "left-wing bias" and "political correctness." Among her criticisms, she claimed the standards overemphasized McCarthyism, the Ku Klux Klan, and Harriet Tubman while failing to reference Robert E. Lee, Paul Revere, Thomas Edison, or the Wright brothers. The document, she said, presented a "warped and distorted version of the American past in which it becomes a story of oppression and failure."

The State Board of Education in Texas is continuing in Cheney's footsteps by seeking to present a triumphant narrative of American history, vigorously conflating religion with patriotism. In order to promote the idea that America is blessedly exceptional, of course, it is necessary to eliminate from the history any facts that might suggest that America is sometimes less than great. So, for example, in order to offset the negative image associated with Joseph McCarthy's anticommunist witch hunts in the 1950s, McLeroy proposes a requirement that students learn about "communist infiltration in the U.S. government" during the Cold War. McLeroy has in fact gone on record with his absurd view that new evidence has "vindicated" McCarthy.

The fact that government-orchestrated propaganda was a factor in the United States' entry into World War I also does not sit well with the board's conservative faction. So the reference to propaganda is voted out. Patricia Hardy—one of the few moderate Republicans on the board and the one with the most comprehensive educational credentials, having taught high school history and world geography for over thirty years—accuses her colleagues of "rewriting history" on this and other matters, but the majority ignores her concern. The majority also decides that US imperialism in the late-nineteenth and early-twentieth centuries wasn't really "imperialism," so they change the word to "expansionism." The United States being exceptional, the majority argues, its policies should not be confused with the similar policies of European countries at the time.

THE BOARD ALSO intends to make America look exceptional by hammering into students' minds the economic ideology that in their view has made America great: namely, the "free enterprise system." The conservatives on the board do not like the word "capitalism." "Capitalism" is a negative term used by "liberal professors in academia," explains Leo. "You know . . . 'capitalist pig!'" she says, waving her hand vaguely. And so Ken Mercer proposes to replace references to capitalism with "the free enterprise system."

At this, the typically stolid Hardy becomes impassioned.

"Please do not do this. I plead you to leave this alone," she begs. "A lot of blood, sweat and tears went into that, and I think this body is just getting a little too specific on certain things." Hardy notes that the scholar who recommended that the terms "capitalism" and "free market" be used in the standards in this context, a professor at Texas A&M University, is "a good Republican . . . not some kind of crazy liberal."

But Terri Leo stands firm in support of Mercer. "I do think words mean things. . . . I see no reason, frankly, to compromise with liberal professors from academia," she reiterates. "Whoever rules the word rules the world . . . Words are important and that's why we wrestle with these words, they do mean something."

Mercer's proposal passes, and the good Republican professor from Texas A&M is overruled.

The conservatives on the board want to make clear that the free enterprise system that makes America great has nothing to do with a universal concern for public policy and the common good—a concern they believe carries the dreaded taint of socialism. On a list of characteristics of good citizenship for grades 1 through 3, the board majority decides to expunge references to "justice" and "responsibility for the common good."

The board's determination to frame American exceptionalism through the promotion of a particular economic ideology reaches a humorous climax in a set of proposed changes offered by board member Barbara Cargill. According to her, students should now be expected to "explain three pro-free-market factors contributing to European technological progress during the rise and decline of the Medieval system." They should also "explain three pro-free-market factors contributing to the success of Europe's Commercial Revolution," and "explain three benefits in the Industrial Revolution." Cargill does not mention which three factors she has in mind in any of these instances; she simply seems to express her desire to impress upon students her conviction that "pro-free-market factors" are always a good thing.

Board member Pat Hardy asks the obvious question: "Would 'pro-free-market factors' as we understand them today have existed in a feudal system in the Middle Ages?"

Indeed, Cargill's standards emerge out of a near-total vacuum of historical knowledge. Cargill seems to imagine that the Middle Ages were just a colorful setting for the eternal struggle between left-wing antimarket Democrats and righteous free-market Republicans. The majority can't quite muster the votes for this new, free-market view of the feudal system, though it passes the other parts of Cargill's proposal.

Another part of making America great involves eliminating all forms of the word "democratic," which in the majority's view might suggest a link between American history and the political party where all of America's haters end up, namely, the Democratic Party. Thus, at

Dunbar's insistence, the board replaces "democratic" and "representative democracy" with "constitutional republic," and "democratic societies" with "societies with representative government."

FOR THE 2008–2009 school year, 47.9 percent of Texas public school children were of Hispanic descent, according to the Texas Education Association. That proportion, which is projected to rise in the coming years, supplies a crucial subtext for much of what is happening on the Texas State Board of Education. The ten-member Republican majority on the board contains no Hispanics, and the proposals of the two Democratic Hispanics on the board, Berlanga and Rick Agosto, are consistently overruled.

"This is all about white anxiety," Paul Henley of the Texas State Teachers's Association tells me over brisket sandwiches at Scholz's Garten, a neighborhood beer hall several blocks away from the Texas Education Agency building. "Fundamentally what they are about is, 'white good, nonwhite bad.'"

A compact man around forty with an impish sense of humor, Henley attends the hearings in order to understand what material the state's teachers will be expected to incorporate into their curricula. The hearings ought to be about meeting children's educational needs, he says, but increasingly they are about race.

"When they show a mural of the Founding Fathers signing the Declaration of Independence, all those guys are white," he says. "Then you have a picture of Martin Luther King off to the side somewhere, so they can say, 'Forget about that, we covered it already.' Look at them," he gestures toward several board members sitting a few tables from us. "They believe that we are a white nation, founded on white, Christian principles."

Back at the hearings, the whitewashing of American history continues. At the behest of board conservatives, the word "slavery" is removed from the standards, replaced by the awkwardly euphemistic term, "Atlantic triangular trade." Students are also required to "learn about the unintended consequences" of affirmative action.

A requirement that American history students learn about conservative icons and heroes such as the Heritage Foundation, the Moral Majority, and Phyllis Schlafly swiftly passes. No similar standard requiring students to learn about liberal organizations or individuals is even introduced.

In the course of the afternoon, Berlanga introduces her proposals, many of which involve the inclusion in the standards of historic figures of African American or Hispanic descent. But each one is viewed with suspicion by the board, and any hint of a left-wing slant brings swift rejection. Dolores Huerta, cofounder of the United Farm-workers Union, for example, is tossed from a grade 3 list of "historical figures who have exemplified good citizenship" because majority members disapprove of her socialist leaning.

The board majority also nixes Oscar Romero, a prominent Roman Catholic archbishop notable for his concern for the poor, who was assassinated in 1980 by right-wing forces in El Salvador. Romero's name had been included in a world history standard about leaders who led resistance to political oppression. One of the board conservatives argues that Romero doesn't belong because "he didn't have his own movie." When someone points out that a film based on the archbishop's life was released in 1989, the board member acknowledges his mistake, but Romero is out in any case.

Berlanga moves to introduce Medal of Honor recipients of Hispanic and African-American origin into one of the standards. McLeroy demurs. "We don't know what happened to them after," he says, questioning whether they are "appropriate role models." It is hard to imagine him asking a similar question about white Medal of Honor recipients.

McLeroy proposes to strike the words "racial, ethnic, gender, and religious groups" in a section on different groups' contributions to American society, saying, "It's redundant and should read, 'Explain actions by people taken to expand opportunities.'"

"You are trying to delete groups," Knight objects.

"It's redundant," McLeroy repeats.

"It is not redundant for me," says Knight, "because the racial and ethnic and gender groups that you are trying to strike out overcame great obstacles to make great contributions to American society. To me, you are sanitizing these groups. So we talk about rewriting history. This board is rewriting history as far as I'm concerned. They want to sanitize anything that may reflect negatively on our country. . . . We are painting a false picture of America. You would have us think that we are in some kind of utopia that does not exist."

Berlanga agrees: "It is painful to sit here in this board meeting and hear people say America is so great to minorities. You are not a minority in this country! We have come a long way because of groups that have fought for our rights."

McLeroy's motion passes.

Board conservatives consistently claim to be resisting pressure to give in to "quotas" and to divide people by their ethnicity or race. But there is one category of activity where they insist on racial division: crime. The board requires that students be taught about crime rates by ethnicity.

Yet board conservatives seem to bristle at the suggestion that there might be racism at play. "I grew up during the Civil Rights times in Memphis, and one of my [presumably black] best friends and I could not go places or we might not be served," reminisces Barbara Cargill. "But we have come a long way. One of my good friends adopted a young black man! She was in the movie, *The Blind Side*. That was my friend!"

Knight offers a calm but frustrated response to this combination of racial condescension and name-dropping: "Since others have been personal, I'm going to get personal. I regret that no member of the board who is not African American has not lived sixty-four years in this country and knows how African Americans are still treated today. Yes we have overcome. But we have not arrived."

The race wars reach a climax when Cargill moves to drop the artist Santa Barraza from a list of Texas artists in the grade 7 Texas history course. Barraza, she claims, once produced an "inappropriate" painting. At this, a dozen reporters simultaneously Google "Barraza." They learn that her work was featured at the state mansion under George W. Bush. Eventually the journalists unearth a blue-toned, somewhat surrealist painting that includes a female torso. "Is this what she's talking about?" one Fox producer says to another.

Berlanga asks, "Should the board now censor Michelangelo because of the nudes in some of his artwork?"

Cargill proposes to replace this "controversial" artist with Tex Avery, an Oscar-winning animator and voice actor who is perhaps most famous as the voice of Frito-Lay's ethnically stereotyped mascot, the Frito Bandito.

The amendments pass. The artist who dared to paint female breasts is out; the voice behind the Frito Bandito is in.

Following Avery's ascension, McLeroy proposes the inclusion of three new white historic figures, including Lawrence Sullivan Ross, a nineteenth-century Texas governor, Confederate general, and college president. "Every Aggie knows him. He's a fine gentleman," McLeroy explains.

Berlanga's frustration finally boils over. Gathering up her papers, she says, "I've done all I can do today, folks. I've listened, tried to work with you, given you names, come back with new amendments to satisfy everyone—and nothing works. You complained about the lists (of Hispanic figures) being too long. . . . And now it looks like you're able to put in the names of all these people, God knows who they are. So I've had it . . . I'm leaving for the evening. Everyone can go ahead and remove the Tejanos who died at the Alamo and we can all pretend that we live in white America and Hispanics don't exist." For the first time in her twenty-eight years of service on the board, Berlanga walks out of the hearings.

WHEN THE SESSION wraps up several hours later, I head out the door with two new acquaintances. With their neat blonde hairstyles and preppy outfits, Lisa and Courtney are schoolteachers and mutual friends from the Dallas-Ft. Worth area. They looked forward to this trip as an opportunity to get a handle on the standards they will be expected to teach their classes and reflect on their roles as educators.

Courtney has a look of visible disgust on her face. "Do they have any idea what a nightmare they are creating for us teachers?" she says, shaking her head. "All those names and facts they added. . . . The standards are too long already. There's barely enough time to teach existing material. Not only do we have to teach all that, but students are tested on it. It's the law!"

Lisa agrees with her friend. "This was all about ego and politics." She scowls. "It should have been about the kids."

I can't help but agree with them. In three days of hearings about textbook standards, I have heard little or nothing about the effectiveness of teaching tools, children's intellectual development, or any of the other issues that preoccupy those who are actually in the business of education. Instead, the debates were about adult anxieties, politics, and ego.

I remember one of the few comments made by Lawrence Allen, the only African-American man on the board and perhaps its most taciturn member. In a rare expressive moment, he had wondered aloud whether the board really knew how to put together a curriculum standards document. He questioned whether "we ought to do a workshop before we go through this process again." It strikes me that a workshop would not begin to address the troublesome issues on display at the State Board of Education hearings.

Whatever the textbook standards that emerge from those hearings, the process will have amounted to a disservice to education, perhaps even a kind of assault on it. The choice is not, as Dunbar seems to think, between one set of ideals and another; it is between educating children and depriving them of education.

BACK IN THE hotel, I tune in to Fox News. Jonathan Saenz appears as a featured guest. He's talking about some of the "outrageous changes" in the textbooks standards demanded by "the liberal left-wing activists."

"We've got some names here," the Fox reporter says. "Who are these people?"

Saenz identifies the pictures on the screen: Kathy Miller, president of the Texas Freedom Network (TFN), an Austin-based research and advocacy group committed to religious neutrality in public education; noted law professor Steven K. Green of Willamette University; and Steven Schafersman, founder of Texas Citizens for Science—all people whose minutes-long testimonials had been entirely ignored by the Board.

"Well, the folks you mention are kind of the group of trouble-makers around this area," says Saenz. "Whether it's social studies, whether it's the evolution battle that took place last year, or Bible curriculum elective courses, they want to attack every aspect of public school. They want to indoctrinate, they want to saturate, and really infiltrate public education and put their liberal ideology. One of the ways you do that is to take out important historical figures that make America great. That's what they're trying to do and that's what they are supporting. Not only that, they're going after Christianity and religion specifically to try to get those things out."

"Man, that is going to be quite a meeting down in Texas," the Fox reporter says.

I pick up the remote control and switch over to the Cartoon Network. I've spent the day watching the board make up the facts about history. I don't need to watch Fox News making up the facts about the board.

8

BIBLE "LITERACY" WARS

ALTHOUGH MANY OF the initiatives by Christian Nationalists to insert religion into public education operate by subterfuge, in some instances the pretenses are so transparent that they hardly count as false. Consider, for example, the "Bible Literacy" class offered as a high school elective by the National Council on Bible Curriculum in Public Schools (NCBCPS). The class, says the NCBCPS, claims to examine the Bible as a work of literature and a historical artifact. But it's hard to see how such a claim could be taken seriously, given what follows in the NCBCPS's self-description. The Constitution, it says, "does not require complete separation of Church and State." "There has been a great social regression since the Bible was removed from our schools," it continues, and so presumably it is time to bring the religion of the Bible back to the classroom.[1]

The National Council on Bible Curriculum in Public Schools was founded by Elizabeth Ridenour, a former paralegal, in 1993. Its mission is, in her words, to "impact our culture, to deal with the moral crises in our society, and reclaim our families and children." The group touts itself as a "conservative Christian organization" and features video endorsements from many of the leading lights of the

Religious Right, including D. James Kennedy of Coral Ridge Ministries and Bill Bright of Campus Crusade for Christ. Not surprisingly, the program is a thinly disguised effort to proselytize.

How that program landed on the ground in Odessa, Texas, is instructive. It shows that even in America's most pious provinces, the introduction of sectarian religious agendas in public schools sets neighbor against neighbor, even Christian against Christian. It divides communities and sways political and professional fortunes. It puts members of religious minorities in particular peril, but its pernicious effects even extend to those who identify with the religion it claims to serve.

MANY RESIDENTS OF West Texas's oil-rich Permian Basin wear their religion with pride. When they say they are the "Buckle of the Bible Belt," they mean it as a boast. The city of Odessa, made famous by a legendary high school football team, the Permian Panthers, is a headquarters for oil-production activities. Former president George Bush senior lived there for several years with his growing family, and the town's fortunes wax and wane with the oil markets.

With 100,000 inhabitants, Odessa's city streets are lined with fast food chains, national franchises, and superstores, but there is no real town center. What geography fails to deliver, faith apparently supplies. Almost everyone in the community comes together in one house of worship or another. For many Odessans church offers fellowship and unity, a core of values, and a place to ponder life's greater purpose.

Yet life in Odessa is more complicated than one might guess from a drive along its endless stretch of commercial centers and housing sprawl. The area prides itself on its religious observance; but it also has one of the highest teen pregnancy rates in the nation.[2] Almost every other street seems to feature a billboard proclaiming the community's faith in the Lord Jesus Christ, and yet the town is not free from religious conflict and division. Until recently, the Ector County School District was still grappling with a desegregation order filed by the US District Court in 1982, and conflicts over sex education and sectarian prayers at school convocations had already consumed many hours of the school board's time.

The religious life of Odessa became a lot more complicated in December 2005, when the school board approved an elective course called "The Bible in History and Literature," created by the National Council on Bible Curriculum in Public Schools. In the following school year, at the request of seven families, the ACLU filed a lawsuit opposing the program.

For Luther Vernon "Butch" Foreman III, a member of the board of Odessa's Ector County School District at the time, the kerfuffle over the Bible literacy program seemed at first to be a non-event. "I don't care what the ACLU does," he scoffed to a fellow board member. "They can kiss my ass!"

Butch and his wife, Jona, are active in their Southern Baptist church, where Butch has served as a deacon. With his sunbeaten complexion, curious blue eyes, and pronounced widow's peak, Butch is a handsome and amiable man, and well liked in the community. He thought that he knew Odessa well, and that Odessa knew him. He had no idea that the conflict over the Bible curriculum would soon dominate the school board's activities, capture national headlines, open bitter fissures across town, and scramble political futures— including his own.

LORI WHITE CUTS a stylish figure in white jeans and a colorful top, auburn hair framing her face in a short, feathered style. An Odessa native, she has served on the Health Committee at Odessa High School. She joined the committee, she says, because she was dismayed over the district's high rates of sexually transmitted disease and out-of-wedlock pregnancies. A challenging pregnancy of her own—she suffered serious health complications while delivering her son—reinforced her belief in the importance of comprehensive reproductive health care. Health education, she feels, is especially necessary for "dispelling all the myths out there . . . like the one that you can't get pregnant on the rhythm method, or you can't get pregnant if you do it in a swimming pool."

When White first heard about the new class sponsored by the National Council on Bible Curriculum in Public Schools, she thought it sounded like a great idea. White was raised in the Southern Baptist tradition, and she and her husband, a lawyer, are both practicing Christians. Faith is important, they believe, and they would like their son to achieve "religious literacy" by learning about a variety of faiths from a neutral standpoint. A former elementary school teacher who enjoys visiting museums in her spare time, White was especially excited to hear that this curriculum promised to explore literary forms used in the Bible, as well as "its influence on history, law, American life and culture," "Biblical Art," and other such meaty subjects.[3]

When White heard that School Board president Randy Rives was a moving force behind the NCBCPS program, her attitude shifted from enthusiasm to concern. She knew that Rives, a rock-ribbed conservative, had recently attempted to disband the health committee because he disfavored any health education program that did not take an abstinence-until-marriage approach. White saw this as an attempt by Rives to impose his own religious beliefs on others.

"Once you let people take over one aspect of your life," she says, "you have given up your freedoms."

When she learned more details about the Bible curriculum's methods of instruction, concern turned to outrage. "It's a curriculum that proselytizes," White says. "The class is almost entirely devotional in nature." It probably didn't help that the instructor was a former Baptist missionary.

White saw the NCBCPS as an instance of right-wing and sectarian politics masquerading as education. "I believe strongly that this violates the separation of church and state," she says. "We should be educating kids in the public schools, not indoctrinating them in one particular creed. Here in Odessa, we have a church on every corner. That type of proselytizing doesn't belong in a public school setting."

White was galled by Rives's characterization of the program as something that was endorsed by the majority of parents. "Maybe he thought that's what the majority of the community would want, but really it's not," she says. "Even though people feel strongly about religion—I'm a Baptist myself—we don't want people putting it in the public schools."

White spoke with other parents who were equally concerned about the NCBCPS, and a group of eight eventually joined with the ACLU in filing a lawsuit, on May 16, 2007, against the Ector County School Board. Partnering in the lawsuit were the People for the American Way Foundation and the law firm of Jenner and Block.

In terms of faith and background, the plaintiffs were a diverse group: in addition to White, a Baptist, there were a Presbyterian couple, two Catholics, and several self-described "free-thinkers," including one whose background is partly Jewish. In the months that followed, nearly all of the plaintiffs came under tremendous pressure, suffering ruptured friendships, social ostracism, and career setbacks. Only one of the plaintiffs, however, received multiple death threats. That distinction was reserved for the one who was identified as a Jew.

ELIZABETH RIDENOUR, THE story goes, was a North Carolina real estate broker and paralegal who once believed that teaching the Bible in public schools was a violation of the principle of church-state separation. But then, some new friends convinced her that church-state separation is a myth propagated by liberals and the ACLU.

Soon after, Elizabeth heard from God himself.

"'I have something important I want you to do,' He said," she reported in a 1998 issue of the *Believer's Voice of Victory*.

"It was easy to imagine God speaking to [other, more important people] and saying He had an important assignment for them," she reported.

"But me?" She laughed. "Me?"

Elizabeth held something called "intercessory prayer meetings," or prayer groups with like-minded folks. With a growing desire to move her Christian convictions into public education, she got involved with "Christian students' rights," including an organization that promotes holding evangelical Christian religious services on public school campuses.

Elizabeth says she wanted to "find out what had happened since the Supreme Court had tried to separate God from the educational system."

"I discovered that since 1963, when the Bible was removed from public schools, the United States has become the world's leader in violent crime, divorce, illegal drug use, and illiteracy," Elizabeth says, practically quoting David Barton, who is in fact on her board of directors. "After the Bible was removed from public schools, SAT scores dropped for nineteen consecutive years."

Elizabeth began to wonder if it was possible to get the Bible back in public schools. Then God spoke to Elizabeth again, apparently telling her to seek aid from a variety of right-wing legal organizations, including the American Center for Law and Justice and the American Family Association (AFA), whose home page states "AFA wants to reach the nations [sic] public schools with the word of God!"[4] She also formed a group called the North Carolina Council on Bible Curriculum in Public Schools.

"I know the Christian community stood silently by when the Bible left our school system in 1963," said Elizabeth, who clearly has a tight definition of who qualifies as a "Christian." "The only way to approach the problem was to get the message of truth out to the public and pray that this time Christians would use their voices."

Contrary to Ridenour's supposition, the Bible has never been left out of school. Courts have made clear that, while teaching the Bible as a sacred text is not permissible according to the Constitution, studying it as literature or history is just fine.

But Ridenour's story conforms to the narrative of paranoia regarding religion and public education that is fashionable among

Christian Nationalists. Affiliated with Regents University, the conservative evangelical institution founded by Pat Robertson in 1978, Ridenour has also been a member of the powerful conservative group, Council on National Policy. NCBCPS's board is made up of prominent social conservatives, including senators, judges, and attorneys affiliated with the Alliance Defense Fund and similar legal entities. Phyllis Schlafly offers an endorsement; and Chuck Norris is its spokesperson.

The NCBCPS asserts that its curriculum has been voted into 563 school districts in 38 states, although the group does not release the list of schools to the public, and some independent experts dispute those claims. What is clear, however, is that the curriculum is being used as a political tool, and is loudly supported by conservative politicians in dozens of states, including Colorado, Oklahoma, Georgia, and Tennessee, which introduce and promote laws mandating its presence in public school systems.

The NCBCPS links to an advisory board of "Bible Scholars," presumably to confer academic or scholarly legitimacy. The board, cited by NCBCPS as "biblescholars.org," is an Austin, Texas–based organization that is "Dedicated to Biblical research and education." The founder and CEO of Bible Scholars is Dr. Roy B. Blizzard Jr., a PhD in Hebrew Studies from the University of Texas who has spent much of his career participating in excavations at ancient sites in the Middle East.

Blizzard's Bible Scholars outfit is stridently sectarian. When a visitor to Blizzard's website poses a question pertaining to the Jehovah's Witness faith, Blizzard writes, "You might as well go out and beat your head against the wall rather than trying to debate with a Jehovah [sic] Witness."

But surprisingly, when I get Dr. Blizzard on the phone and ask him what he thinks of the NCBCPS curriculum, he exclaims, "When they first sent it to me, it was just awful!" Asserting that one can't correctly interpret the Bible without being able to read and contextualize ancient Hebrew, he says he has doubts that a program such as the NCBCPS could offer students a true understanding of the ancient scriptures.

Were the problems with the NCBCPS eventually corrected, I ask Blizzard?

"I was able to correct some of the worst problems," the program's expert scholar says doubtfully, "but it is still full of errors." Independent observers are even more critical of the program. In fact, they overwhelmingly agree that the Bible curriculum is sectarian to its core. Mark A. Chancey, professor of Biblical Studies at Southern Methodist University, released a study of the curriculum in 2005 through the Texas Freedom Network (TFN). "Not only does [the NCBCPS] treat the Bible as an inspired book and as literal history," he wrote, "it implies that the Bible is completely accurate in its historical claims, claims that this accuracy is confirmed by archaeology and the hard sciences, and argues that the words of the biblical books have been transmitted from the original authors to the present day without error or change." "Distinctively sectarian claims," he found, permeated the classrooms. The NCBCPS course, he concluded, represents "an attempt to promote particular religious views about the Bible, namely those of some conservative Protestants."[5]

Citing factual errors, fringe scholarship, and plagiarism, Chancey writes, "With its promotion of a fundamentalist Protestant understanding of the Bible and a revisionist history of the United States as a distinctively (Protestant) Christian nation, its growing use reflects the increasing influence of Christian Americanist ideology as well as the need for greater involvement of religious studies scholars in the issue of religion and public education."

State education officials' endorsement of the program, the Texas Freedom Network adds, "recklessly encourag[es] school districts to adopt a curriculum that will put those districts and their taxpayers in legal jeopardy and threaten the religious freedom of families to pass on their own faith beliefs to their children." The introduction of such programs, the TFN concludes, "betray[s] the faith families place in public schools by misusing Bible courses to promote their own narrow religious beliefs over all others."[6]

A quick perusal of the NCBCPS's own materials makes it clear that teaching the Bible from a secular perspective was never their intention. "It's coming back . . . and it's our constitutional right!" screams the website testimonial of the group's president, Elizabeth Ridenour. Promotional videos from Charlie Daniels, D. James Kennedy, Bill Bright, and others drive home the notion that America's founding fathers were Bible-thumping Christians.

"The Bible was the foundation and blueprint for our Constitution, Declaration of Independence, our educational system, and our entire history until the last 20 to 30 years," Ridenour declares. She also asserts that "94 percent of the documents that went into the Founding era [which it describes as the period from 1760 to 1805] were based on the Bible, and of that 34 percent of the contents were direct quotations from the Bible." This bizarre and confused claim is, of course, nearly identical to one that Texas State Board of Education member Cynthia Dunbar cites in her book. Its ultimate source is David Barton.

Following Barton's lead, the NCBCPS website prominently features a quote from Thomas Jefferson that no one has ever discovered in any of Jefferson's writings. Even Barton, who includes the same quote in his books and on his website, has felt compelled to describe its source as "unconfirmed."

History could have predicted the conflict that would ensue over such an overtly sectarian outfit operating in a public school. But nobody predicted the extent to which the resulting lawsuit would roil this devout West Texas community—angering Christians on both sides of the dispute.

KAREN AND DOUG Hildebrand have lived for many years in an Odessa neighborhood that was built during the oil-boom years. Identically spaced lots boast solid, comfortable, single-family homes.

Their house is neatly tended, with a religious statuette on the lawn and a collection of decorative crosses in the foyer. A table in the dining room is adorned with hand-blown glass sculptures containing positive exhortations to "Believe!" and "Celebrate!"

Karen, a petite blonde mother of three, is the CEO of Permian Basin Planned Parenthood. Working in women's health care is an extension of her Presbyterian faith, "the hands-and-feet work of serving the Lord," as she describes it. "Ector County has one of the highest teen pregnancy rates in the country," she reminds me. "These girls get no good information on how to protect themselves from pregnancy and disease. We offer abortion services as well as birth control, prenatal care, and STD testing and treatment."

Karen decided to become a plaintiff in the ACLU case because she strongly believes that religious teaching should be the province of religious institutions, not public schools. She wasn't all that nervous about reprisals from the community because she was already accustomed to them.

"I got a death threat once," she recalls sardonically over tea and homemade cookies in the family kitchen. "The timing was terrible! It was during one of my son's sleepover parties. I knew if I reported it to the police, none of those parents would ever send their kids to my house again. My kids would have no social life!"

Karen's husband, Doug, who serves as an ordained deacon and elder at his Presbyterian church and works as a director of Equipment Services for the City of Odessa, had always quietly supported his wife's work with Planned Parenthood, and figured the blowback she received from antiabortion activists was an inevitable consequence.

But this time, even the Hildebrands encountered more conflict than they expected. Soon after they joined in the ACLU lawsuit, the community around them seemed to explode in rage. Pastors around town delivered sermons supporting the NCBCPS and decrying the ACLU. Some churches, such as the Life Challenge Church, a New Apostolic Reformation congregation (which is in the Pentecostal vein), sent busloads of congregants to school board meetings to pray

en masse, lending a circus-like atmosphere to the traditionally anodyne proceedings.

One father, James Cook, felt so strongly that the class should remain in place that he printed up 1,500 bumper stickers with the slo-
gan, "We support the Bible Curriculum," and distributed his fender
manifestos from his machine-shop storefront. The flyers were also carried by sympathetic businesses around town, such as Walter's Family
Restaurant and J. Bradley Salon.

Another Odessa resident, John Waggoner, was involved in a
massive signature-gathering effort in support of the curriculum.

"I think I delivered to the school board something like six or seven
thousand signatures," Waggoner recalls. "When I was in high school,
you did not have people running around trying to take the name of
God off currency." (In fact, the phrase "In God We Trust" was not included on paper currency until 1957, which may be around the time
Waggoner attended high school.) His tone turns conspiratorial. "I
think that there is a serious movement out there to eradicate Christianity," he confides.

The local newspaper, the *Odessa American*, also weighed in with
a series of editorials, news stories, and letters to the editor from all
sides.

For Doug and Karen, it soon became personal. Doug received numerous e-mails challenging his involvement in the suit. Even his
friends questioned his motives. "I have lunch every Monday with
three guys who are pretty conservative," he says. "One of them went
to Baptist seminary. He said to me, 'This is wrong,' and I said, 'No
it's not.' He said, 'Why have you dragged the community through
this?' And I said, 'Me and those seven others, we have made this
community a better place to live.'"

However, Doug says, even greater numbers of colleagues approached him and quietly thanked him for his participation in the
ACLU case. They almost invariably wanted to keep their support
private. "They'd say, 'I support what you're doing. But don't tell anyone we talked about it.'"

Doug still wonders whether his involvement in the ACLU case had an impact on his professional future. "I had applied for an assistant city manager job," he says hesitantly. "And . . . I didn't get it. My colleagues said, 'You know, it's because of the lawsuit.' But I don't know . . . I don't think so. But some of 'em did . . . a lot of 'em did."

RAY BEATY IS the only surviving school board member from the period of the NCBCPS Bible curriculum. A sturdy, bearded man with light brown hair and watchful eyes, his enthusiasm for his evangelical Christian faith is apparent from a glance at the wood-paneled waiting room of his chiropractic office. Two Gideons Bibles lie open on side tables by the chairs and couch. There is a card offering "How to Be Saved," instructing readers to recite:

> Dear Father I acknowledge that I have sinned and walked away from you. I now turn to you and confess The Lord Jesus as my Savior. I believe that His precious blood cleanses me from all sin. Come into my life Lord Jesus. In Jesus name, Amen.

A hardboard flyer pasted to the wall also offers step-by-step instructions on "How to be saved" in English and Spanish. Christian magazines are piled atop the end tables.

In Beaty's personal office I count four more Bibles as well as innumerable patriotic works of art, such as a painting of a pair of hands manipulating a needle and thread to repair an American flag. Statuettes of American eagles, with Bibles and American flags sprouting at their feet, rest beside framed plaques of the Declaration of Independence and the Constitution. There's a quote from former president Ronald Reagan, "If we ever forget we are One Nation Under God, then we will be a nation gone under," and a letter from comedian Red Skelton, extolling the virtues of the Pledge of Allegiance. Beaty clearly has a deep passion for a certain version of American history, a version that becomes quite familiar to anyone who travels in these waters.

"If you are studying the Bible, what better tool to use than the Bible itself?" Beaty asks. "That has worked from the beginning. It was a very strong tool, the process was very much a part of the beginnings of our country. We can recover what we once had as a nation. . . . We have to stand on our foundation."

Beaty continues, occasionally slipping into inexact phrasings that nevertheless effectively convey the essence of his viewpoint: "The Bible used to be the textbook of schools," he says. "It was a tool to utilize in practical purposes, and a set of rules from a common standpoint. It was a common bond—we used to base our laws on it. Now we have a sliding scale. It seems to be more man's decision on what a particular outcome is going to be, instead of a solid foundational area. I think that's why confusion has stepped in.

"If you look at Harvard and Yale and all of those schools, they originally had a foundation of a religious nature and a spiritual area," he continues. "At some point it was man's decision they could do it better, and stepped away from some things that they were solid grounding. And the more you step away from that, there's no respect for authority. That's man's push."

These days, Beaty feels, our society has become altogether too lenient.

"It all boils down again to the family, for a big part, because from a spiritual standpoint the institution of the family came from God, and then that changed," he says. "It's important from generation to generation, but from the breakdown it is evident that we have not performed that procedure well."

Beaty has little respect for the notion of the separation of church and state. "We've gone too far the other way," he says.

"I feel that the America of today is not the one I grew up with," Beaty recalls his Odessa childhood. "I was born in 1955; back then, issues seemed black and white. Once I got into junior high and high school, I thought things hadn't changed that much. But in the last ten years or less I have seen more changes than I'd seen in my entire life."

As our conversation ranges from the corrosive effects of poverty to the breakdown of ethics in society, I find myself nodding in agreement more than I would have expected. I begin to suspect that Beaty and I have more in common than either of us might like to imagine. I, too, am dismayed by the general coarsening of public discourse. I, too, worry about the garish sexual imagery that has become a normalized part of our culture, such as the ads for "Gentleman's Clubs" plastered on some of New York City's bus stops, and wonder how such advertisements will affect my children's inner lives. I often wonder whether shifting family arrangements in modern society are the best way to serve the needs of children. And, like Beaty, when I look to the future, I sometimes see only a chaos of uncertainty amid the overwhelming flood of social and technological changes.

It's only when Beaty starts to talk about solutions that I see how far apart we remain. Beaty will never know how much he and I agree about the troubles facing modern society for the simple reason that, in his view, people like me are the problem because we are of the "wrong" religion. "You can see many things would be healed up if we reclaimed our Christian heritage," he says. "America was founded as a Christian nation."

ANOTHER VOCAL SUPPORTER of the NCBCPS was the Life Challenge Church, which sent buses of "prayer warriors" to the school board meetings. The Life Challenge Church is part of a fast-growing movement within Pentecostal Christianity called the New Apostolic Reformation, of which Morning Star New York, the church installed in P.S. 6, is also a part (see Chapter 5). Life Challenge women favor long skirts and very long hair, which is sometimes poufed up in the back. Churchgoers are largely working class, and the racially integrated services are warm and welcoming.

The attitude toward education at Life Challenge seems ambivalent. During a recent sermon, lead pastor Daniel Smesler, a tall, stern white man, said, with a note of menace in his voice, "We do support you going to college . . . but don't let it make you so analytic that it ruins your faith. Get your degree, and then get victory over your degree."

One Sunday after church, I share lunch at Furr's Buffet with another one of Life Challenge's pastors, Pastor Sotilo, who had taught that morning's Bible class. He is a gentle, soft-spoken man with a ready smile who frequently punctuates his speech with "Praise God." His wife, Evelyn, a doe-like woman of perhaps fifty, has black hair that falls to the back of her knees.

"With what's happening in the culture today, they *should* teach the Bible in schools," he says, voicing his support of the NCBCPS. "They're teaching evolution and all kinds of stuff," he adds, disapprovingly. If Sotilo had his way, all public schools would teach sectarian interpretations of the Bible. "How can you teach the Bible as a secular document?" he asks incredulously. "That's not possible. It is matter of faith." Then, his tone turning conspiratorial, he says, "You know who was behind all this ACLU stuff?" He lowers his head and gives me a significant look. "A Jew."

NEWMAN DESCRIBES HIMSELF as a nontheist of mixed ancestry, some of it Jewish. His wife and daughter are Jewish, however, and that is generally how people in the community see him. Even before the NCBCPS came to town, Newman was concerned about the atmosphere in his daughter's school; she has been repeatedly bullied for her faith.

A slim, athletic man of about forty, Newman is an English professor at Odessa College. He has enjoyed studying religion in the past, and insists that he is eager to support genuine scholarship about the Bible. It was the shoddy and fake scholarship behind the NCBCPS Bible curriculum, he says, that first drew his attention. A pseudo-scholarly, crypto-sectarian course, he thought, was the last thing the Odessa high school needed—and it wouldn't make life any easier for his daughter.

Newman tackled the issue with an academic researcher's attention to detail. He undertook a meticulous, page-by-page analysis of the 270-page syllabus for the NCBCPS course, itemizing the ways in which sectarian claims pervaded the curriculum. He also sent e-mails to multiple Texas school districts to publicize his findings.

"Christianity is presented not as a subject for study by mythologists, literary critics, or anthropologist, but as a cultural and metaphysical fact," Newman says of the course. "This last point is made repeatedly in insinuations that one can find in the course's main objectives. The word 'religion' is endlessly conflated with a certain interpretation of Christianity, so that in the abstract one may believe students are being challenged to think critically about comparative religious doctrines. In practice, students are not asked to think critically at all. In the questions that accompany the lessons, for instance, students are asked to 'defend what Moses did' or 'justify Christ's attitude toward' something, rather than 'analyze this' or, heaven forbid, 'challenge that.'"

The ACLU case and its aftermath consumed Newman for years. "I wrote dozens of letters," he sighs. "Education matters to me." I skim through some. "I'm also begging for the courtesy of response, even if it is hostile," I read in one letter. "Indifference is more worrisome to me than any other kind of reaction."

In the end, Newman did not receive many responses to his letters; but he did not experience indifference, either. Some members of the community hit back, and they hit back hard.

He refuses to tell me anything about it. When I press him to explain what happened, his conversation becomes incoherent, then dissolves into silence. From others, however, I learn that he received many threatening letters and telephone calls, and that his daughter was the target of anti-Semitic bullying at school.

Newman does confess that he has wondered if he ought to leave Odessa. But he reasons that he and his wife enjoy their work and the lives they have built for themselves here. Academic jobs like his are hard to come by these days. He tells me—though it sounds like he's just telling himself—that it's best to tough it out.

"WE SHOULDN'T BE afraid of conflict," says Randy Rives from his office at the Clay Desta building in Midland, the town adjacent to Odessa. "Controversy gets people to think. Would [bringing religion into the classroom] cause controversy? Probably. Is that a bad thing? No."

Rives, a tall man of around sixty, has the rugged good looks of a well-aged leading man. A former oilman who became involved in politics while running for the Ector County School Board, Rives is nostalgic for the world in which he grew up: small-town Texas, where family and church were the pillars of the community, where pregnant unmarrieds were shunned, and children respected their elders.

"My mama was schoolteacher; she only whupped two students a year!" he quips. "She only had to whup two. . . . When you saw those whuppings, you didn't do anything wrong after that!"

Kids these days don't behave the way they used to, he claims, and much of that is due to what he sees as a decline in conservative Christian values.

"We're not trying to make Christians out of 'em," he says, referring to non-Christian kids who might be exposed to the Bible in public schools. "We're just trying to tell them, you know, there's values in this book and maybe you really ought to think about 'em."

Rives links taking prayer out of the schools to everything from a rise in teen pregnancy to the shootings at Columbine. "Somebody asked a woman, 'Why wasn't God protecting the [Columbine] kids?' and she said, 'I think we told God to get out of the public schools,'" says Rives. "If you want God's protection, you can't have it both ways."

When it comes to the NCBCPS curriculum, Rives simply can't fathom why parents might have opposed its presence in the public schools.

"The course was elective and nobody was forcing anybody to take it," he says. "I think," he concludes, "that they should just allow the parents and the students to decide, and not allow this issue to be dictated by the state."

ON MARCH 5, 2008, the lawsuit was settled in Midland Federal Court. The settlement agreement mandated that the NCBCPS curriculum not be used after the current school year. It also allowed that a different Bible curriculum, one widely considered to have less of a sectarian bias, would be offered in its place.

Rives says he is happy with the outcome. There's a Bible curriculum being taught in the schools after all, which is how it should be. But by all accounts, Rives paid a high price for his involvement in the case.

Although opinions about the Bible curriculum were and remain divided, almost everyone in Odessa agreed on one thing: that the entire episode was a colossal waste of energy and time. Even in the Bible Belt, it turns out, people elect school board members to run schools, not to start needless religious wars. The high-profile controversy also put the skills and experience of the board members under intense public scrutiny—and the wider public, whatever its views about the curriculum, did not always like what it saw. When Rives ran for reelection, the voters rejected him. In 2010, when he attempted to unseat State Board of Education moderate Republican Bob Craig, he was trounced.

Dr. Roland Spickermann, chair of the Department of History at the University of Texas of the Permian Basin and another one of the seven ACLU plaintiffs, observes that the fallout of the NCBCPS was a total fiasco for the school board.

"One of the hard-line members, Mary Hill, was discovered to not be living in the district that she represented," Spickermann says. "Randy Rives got totally pasted in the State Representative election. And Butch Foreman finished third, which I think was a great shock to him."

"It ruined Randy Rives's career," says Lori White. "I think that speaks for itself."

The plaintiffs' victory did not bring them much happiness, either. The settlement was achieved by mediation, which most of them felt was a waste of time.

"The judge just did not want this case coming to his court," says Doug Hildebrand, referring to the fact that the case was settled by mediation rather than at trial, "and I think that hurt the nation. Had it gone to trial, we would have won and it would have set precedents for all other states."

"Nobody suffered more than David (Newman)," says White. "I think it has affected him deeply. Even to this day."

BUTCH FOREMAN IS sanguine about losing his bid for re-election. "It was just as well," he says with a game smile. "It took a lot of time away from the family." But when Foreman thinks hard about the story of the NCBCPS in Odessa, it unsettles him. Sure, both sides eventually settled. Sure, time has healed the community fissures that erupted when the suit was coming to a head. But still.

"Christians wouldn't mind a class like this taught by any other faith in the school," he asserts—disingenuously, perhaps, because classes like these are not taught by any other faith—"so why should they care when we want to teach one?"

Butch shrugs and gives a smile, cheerful but quizzical. "I don't know," he says, with his easy grin. "I guess I still don't get it."

NEITHER THIS LOCAL defeat nor any of the apparent issues concerning the intellectual credibility and intentions of the Bible curriculum, however, appears to have put a dent in the NCBCPS's stealthy expansion across the nation's public schools. According to the NCBCPS website, its course has been approved in over 2,000 high schools, and has already reached 353,000 high school students, "during school hours, for credit!"

So in spite of its weaknesses, or more accurately because of them, the NCBCPS has become especially popular in the past few years among politicians in a variety of states, which have passed laws mandating that it be taught.

In March 2010, the Oklahoma Senate passed a measure requiring that course materials for elective courses on the Bible must come from the National Council on Bible Curriculum in Public Schools. The Senate bill 1338, which was introduced by Senator Tom Ivester, passed by a vote of 38 to 4 and now heads to the House. Ivester defended his selection of the NCBCPS by saying he selected the curriculum "to head off controversy" and asserted the curriculum will provide students with "a more well-rounded education."

In Texas, House bill 1287 from the 2007 legislature requires Texas school districts to offer the courses to high school students if fifteen or more students show an interest in taking them. In Lubbock, Monterey, and Coronado, over one hundred students signed up for the NCBCPS courses when they were offered in the public school, and some schools are offering more than one section.

In Alabama, the State Board of Education voted unanimously to provide state funding and approval for the NCBCPS curriculum. The curriculum is already being used in several school districts across Alabama, but state board approval means that local districts can now be reimbursed by the state for the cost of the course materials.

In Georgia, the state legislature passed a bill calling for a Bible class to be taught in the public schools—and recommended that schools choose the NCBCPS curriculum. A similar bill passed in Tennessee, and the state Department of Education has collected information on the NCBCPS curriculum and others, to share with districts that don't have a Bible curriculum in place.

Support for the NCBCPS, it seems, has become a way for folks to demonstrate their faithful allegiance to a particular creed. Numerous residents of the city of Craig, Colorado, for instance, have signed a petition asking the NCBCPS to be added to the curriculum at Moffat County High School.

"The world is watching to see if we will be motivated to impact our culture, to deal with the moral crises in our society, and reclaim our families and children," the NCBCPS's website proclaims.

But really, the point is to claim the children of other families.

9

PACKAGING PROSELYTIZING
AS EDUCATION

ON A CRISP Tuesday evening, I trundled into P.S. 6's art-filled auditorium with a crowd of fellow parents for the PTA's Back to School night. It was the first time I had been able to enter the building after attending the Morning Star New York church service a week and a half previously, but as a new parent I was excited to be here, at my first PTA meeting, and to observe some of the inner workings of our new school. Most of the moms and dads arrived in business attire. They had the respectable yet slightly frayed look of people starting the second shift of the day. Yet the wide attendance spoke to the degree of passion and commitment this community feels for their children's education. They listened closely as the cheerful PTA president described her ambitious plans for the coming year and presented the projected 2010–2011 budget.

My daughter was entering the third grade, and so I took particular notice of one budget item: the PTA had set aside $10,000 to pay for a weekly, in-school program for all third graders under the name "SFK." The initials, I learned, stood for "Success for Kids," and the purpose of the program, as far as I could tell from the PTA leader's brief commentary, had something to do with "character education."

When I got home that evening, I looked into the mysterious SFK program in which my daughter would now be enrolled. I quickly discovered that Success for Kids is the new name for Spirituality for Kids, also shortened to SFK—a program that originated with and remains controlled by the Kabbalah Centre.

The Kabbalah Centre's roots can be traced back to 1971, when a Brooklyn-born insurance salesman named Shraga Feivel Gruberger began preaching unusual ideas about mystical enlightenment to a small group of students in Israel. Gruberger soon left his first wife, married his secretary, Karen, renamed himself Philip Berg, and moved to the United States, where he and Karen created a religious sect that they claim to be based on arcane Jewish teachings called "Kabbalah."

Lavish community centers, self-improvement courses, and pricy accessories soon followed. The Kabbalah Centre is known for selling red strings to be tied around the wrist in order to ward off the "Evil Eye." Price: $26 dollars. Another product is "Kabbalah Water"— bottled water that has been blessed by the Kabbalah Centre leaders and that is said to possess astonishing curative powers. The Kabbalah Centre is widely associated with its most famous member, Madonna, and boasts a number of other celebrity supporters, including Demi Moore, Ashton Kutcher, and Roseanne Barr.

In its official documents, SFK makes no mention of the Kabbalah Centre. A representative of the group later assured me that the SFK program is entirely independent of its original sponsoring group. My research told a very different story. When I consulted SFK's website, it listed one and only one member on its board of directors: Michal Berg. Michal turned out to be the wife of Yehuda Berg, who is the son of the center's founders. Both Michal and Yehuda are also teachers at the Kabbalah Centre in Los Angeles. The CEO of SFK, a Dr. Heath Grant, had been associated with Madonna's Raising Malawi program—a disastrous effort to spread the word of the Kabbalah Centre in that African country. The individual named as SFK's "Training Specialist," reportedly in charge of all the preparation of SFK teachers, was the sister of celebrity Kabbalah Centre member Ashton Kutcher. SFK is an aggressive fund-raiser, and its head of Donor Relations, Elisa Pittman, turned out to be an employee of the Kabbalah Centre. SFK, in short, was simply the Kabbalah Centre by another name.

SFK also appeared to share with the Kabbalah Centre a tendency to get caught up in controversies over alleged financial improprieties. In May 2011, according to the *Los Angeles Times*, the Los Angeles–based Kabbalah Centre released a statement acknowledging that they, along with Spirituality for Kids, had "received subpoenas from the government concerning tax-related issues." According to the *Times*, the IRS was seeking to determine whether nonprofit funds were used for the personal enrichment of the Berg family.[1]

Exactly what SFK teaches children is hard to say with precision, since the program published no formal curriculum. On our school's website, however, SFK did post a two-page document describing the program. Even from this brief overview it was easy to see that the course did not stray very far from its origins in the Kabbalah Centre. For example, according to that document, SFK teaches children that they possess an "Inner Light"–a concept that is a centerpiece of the religious doctrines of the Kabbalah Centre. SFK also defines "Spiritual Powers" as "good feelings that we really want, cannot be measured, weighed, counted or touched." It contrasts these spiritual powers with "material things," of which it apparently does not approve.

AT AROUND MIDNIGHT on my first evening of research into the new course that was about to enter my daughter's life, with glass of wine firmly in hand, I began to do some digging on the SFK instructor assigned to our school. The bio posted on the SFK website looked promising: she was an experienced public school teacher, a Peace Corps Fellow, and had a Masters degree from Columbia University.

But her bio neglected to mention something that I quickly discovered: just before taking her position with SFK, in 2008 and 2009,
she was a fellow in the Developing Teachers Fellowship Program at
an organization called the East Side Institute.

The East Side Institute, and its founder, Fred Newman, who died
in July 2011, have been widely written about by many investigative
reporters, cult researchers, and political analysts. Newman was an
avowed Marxist and the creator of a form of psychotherapy in which
he alleged that there is nothing wrong with psychotherapists having
sex with their patients. He required his followers to engage in frequent group therapy meetings and encouraged them to sleep with
one another, an activity he called "friendosexuality." His East Side
Institute's annual Performing the World program contains videos
offering praise for "revolutionaries" and deriding the "individualistic
bias" in the field of psychology.

At this point in my first evening of research into SFK, the situation seemed worth the risk of waking my husband. As he grumbled
out of bed, I tried to explain that our daughter would now be receiving "character education" from Madonna's spiritual friends and
others whose educational experience centered around selling red
strings for $26, and that her instructor would be a woman who
thought it important to be a member of not just one but two separate sects. All of this would be taking place in our public school during the school day, with the financial support of the same PTA to
which we were about to donate some money.

My husband stopped grumbling. He looked at my research, just
to make certain I wasn't hallucinating, then poured a glass of wine
for himself, too. We agreed that the situation was so absurd and par-
adoxical that it should sit on the computer for a day. Then, after
doing a bit more research, we assembled our findings and concerns
in a letter and gave it to the principal of our school.

What followed was instructive. For example, I learned more about
the Kabbalah Centre religion and the SFK program. I also got a taste

of what happens to parents who raise troubling issues on which not everyone shares the same viewpoint.

THE KABBALAH CENTRE is far from the only religious group to realize that it need not send volunteers on after-school missions in order to gain access to America's public school children. Religious groups can now get paid to do their work during the school day, as part of the children's mandated curriculum. The only catch—not a very big one, as it turns out—is that they must misrepresent the nature of their activities. More tactfully put, they need to package their proselytizing missions as teaching on secular subjects: as character or health education, as substance abuse prevention, as self-esteem or personal development workshops.

The new opportunity has resulted from the convergence of three trends. One is the growing tendency of overworked and underfunded school administrators to rely on outside suppliers to develop and run courses that previously originated inside the school. A second important factor is an increasingly lax legal environment, already familiar to us, that simultaneously sets a very high threshold for Establishment Clause concerns and a very low threshold for viewpoint-discrimination lawsuits. The third and perhaps more fundamental force at work is the very long-term trend, operating across more than a century, that has led schools to assume increasing responsibility for instruction governing student behavior in areas that were in earlier times thought to be the province of religious institutions and the family.

A century ago, no school in America offered sex education, and very few people would have thought the subject appropriate for a classroom. Substance abuse—or "sin," as it was then called—was something to be addressed with religious faith and possibly laws, not with textbooks.

The dramatic change in the scope of education is to some degree part of the process of modernization, according to which more and more areas of life are addressed in a systematized fashion. By the start of the twentieth century, with industrialization steaming ahead, supporters of the common school movement stressed the necessity of creating a property-respecting, law-abiding, productive work force, and children were taught skills such as woodwork, cooking, building, and gardening in addition to their academic subjects.

This shift also reflects significant social changes taking place throughout the twentieth century. With extended families dispersing geographically and youth culture acquiring a momentum of its own, schools have been called upon to assume new socializing roles. Perhaps the biggest single factor behind the expansion of the schools' social role, however, has been the drive to deal with public health concerns.

Sex education made its first gains in America with the epidemic of STDs that broke out during World War I. Educating the troops about sex became a matter of public health, and the same was true by extension of America's adolescents in general. National vaccination programs vanquished such scourges as polio and diphtheria, and educating the public about the dangers of such diseases and effective means of prevention was a key to their success. Indeed, children in public schools were often lined up in the hallways and vaccinated one by one.

In the 1980s, the outbreak of AIDS/HIV reinforced claims that sex education was a public health concern, and an especially important one. Drug abuse, too, had come to be seen as a social problem, particularly for adolescents, and schools decided they had a constructive role to play.

Religious conservatives objected from the start, and have not stopped in their efforts to reverse the clock. In the 1920s, they called it "smut in the classroom." In the 1960s, the vitriol reached feverish levels. In a widely distributed 1968 pamphlet titled "Is the School House the Proper Place to Teach Raw Sex?" James Hargis and Gordon Drake argued that sex education is really a kind of communist indoctrination: "If the new morality is affirmed, our children will become easy targets for Marxism and other amoral, nihilistic philosophies—as well as V.D!" Rumors were circulated that instructors were having sex in front of their classes or encouraging kids to become gay. The John Birch Society linked sex education to a devilish conspiracy against American moral values, and across the country, groups formed to protest. "Religious conservatives began using sex ed to their political advantage," says Janice M. Irvine, who wrote *Talk About Sex: The Battles of Sex Education in the United States.*[2]

The current battles over sex education and related subjects might be seen as simply a continuation of this culture war, and to some degree that is what they are. "Sex education classes in our public schools are promoting incest," asserted Jimmy Swaggart, speaking for the unanimous chorus of disapproval on the Religious Right in the years before he admitted to involvement with prostitutes.[3] "The results [of public school sex education] are rampant immorality, illegitimacy, abortions, venereal diseases, infertility and teen age emotional drama that often follows them through their entire lives," said Phyllis Schlafly.[4]

Yet changes in the public school environment have scrambled the logic of the struggle in important ways. Rather than attempt to keep programs about sex and drugs out of the schools, religious activists now see such courses as opportunities for entering the schools. Sex education and substance abuse programs are religiously righteous after all—as long as they are done from the correct viewpoint. Doing it from the right viewpoint, in this case, however, involves dropping most of the education and focusing on the correct religious message.

ABSTINENCE EDUCATION POSITS the idea that the proper way to educate adolescents about sex is to instruct them to refrain from sexual activity until marriage. The way to avoid contracting an STD or an unwanted pregnancy, a typical program tells its students, is to follow a few simple rules: "Respect yourself. Choose friends who are positive influences. Go out as a group. Get plenty of rest." Doug Herman, a popular abstinence-until-marriage speaker at public high schools across the United States, sums up the message this way: "If the sun don't touch it, nobody else better, either."[5]

The typical abstinence program, however, is not against sex per se. Abstinence instructors often make a point of telling teenagers that they know how hard it is to refrain from sexual activity. Sex is wonderful, it is incredible, it is mind-blowing—*if* you are married. The principal goal of most such programs, in fact, is to imbue children with a certain view about the proper relationship between sex and marriage. Sex within marriage is a source of fulfillment and even ecstasy; sex in all other contexts is degrading and shameful.

Abstinence educators frequently promote this view by representing all sex that occurs outside the marital bed as harmful. Premarital sex is dangerous and dirty, they say—a gateway to decadence, depression, broken lives, and an early grave, especially for women. If you have sex outside of marriage, says Pam Stenzel, a nationally recognized "abstinence proponent" who delivers talks to public school students around the country, "*then you will pay.*"

Not having premarital sex, on the other hand, is always posited as beneficial. Game Plan, an abstinence course developed by A&M Partnership (formerly Project Reality) and taught in public schools around the country, offers as evidence the instructive tale of Steve, who resisted his girlfriend Tina's sexual overtures. Tina, the little tramp, was already pregnant when she asked Steve to have sex with her, and faced a dead-end future as a single teenage mother. Steve, however, met his future wife, the virginal Karen, six years later at college.

"Steve and Karen have now been married for over seventeen years and have four children. Steve is a teacher, and Karen enjoys caring for the children. Steve and Karen never have to worry about sexually transmitted diseases or unwanted pregnancy. Sex is a normal, natural, and exciting part of their lives together."

Of course, Steve wouldn't have considered using protection when he had sex with Karen or Tina—A&M Partnership strongly opposes the idea that discussion about condoms and other methods of contra-ception belongs in sex education programs.

The real lesson of abstinence-only education is associating sexual feelings with guilt and shame, of course. Choosing the Best, Inc., a Marietta, Georgia, based program that received a half million dol-lars in federal funding and whose curriculum was written by a former National Director for Campus Crusade for Christ, has a particularly gripping way of communicating its message of sexual disgust.

> *Boys and girls are invited to chew cheese-flavored snacks and then sip some water, after which they are to spit the resulting "bodily fluids" into a cup. After a game in which the fluids are combined with those of other students, ultimately all cups are poured into a pitcher labeled "multiple partners" sitting adjacent to a pitcher of water labeled "pure fluids." In the final segment, each boy and girl is asked to fill a cup labeled either "future husband" or "future wife" with the contents from one of the pitchers.[6]*

Many abstinence education programs make cheerful use of gender stereotypes. The Just Say Yes curriculum, used by twelve public school districts including Dallas's exclusive Highland Park Independent School District, tells teens that abstinence means "you make a con-scious decision to avoid turning others on," and continues to explain that "if a guy is breathing, then he's probably turned on." The text continues by advising girls "to think long and hard about the way you dress and the way you come on to guys." A woman who "shows a lot of skin" is either "ignorant when it comes to guys," is cruelly "teasing" men, or is "giving her boyfriend an open invitation" to have sex with her. The responsibility for policing the boundaries of sexual behavior, evidently, rests on women alone; men, according to the Just Say Yes way of thinking, can hardly be expected to control themselves.

The "No Apologies" program, produced by Focus on the Family and used in at least five public districts, waxes nostalgic about gender arrangements of yore. Girls used to be modest, it posits approvingly, and were given written instructions on what "a lady should do if she had bad breath, bad teeth or an offensive laugh."

South Carolina's Heritage program, which has been taught in public schools around the state and has received millions of taxpayer dollars in funding, suggests that "girls have a responsibility to wear modest clothing that doesn't invite lustful thoughts."

Abstinence-until-marriage sex education courses are taught by a wide variety of outfits. Some operate on a large scale, serving multiple communities in dozens of states. Others work with a single school district. In almost all cases, however, the sponsoring organizations are religious in nature or have thrown themselves into the business of sex education for transparently religious purposes.

DRESSED IN BLUE jeans, layered T-shirts, and sneakers, Jeffrey Dean teaches abstinence education to public school students in Wise County, Texas. He is also the founder of the Jeffrey Dean Ministries, which established the Wise Choices Pregnancy Center in order to dissuade women with unwanted pregnancies from obtaining abortions. The center's mission, as per their website, is to "show the young woman the first picture of the life she is carrying inside her through Ultrasound technology," "impact [the client's] ability to end destructive patterns of living," and "encounter a one-on-one evangelist message of the love, mercy, and forgiveness of Jesus Christ."

Youth for Christ, which receives federal funds to teach abstinence education in public schools all over the country, makes no effort to disguise its agenda. "YFC goes where kids are," says text on the Youth for Christ website. "With programs like Campus Life [reaching public high school and middle school campuses] . . . YFC carries the Love of Jesus Christ to all different kinds of kids in many different situations."

Pam Stenzel, of "you will pay" fame, has developed several abstinence curricula. There is an overtly religious one, but also a "secular" version that is specifically for use in the public schools. The basic message, and the underlying sectarian agenda, is the same in both.

As Michelle Goldberg reports in *Kingdom Coming: The Rise of Christian Nationalism*, Stenzel attended a 2003 Reclaiming American for Christ conference, sponsored by D. James Kennedy's Coral Ridge Ministries (now Truth in Action Ministries), at which she loudly decried premarital sex as "stinking, filthy, dirty, rotten sin!" There, she made clear her goal in spreading the news about abstinence among public school teenagers. As she stood at the podium, she related a conversation she had had with an airplane seatmate who had expressed skepticism as to whether abstinence education really works. "People of God," she cried, "can I beg you, to commit yourself to truth, not to what works! To truth! I don't care if it works, because at the end of the day I'm not answering to you. I'm answering to God! . . . I will not teach my child they can sin safely."[7]

When asked to defend their claims about the attributes of abstinence, many abstinence instructors cite their personal sexual histories, which more often than not involve personal and sexual choices that went awry. Leslee Unrah, for example, deeply regretted having an abortion in her early twenties; she has since parlayed that early setback into a triumphant career in abstinence education. The founder of the nonprofit Abstinence Clearinghouse ("Your Source for All Things Abstinence"), she delivers programs for public high schools around the country along with books, DVDs, presentation materials, personal safety products, and even a line of "Pet Your Dog, Not Your Date" T-shirts.

Unrah's advisory board has included prominent Christian Nationalists such as Beverly LaHaye and D. James Kennedy before his death in 2007. She hobnobs with James Dobson and Summit Ministries's David Noebel. Based in Sioux Falls, South Dakota, her Abstinence Clearinghouse has a sanctuary for women grieving past abortions, including a "memorial for the unborn." Needless to say, Unrah's opposition to premarital sex is anchored in her religious beliefs. Even her "secular" materials for the public schools have a religious overlay of rhetoric, ideas, and value judgments. Abstinence Clearinghouse, for example, promotes a program that asserts that

AIDS can be transmitted through tears and sweat; claims that women derive their happiness from relationships, while men become fulfilled through their accomplishments; and characterizes masturbation as "the first stage of sexual addiction for sex addicts." Researchers for Representative Henry Waxman, who assessed textbooks and other materials created by Unrah and her cohorts, determined that about 80 percent of their data on reproductive health is misleading or untrue.[8]

True Love Waits, a program created by a group called Lifeway Christian Resources, creates a climate of pro-chastity peer pressure and encourages teens to take public vows of abstinence until marriage with slogans like, "Wait for the ring." The pressure is especially acute for girls, many of whom don silver rings on their fourth finger of their left hand to symbolize their "purity" as well as their "personal relationship with Jesus Christ as the best way to live a sexually pure life." The program, which received well over $1 million dollars in federal funding, was used in public schools until the ACLU filed a lawsuit with the Department of Health and Human Services in 2002. The evangelical initiative went a step too far in making the links between their religious views and curriculum explicit. Other funded groups simply do a better job of disguising those links.

One such group is Friends First, a federally funded "non-sectarian" program and one of the most prominent abstinence programs in America, taught in numerous states. Friends First targets Latino youth with a Quinceañera Program, which claims to "reinforce the traditional *quinceañera* values of purity and virginity until marriage." The program includes a graduation ceremony at which girls pledge their commitment to abstinence until marriage. In an incestuous bit of pageantry, each participant's father places a "purity ring" on her finger "as a reminder of her promise to save her virginity for her future husband."

This ritual, not practiced in traditional *quinceañeras*, is taken straight from the religious programming of True Love Waits. In spite of their nonsectarian claims, Friends First echoes conservative religious views in advancing a narrow idea of what constitutes an acceptable and moral life. Friends First promotes gender stereotypes, elevates marriage as the only responsible relationship goal, demonizes abortion, and marginalizes gay and lesbian youth and their families. It describes nonmarried sexual relationships as "broken," coded language that signifies Godlessness within the evangelical Christian community. It also presents the notion, contradicted by all the available data on the subject, that a marriage between two virgins is less likely to fail than any other.

Some abstinence education programs do allow for discussion of the role of contraception and safe sex practices in preventing unintended pregnancies and sexually transmitted diseases. In many cases, however, these "abstinence-plus" programs, as they are known, spread disinformation rather than information about sex. According to a report by the Texas Freedom Network, factual errors are taught in the health programs of 41 percent of Texas public school districts. The most common errors concern condoms and their efficacy, such as the notion that the HIV virus can pass through latex. In a theatrical exercise from the Brady Independent School District in Brady, Texas, students are told that condoms have a 30 percent failure rate in "preventing most STDs" and that "HPV and syphilis are so small that they can slip through condoms." One character in the theatrical production says, "Giving a condom to a teen is just like saying, 'Well if you insist on killing yourself by jumping off a bridge, at least wear these elbow pads—they may protect you some?'"[9]

Misinformation about other STDs is also pervasive. Programs such as the Austin LifeGuard Character and Sexuality Education, used in ten school districts, teaches that there is "virtually no evidence" that condoms reduce the risk of HPV (human papillomavirus) infection and alleges that "about a third" of all in vitro fertilizations can be linked to infertility caused by STD infections[10]—in spite of evidence to the contrary from the American Society of Reproductive Medicine. At least one Texas curriculum, Wonderful Days, taught the dangerously false notion that "natural fertility regulation"—the rhythm method—has the "highest . . . user effectiveness rate." In an attempt to help students understand fertility, Wonderful Days offered an outlandish little rhyme: "If a woman is dry, the sperm will die. If a woman is wet, a baby she may get!"

Abstinence programs have now been running for long enough to have accumulated a fair degree of evidence with which to judge their effectiveness—and the evidence is damning. A January 2009 study in the journal *Pediatrics* found that teens who take virginity pledges are just as likely to have sex before marriage as their peers who didn't take pledges, but they are less likely to use condoms or birth control when they do become sexually active. It is thus not surprising that communities with the highest concentration of state-mandated, abstinence-only education have some of the highest rates of teen pregnancy and STDs in the country. In Lubbock, Texas, for instance, where the state has mandated abstinence-only education since 1995, the level of gonorrhea has risen to double the national level, and teen pregnancy rates are among the highest in the nation.

The alarming evidence concerning the ineffectiveness and even harmful effects of abstinence-until-marriage education did little to stop the clamor from conservative groups in support of such programs, nor did it stanch the flow of money from the federal government. Publicly funded abstinence education programs were introduced to the United States in 1981, when $11 million was appropriated under the Adolescent and Family Life Act. Under George W. Bush, the amount of money mushroomed, and the president's 2006 budget asked for $206 million for abstinence education, an increase of $39 million from the year before. By the end of Bush's first term, the government had spent nearly a billion dollars on chastity programs, and nearly a third of public schools with sex education programs took an abstinence-only approach. A typical recipient of this federal largesse has been Leslee Unrah, whose Abstinence Clearinghouse took in millions of dollars in grants from former president Bush's Health and Human Services Department.

When Democrats seized control of Congress in 2006, they failed to defund abstinence education, although they did make it easier to opt out of the Title V funding that mandated the discredited programs. In June 2008, twenty-two states had chosen to opt out of abstinence-until-marriage education, and in May 2009, President Obama eliminated funding for it from the federal budget, citing numerous studies that show such programs may erode public health. Meanwhile, proponents responded by forming a trade association, the National Abstinence Education Association, to pressure legislators for a slice of the federal funds. In October 2009, their efforts paid off when the Senate Finance Committee, in a 12-11 vote, restored $50 million in abstinence funding in a rider on the health insurance reform legislation. And with Republicans once again taking control of the house in 2010, the future of abstinence education looks bright.

Abstinence education may not have stopped young people from having nonmarital sex or diminished the rates of unwanted pregnancies or STDs, but it has benefited at least one constituency: evangelical religious organizations. It has resulted in a generous flow of funds from the federal government to these organizations, representing a significant part of the billions of taxpayer dollars diverted from secular social service organizations to "faith-based" charities over the past decade.

When money flows into these faith-based organizations, as Michelle Goldberg points out, it is all but impossible to track where it goes. Multiple repositories for money are administered by several government agencies and distributed in ways that are generally opaque to the public. Some grants go to the states, who then funnel them to local faith-based groups that operate in the public schools. Millions more go through something called the Compassion Capital Fund to intermediary groups, such as one run by leading televangelist Pat Robertson, who then disperse those funds to operations of their choice. Some funds go directly to evangelical groups, such as Youth for Christ, whose declared mission is entirely religious.

Public school students who are the pretended beneficiaries of this kind of sex education may learn little about the sexual health issues that are the main motivation for having such programs in the schools in the first place. But they learn something else, which is perhaps the intent of the programs: that there is a "right" group in society, one with the correct attitudes and convictions, and a "wrong" group. Like the young women who make their virginity pledges before engaging in unprotected sex, they learn just enough to understand the importance of putting on the ring that signals their membership in the right group.

IF SEX FAILS to reach the kids, one can always try drugs. A group called Narconon, founded in 1966 as a drug rehabilitation program, found a reception for its anti-drug message in a handful of public schools in California. Parents soon discovered, however, that the program was largely based on the teachings of L. Ron Hubbard, author of *The Fundamentals of Thought* and founder of the Church of Scientology. Controversy followed and eventually school districts in San Francisco and Los Angeles expelled the program in 2005.

A Los Angeles Unified School District (LAUSD) spokeswoman said the school district contracts with several enrichment companies, some of which bring in programming with known religious affiliations.

"The Los Angeles Unified School District accepts and supports having programs such as Spirituality for Kids on LAUSD campuses," said Sharon Thomas, assistant general counsel to the district, in a statement. The district, she acknowledged, must abide by the Establishment Clause of the First Amendment by maintaining "strict neutrality in religious matters," she said, and any program is acceptable "as long as it does not run afoul of that."

While the Scientology-based program apparently failed to meet the test, programs run by representatives of more widely accepted religions have had better luck. Particularly successful, as usual, have been the efforts by evangelical groups. The practice of proselytizing public school children under the guise of offering educational programs concerning substance abuse or other forms of "character" or "moral" education is now so common that the activist groups have given it a nickname: Pizza Evangelism, because the presentations on "character" are occasionally accompanied by pizza parties. These are generally one-off spectacles (though many of them appear at schools on multiple occasions) that offer messages about drug abuse, peer pressure, and the like. Their ultimate goal is to evangelize children—though in order to do so, they have to be a little tricky about how they operate.

"They have someone come into the school and give the kids something—pizza, special activities, whatever it takes in order to enter in and present oneself as being about teaching," says Richard B. Katskee, former assistant legal director of Americans United for the Separation of Church and State. "They claim to offer something neutral, something secular, in order to get access to the kids."

Katskee, who currently works for the Office of Civil Rights at the US Department of Education, says he received many complaints about such groups from around the country. "'Team Impact,' 'Commandos! USA,' the 'Strength Team,' there are a whole bunch of them."

The way such groups typically operate is that they approach the schools offering to give an assembly on leadership, good citizenship, or self-esteem. Often the group stages a muscle-man show, martial arts demonstration, or other type of spectacle with a broad appeal.

"They put on this kind of impressive show for the kids, and then at the end they say, 'If you like what you saw and want to see even more of this great stuff, come see this show we are doing on Saturday night,' and the address is for a fundamentalist church in the area," says Katskee. "And this is where the evangelism happens." By exploiting their access to the students, such groups find roundabout ways to pull them in.

"Sometimes school officials clearly approve of it," Katskee says, "but often they don't have a clue."

The Power Team, a Dallas, Texas–based group of former college and professional athletes, snap baseball bats, roll up frying pans, and rip phonebooks in half in order to teach children "positive character development." The Power Team claims that it has performed for millions of youth, many in public schools. An open letter on their website, addressed to school principals and administrators, boasts, "With over 30 years experience and over 30,000 school assemblies performed, the Power Team would be honored to encourage your students to reach their goals and dreams," and cites "hundreds of recommendations from teachers, principals, administrators, mayors, governors, congressmen and women, senators, and Presidents."[11]

It doesn't take much digging to figure out what the Power Team is really about. "Capturing the Hearts of Your Community for Jesus Christ!" proclaims the Power Team website. The group's stated mission is "to reach people of all ages, who would typically not ever attend an event in a church setting, with the gospel of Jesus Christ. Drawing people from all walks of life together into one setting, through the use of performing visually explosive feats of strength, by incredible athletes, who share the life-changing message of the Cross." Of course, the "Schools" page of their website carefully scrubs all mention of this overarching religious agenda.

Another group that presents assemblies on "positive life choices" to public school students is Answering the Cries. The New Orleans–based group is committed to "reaching the lost, with our mission 'to win souls and raise up soul winners,'" according to their website. "Our evangelists travel thousands of miles to speak to students that need the hope of Jesus."[12]

Under the pretext of treating drug addiction and other self-destructive behaviors, ATC is eager to bring its message to the "lost" of the public schools. "We believe strongly in the commitment of our public schools and coming along side them, affirming their teachers and administrators," they proclaim. "We discuss the choices students face every day, and how their past doesn't have to determine their future. The same compelling positive messages are presented in a way that is suitable for the public school setting."

Go Tell Ministries, an anti-drug group based in Duluth, Georgia, claims to have addressed two million students in public schools. The ministry is led by a former Liberty University assistant football coach, Rick Gage, who boasts that he "has led thousands of people—young and old, rich and poor of all ethnic backgrounds—to make personal decisions to live for Christ."[13]

Yet another group is the Nebraska-based Todd Becker Foundation, which has delivered hundreds of anti-drunk-driving assemblies to tens of thousands of students in public high schools. The group follows up dramatic and emotional stage presentations with one-on-one chats with "team members," who then "typically . . . share with the student the gospel of Jesus Christ and point them to the new life found in Christ." The foundation's "sole purpose," they boast, is "to motivate high school students to discover their potentials and ultimately discover themselves by placing their faith in Jesus Christ as Lord and Savior." On the "Support" page of their website, they urged supporters to "Pray that this ministry would continue to have the opportunities to share Christ in public schools across the mid-west."[14]

AFTER SENDING OUR letter concerning SFK to the principal, it occurred to me that other parents of third-graders might want to know what I had discovered about the group that would now be offering "character education" to our children. It seemed reasonable to suppose that they would find the information just as interesting as we did. As a newcomer to the community, however, I was reluctant to engage in any kind of mass mailing and make my first mark as a troublemaker. I was at the time making some effort to volunteer my services to the PTA—although, strangely, I hadn't yet been called upon to do anything, despite responding to an all-points plea for volunteers. I decided to approach the school's parent coordinator first.

"Please do not send this to other parents!" she said when I showed her the letter in her office. She did not quite explain why I should hold back, though it was easy to guess that she thought it important to give the administration time to look into the matter before getting caught up in controversy. I saw her point, and yet, as I told her, I also felt a certain responsibility to my fellow parents. In the end, I shared the letter with just two other mothers. I had had brief earlier conversations with both of them about the topic, and they both asked to see it.

In the meantime, the principal called us and requested that we meet with her in her office in order to discuss our concerns. I assumed our conference would include school officials alone. However, several minutes into the meeting, she announced that she had invited the new SFK director, Jenny Weil, to join us. Weil, who had been waiting just outside the principal's office, then entered the room. Unbeknownst to us, the principal had forwarded our letter to Weil. She had also shared our letter with the New York City Department of Education's legal department.

Weil, who was attractive and personable, was disarming. She had held her position with SFK for only a few months, but assured us that she, too, had found the Kabbalah Centre connection "a little strange at first" and "not my thing." She sought to assure us that "SFK and the Kabbalah Centre *are* separate," and "SFK is in the process of filing for independent tax status." She also told us that the information on the SFK website at that time was "misleading" and "incomplete."

Indeed, two days after our meeting, I discovered that the SFK website had been completely redesigned and beefed up, in an apparent effort to address many of the concerns we and presumably others might share. Some staff members with skimpy qualifications had been replaced with more credentialed candidates; the board of directors now had seven members (including celebrity Kabbalah Centre members Madonna and Ashton Kutcher) instead of just one. In the end, I realized, our letter to our principal enumerating our concerns about SFK had probably been very helpful . . . to SFK. It offered paint-by-number tips on the steps the organization might need to take in order to rebrand themselves, assume the appearance of legitimacy, and hide their connections with the Kabbalah Centre more effectively.

While only a small number of parents at our school were connected in some way with the Kabbalah Centre, I soon learned, one of them happened to be the president of our PTA. She said she had brought in the program at the recommendation of her sister, who had been a member of the Kabbalah Centre for a decade. The school also boasted a minor celebrity, a TV personality, whom the principal gave me to understand had approved of the presence of SFK in the school.

The principal was not going to change the program, I gathered; the PTA was going to continue to back it, and I now had some idea why I was not likely to be called upon as a PTA volunteer any time soon.

It wasn't much of an ostracism. As social snubs go, my exclusion from the school's PTA scene was as mild as could be. Nothing like the kind of backlash one might face in confronting a majority culture over its cherished rites and rituals, and certainly not worth comparing to what David Newman faced when he objected to the sectarian Bible curriculum in his daughter's public school. Yet it was there, the sharp glances and sidelong whispers, this hard nut of disapproval grimly handed out to those who stick their hand up when everyone prefers that questions not be asked.

While all this was happening, however, unbeknownst to me, my letter was lighting up the inboxes around the parent body. Apparently, the two parents with whom I had shared it thought it was indeed of interest, and they had passed the letter along to others, who passed it along to others. Enough heat was reflected back on the administration that, a week after it started, the SFK program quietly disappeared from our school, with no fanfare or announcement. Minority religions, in this kind of marketplace, generally don't stand a chance.

10

THE PEER-TO-PEER
EVANGELISM LOOPHOLE

Warning!
What you are about to read may be the most Radical approach to Evangelism in Public Schools you have ever heard of.
IS IT LEGAL? No—not for adults. But it is completely legal for
students! It is a God-given loophole!

—THE LIFE BOOK MOVEMENT WEBSITE, A PROJECT OF
THE GIDEONS INTERNATIONAL, WHICH HAS DISTRIBUTED
NEARLY 1.5 MILLION RELIGIOUS TRACTS TO
HIGH SCHOOL STUDENTS SINCE LAUNCHING IN 2009.

"GOD TRULY MOVED in such a mighty way. I just felt the presence of
God and the Holy Spirit in our school today," wrote Rachel Haley.
Another participant, Olga Cossey, said that witnessing the symbolic
pieces of paper being nailed to the cross was a "very emotional" moment for her. About 150 students took part in the event around
the flagpole at Edmond North High School in Edmond, Oklahoma.
Students prayed together and sang hymns as they nailed the paper
to the cross. On each piece was written the name of one of their
non-Christian classmates.

Like many of the religious initiatives now taking place in America's public schools, "See You at the Pole" represents itself as a student-led program. It began when a group of students gathered around a flagpole in 1990 in Burleson, Texas, a small town just south of Forth Worth, and now claims to reach two million students at 50,000 schools. The events take place annually, usually at 7 a.m. on the fourth Wednesday of September at schools across the nation, and students often bring sophisticated sound systems, rock bands, and other accessories of the megachurch movement onto their public school campuses. The ceremony involving nailing pieces of paper to a cross has been recorded in at least one other instance, at a high school in Kaufman, Texas.

In the technical terms of the public school missionary movement, "See You at the Pole" is an example of "peer-to-peer evangelism." The important thing about peer-to-peer evangelism is that, from a legal perspective, it is "private speech" by students, of the sort that is protected by the Free Speech Clause of the First Amendment. So, as the national leaders of the movement are fond of repeating, it's perfectly legal.

But the reality is much more complicated than the legal theory. At the Edmond High School, the people nailing names to the cross were indeed students; but the cross actually belonged to Darrell Haley, Rachel's father and a youth pastor at a local church, who had brought it along for the occasion. At other schools—such as Harrison High School in Evansville, Indiana, and Lakeview Elementary School in Wilson County, Tennessee—pastors, teachers, administrators, and parents have organized and participated in the events. In these and in countless other instances, peer-to-peer evangelism is just a complicated and increasingly popular way in which adults use children to do what they're not allowed to do on their own.

ON THE YOUTUBE video, the person you do not want to be is Nicole Smalkowski. Fifteen years old, a gifted athlete, and an enthusiastic member of the basketball team at her high school in Hardesty, Oklahoma, Nicole is also, as it happens, the daughter of Jewish parents with a nontheistic worldview. In the 2004 video of a home game, Nicole's teammates gather in a circle before the game to recite the "Lord's Prayer." While hundreds of spectators look on, Nicole stands alone, outside the group, not quite knowing what to do with her hands.

Following her performance, Nicole became the subject of a smear campaign.[1] Like the prayer rituals before the game, the initiative ostensibly came from the students themselves. But according to Nicole, adults were moving forces behind both the prayers and the smears. "This is a Christian country, and if you don't like it, get out," she remembers one teacher telling her. School officials not only did not stop the verbal campaign, according to Nicole, but also falsely accused her of "threatening another student" and suspended her from the team.

When Mr. Smalkowski obtained evidence that school officials had lied in their effort to remove his daughter from the team, he decided to take the matter up with the school principal. In the company of his wife and daughter, he approached the principal at his home.

Shortly after answering the door, according to allegations made in a federal suit, the principal "struck [Smalkowski] repeatedly without warning or provocation."[2] The Smalkowski family retreated.

In the next days, Mr. Smalkowski complained about what had happened to the principal and to other members of the community. The principal claimed that he had been hit first and took out misdemeanor criminal charges. The principal then offered to drop the charges—provided the Smalkowski family would leave the state.

The Smalkowskis refused to be run out of town. They chose instead to fight the allegations. In a swift and easy decision, a jury awarded them a small victory by tossing out the principal's charges.

Nicole doesn't play basketball anymore. But her team is still praying. And so are student athletes all across the country. We know about Nicole only because she stood her ground. But few fifteen-year-olds have the courage to stand alone, outside the prayer circle, with the entire community watching, in defense of their principles. And few parents and school administrators are foolish enough to draw national attention to the situation (and put their livelihoods and community standing at risk) by bringing a case to court. For every Nicole, there are perhaps thousands who quietly join the circle and mumble the words. Many students praying at their sporting endeavors are themselves nontheists or members of other religious traditions. But they know that the locker room is no place for dissent, and that a refusal to participate could easily be construed as a sign of lack of commitment to the team. They have learned that they have to pray to play.

Student athletics have become one of the most active targets for peer-to-peer evangelism in public schools today. The largest of the student athletics programs is the Fellowship of Christian Athletes, which specializes in instructing children on how to establish Christian prayers as a regular part of their school sports activities. The FCA was founded in 1954 by sports enthusiast Don McClanen, taking its place alongside some other youth-oriented ministries such as Young Life and the Campus Crusade for Christ that were forming around the same time.

The FCA seeks to project an open face of toleration on religious perspectives, thereby drawing in Christians of a variety of persuasions. But liberal religionists are conspicuously absent from the FCA, and its leadership and support are hard-line evangelical. Truett Cathy, a major funder and the founder of the Chick-Fil-A corporation, also contributes to the highly conservative Focus on the Family and an organization called All Pro Dad, best known for its promotion of "covenant marriage," in which marrying couples accept more limited grounds for divorce. The FCA also receives support from the Bradley Foundation, one of the largest philanthropic foundations responsible for the financial backing of the right-wing agenda and a major promoter of school voucher programs, which funnel public money to religious schools.

The move to Christianize the playing fields of public schools is an extension of the push at all levels of sport to "turn ballparks into pulpits and players into preachers," says Tom Krattenmaker, who writes on religion and public life for *USA Today*. In his 2009 book, *Onward Christian Athletes*, Krattenmaker details the systematic, well-funded, and highly successful effort to insert crusader overtones into the sports arena by drenching pro sports in a conservative version of the Christian religion. He explains that while liberal Christians and people of other faiths have stood idly by, hard-line evangelicals have "seized control of religion in the game," merging piety and aggression and separating both players and spectators into opposing sides—one "right" and the other "wrong." Players on high school sports teams thus imitate their heroes on the pro sports circuit by joining hands at midfield; forming "huddles," or group meetings that explore the Bible from a conservative Christian viewpoint; and pointing skyward as they cross home plate.

Such showy displays of piety in sports are far from spontaneous, as Krattenmaker points out. More often than not, there's a "faith coach" behind the game-time prayers and testimonies. In the case of the Philadelphia 76ers, it's Kevin Harvey, the team's volunteer Christian chaplain. Chaplains like Harvey are embedded inside each of the nearly one hundred teams in the "big three" major league sports. Many see themselves as sports world missionaries, target-marketing their version of "muscular Christianity" to impressionable young men. Harvey's day job is handling outreach for the Fellowship of Christian Athletes in southern New Jersey, which has established "huddles" at over sixty area schools.

The FCA has been spectacularly successful, and much of its growth has taken place in the past twenty years. In 1990, it claimed to have approximately 100,000 students involved in its programs. As of 2009, the FCA was the largest Christian sports organization in America, reporting a full-time staff of 600, 33,000 events, and nearly 1.8 million children "reached" at public school campuses and events, as well as at FCA-sponsored sports camps and activities.

According to many religious conservatives, the religion on the public school playing fields merely represents a return to the good old days, back before the courts kicked God out of the schools. In fact, so far as the use of school athletics for proselytizing goes, there is no time like the present. In San Diego, California, a long-serving vice principal who wishes to remain anonymous observes that thirty years ago, prayer played a peripheral role in high school sports. Now, he says, there are FCA huddles at nearly every high school in the region. "They have a more prominent presence today than they did in the past," he asserts.

The impact of this organized sports ministry, and others like it, can be seen in public schools nationwide. From the New Brunswick Bears, a football team in New Jersey, to the Celina Bobcats, a Texas football team, to the Tigers, a girls' basketball team in Wheaton, Illinois, players in public schools across the country gather to "pray before play." They join hands, praise Jesus, assert their identity as Christians, then break huddle to play ball.

WHEN RELIGIOUS CONSERVATIVES tell the story, it's all about little Johnnie who wants to sing about Jesus at the school talent show, or little Anna who wants to hand out candy canes with scriptural messages to her classmates at Christmastime, or football team members being so moved by their love for Jesus that they spontaneously burst into pre-game prayer. Sometimes that is what the story is about, and everyone can agree that, within an appropriate framework, students should always have the freedom to express their views. Considered on the whole, however, the mini-Awakening on the playing fields and in the classrooms of America's public schools is mainly an accomplishment of lawyers and judges.

Principal credit should go to the Christian Nationalist legal establishment: the American Center for Law and Justice (ACLJ), the Alliance Defense Fund (ADF), and their allies. The Justices of the Supreme Court deserve credit, too. Sandra Day O'Connor's distinction between public and private speech in the 1990 Supreme Court Decision *Westside School District v. Mergens* has an elegant and logical sound to it. Translated into the real world of playgrounds and classrooms, however, its real meaning is expressed in the conviction that "as long as it's coming from the kids, it's okay." Justices Thomas and Scalia, by all but dismissing the coercion thesis—the notion that school children are especially susceptible to peer pressure and school authority—have rendered the potentially coercive aspects of peer-to-peer proselytizing legally invisible.

The main actors on the Christian Right see peer-to-peer proselytizing as a legal loophole because that's exactly what it is—a way of getting around the spirit of the law without incurring any technical violations. In fact, the Sacramento, California–based Pacific Justice Institute (PJI) has produced a primer on the subject in its 2002 book, *Reclaim Your School: Ten Strategies to Practically and Legally Evangelize Your School*, published in very high spirits after the 2001 *Good News Club v. Milford Central School* decision.

Reclaim Your School lists the myriad ways that conservative Christian students may evangelize their peers on public school campuses. The list is long: start a "student-led" Bible club; wear Christian-themed T-shirts; or sing Christian songs at talent shows. "Choosing to use a talent show or lip synch to spread the Gospel is a great plan!" The book suggests that students find ways to infuse their academic subjects with religion. "Book reports, especially ones that are done orally, provide a tremendous opportunity for evangelism." Students might include religious messages or iconography in their arts-and-crafts projects such as Valentine's Day cards and Mother's Day cards. And "reaching" teachers is actively encouraged. "When the student writes a paper expressing his or her faith," the book states, "*the teacher has to read it*. But students can also be creative. Some students may (with parental consent) invite their teacher over for dinner," where presumably the family will proselytize them. "Students may also give their teachers holiday cards with a distinct religious message."[3]

The fun doesn't stop with public school teachers and administrators. In addition to delivering faith-infused graduation speeches, handing out religious tracts on campus, and just plain "sharing their faith," the book encourages "students" to organize "revival rallies" on campus.

"The idea of having revival rallies at public schools is very close to our hearts. . . . Organizing revival rallies on public school campuses will no doubt multiply youth ministries," the authors advise.

Whether you are a student, youth minister, or parent reading this book, we strongly encourage you to consider this exciting opportunity. It is an opportunity to bring in worship bands, dynamic speakers, and testimonies from people who previously dealt with drug addiction, promiscuity, or homosexuality before they found the Lord. Does this sound overwhelming to you? Well, you do not have to do it on your own! Talk to others in your church. Talk to your pastor. Help them see a vision of young people gathering after school, in their school, to hear the Gospel creatively presented through music, testimonies and speakers![4]

The basic idea behind the PJI primer is that children in schools can effectively set up miniature missionary operations within the schools. One group that has taken this message to heart is Kids for Christ USA, a group formed in 2001 to assist students and parents who wish to "plant" Bible clubs in public schools. Kids for Christ USA makes no bones about the fact that it sees its kids as a means to reach other kids. One of its principal missions, it says, is to "train and equip young believers with what they need to win others to God." "Bible clubs which are done well look like full-blown kids' church or youth church—de-churchified—and condensed to 30 to 40 minutes before or after the bell, right inside public schools," the group's leader declares. "Our purpose is simple: Reach children in the public schools with the Good News of Jesus Christ. . . . I would venture to say that it is entirely possible that we are seeing more unchurched kids than anyone else in the USA."[5]

The ADF, eager to capitalize on the new form of access to America's public schoolchildren, has moved in on the peer-to-peer action with its own initiatives. Partnering with a group called Gateways to Better Education, a group allied with Focus on the Family and others, it now backs a project called Religious Freedom Day and publishes *A Guide for Commemorating Religious Freedom at School.* The guide is intended to "promote religious freedom for America's public school children" by helping churches to equip their members with "vital information regarding religious freedom in public schools."[6]

The freedom that the ADF and its partners have in mind, it would appear, applies only to those who share their religion. "Religious Freedom Day is not 'celebrate our diversity day,'" the Gateways group cautions. The guide teaches children "a Biblical approach to tolerance"—which mainly describes their intolerance for what they call "pro-homosexual education" and the "gay activist agenda." Gateways also embraces creationism, and seeks to cast the issue as one of "tolerance" for a "Biblical" point of view. The number-one goal, they say, should be to "encourage your children to be bolder in living their faith at school because you, and they, know their freedom of religious expression."[7]

In his critique of peer-to-peer initiatives, Krattenmaker notes that "Proponents of the majority religion may fail to see that 'sharing their faith' starts to feel like 'religious bludgeoning.'" But the lawyers behind the movement seem well aware that the kind of "tolerance" and "expression" they wish to promote will be experienced by others as insulting or coercive. Indeed, it can only be on that account that Gateways has made sure to insert language in its Religious Freedom Day program that promises to "promote clarity and respect by providing its staff and students with information on freedom of religious expression in our schools." The way to bring clarity, it turns out, is to send a "detailed letter" from the ADF's litigators, who will make sure that school administrators know whose side the law is on.

FOR YEARS, THE Gideons International was best known for placing Bibles in nearly every hotel room in America. It also sought to find different ways of distributing the Good Book in America's public school classrooms and at school-related events, from walking into the school with boxfuls of Bibles and putting one in each classroom, to handing out Bibles at school fairs and back-to-school nights. Results have been mixed. Some school teachers and administrators, perhaps favorably disposed to the Gideons's evangelistic message, welcome them in; others, recognizing that our courts deem it unconstitutional for a school to distribute sectarian religious material, do not. Court battles over Bible distribution have erupted in dozens of communities—in Collier County Florida; in Upshur County, West Virginia; in eastern Missouri—and while its illegality has been reaffirmed by the courts numerous times, the practice continues.

But a glance at the Gideons's latest initiative, the Life Book Movement, which debuted in 2009, shows that they too have discovered the loophole in judicial reasoning about religion in public schools. Their stated goal is to "Saturate 91,957 high schools with God's word," and the basic plan is to persuade *students*, rather than adult missionaries, to give copies of the Good Book to their friends and classmates. That way, they say, it's perfectly legal.

The Life Book is a bite-sized, Cliff Notes–type summary of the evangelical Gospel, complete with "real teen" handwriting scribbled in the margins. Participating "student missionaries" are provided with enough Life Books to hand out to every child in their class, or even at their school. "Through strategic counter-insurgency," says Carl Blunt, one of the key leaders of the movement, "students give classmates a copy of the Life Book at school to introduce them to Jesus Christ."

The Life Book Movement is also referred to as "Bible Smuggling 101." Touted as "an innovative strategy to reach public school students," in the words of a Life Book movement participant, it "brilliantly threads a separation of church and state loophole." "It's like we're helping students smuggle God's word into a closed country [public high schools] to reach an unreached people group," boasts Blunt, striking a note of gleeful defiance. At least by its own account, the group has been an enormous success. While "flying under the radar," they have distributed over a half million copies in two dozen states.[8]

One of the Life Book's partners is the California Schools Project (CSP), a nonprofit that "helps to promote God, the Bible, and Prayer in California public schools." It was founded in 2004 by Warren Willis, who served for forty-four years with the Campus Crusade for Christ (the organization recently renamed itself Cru). The CSP claims to have forged relationships with teens on sixty-six campuses in the Golden State to date. CSP enables college students to mentor high school students in becoming evangelizers on their public school campuses. Participating high school students then carry out those missions through "student initiative." That includes "giving out Bibles to the entire campus," "students praying in the Quad," and "personal witnessing on campus." In every instance, the religious activity is ostensibly student-led, bypassing the strictures of First Amendment prohibitions. The California School Project website boasts a map with small blue flags to indicate conquests, which appear to be mostly in California's southern and inland areas. Partnering organizations include California's evangelical Christian, "Bible-centered" colleges such as Azusa Pacific University and Biola University, whose students act as mentors to evangelical high school students seeking to "reach" their public schoolmates.

"We really felt like God wanted us to push out from our comfort zone this semester," said Michael Towson, director of Biola's California Schools Project chapter.

"In the US alone, there are 25 million middle school and high school students," says a thirtysomething man on the video named Chad, who is identified as a leader of the North American Mission Board. "The odds of reaching all of them are staggering."[9]

The screen switches to Greg, a fresh-faced youth representing a peer-evangelism organization called Dare 2 Share. "See, the vision is we all go together to make disciples who make disciples," he says. "We're talking about a self-replicating cycle of teenagers in every high school and middle school in America, because they can do it."

Steve, from Youth Alive/Assemblies of God, chimes in: "A student can reach their friend for Jesus more effectively than me as a youth pastor or even a parent can."

"Lock arms with people with a common vision!" enthuses Dan from the Fellowship of Christian Athletes.

The promotional video is intended to support what is surely the most ambitious peer-to-peer project to date. Launched in 2011, "Every Student Every School" intends to live up to its name by establishing student "ministries" in every public middle and high school in the country. "The goal is to see a ministry to every school so that every student has the chance to hear about and see God's love and forgiveness in action. . . . Great movements have always been driven by the young."

The video is slick and expertly produced. This is clearly a group with a lot of backing. Its roster of supporters proves that the peer-to-peer proselytizing business has moved into the big leagues. ESES's sponsoring group, the CampusAlliance, represents an all-star coalition of forty-nine powerful conservative and fundamentalist organizations and religious groups, including Youth for Christ (USA), Church of God, Christian Educators Association Int'l., Josh Mc-Dowell Ministries, Gateways to Better Education, Fellowship of Christian Athletes, Young Life, Youth with a Mission, the Life Book Movement, the Evangelical Free Church in America, General Baptist Conference, Joshua Force, Student Venture/Campus Crusade for Christ (or Cru), Intercessors for America, and the Church of the Nazarene.

The keynote sound bite in the fast-paced video comes from a pastor named Mark. "What is stopping us from doing this?" he asks. "What is stopping us from looking at the one place that everyone has to go?"

11

Enlisting in the Army

How to Join the Good News Club

I DON'T LIVE in Brookline anymore, but I return often to see my mother, who still lives in the creaky Victorian home where I grew up. I like to check in with old friends and stroll through the neighborhood, counting off the fading memories: Karen's house, where I had my first sleepover; the Barnets, who hosted the annual neighborhood Easter egg hunt; Emma's house, where I spent many an afternoon poring over *Tiger Beat* magazine.

I usually find myself drifting past the anchor of our community—the John D. Runkle public elementary school. When my kids are with me, I point out the familiar red brick classroom where I learned my letters and the grassy field where I ran my first race. From time to time I step inside to check out the new sports trophies in the old display cases, or peek into the seventh graders' classroom, where my favorite teacher taught us about world history. I take note of any structural changes— an expanded playground, a renovated auditorium—which sometimes seem inexplicably like a betrayal, at other times a comforting reminder that the school remains alive. The familiar echo of children's voices in those hallways whispers to me of how much I have changed, but also of how much remains the same.

In the summer of 2010 I returned to find the neighborhood busy with the usual activities. The parks were noisy with kids, its reservoirs ringed with runners sweating through the humid afternoons. On this visit, however, my plan was different. I set about to join the CEF and participate in the massive Good News Club initiative it has launched in the Boston area.

THE BOSTON INITIATIVE is part of CEF Across America, one of the CEF's most forceful means of expansion. For each of the past three summers, CEF Across America has convened at a different city to "Jump start an evangelistic outreach to children in a target city," and thus "Capture a City for Christ!"[1] The first such initiative took place in Chicago 2008, followed by Little Rock in 2009. In 2010, it's Boston's turn.

I've found the Countryside Bible Chapel in Lexington, Massachusetts, and I am ready to apply. The CEF has solidified partnerships with forty Boston-area churches that are theologically aligned with their mission. Many of them are in the city's outlying areas such as Franklin, Framingham, Quincy, Chelsea, Everett, Dedham, and Norwood. A handful are in Boston proper, generally concentrated in some of Boston's historically working class neighborhoods. Three are in Dorchester, where my mother was born and raised.

By now it's mid-July, and several hundred seasoned CEF missionaries have recently descended upon the city to help to train volunteers from the partnering churches. The missionaries have come from all across the country, and are based at the Boston Baptist College. They will teach the volunteers how to lead a Good News Club and "counsel children for salvation."

In order to sign up as a volunteer, the CEF requires that we fill out some paperwork. As I flip through the handout, I discover that the CEF has an awful lot of questions.

The first page of the questionnaire requests the information required by state law of all child workers: a Criminal Offenders Request Information, or CORI, form. The Child Evangelism Fellowship has been certified by the Criminal History Systems Board for access to conviction and pending criminal case data, and those who wish to work or volunteer with the organization must submit their name, date of birth, place of birth, and Social Security number, as well as their mother's maiden name, current and former addresses, information on height, weight, eye color, and a state driver's license number. They must also offer a government-issued photo ID.

The next round of questions is much more personal and in-depth. The CEF wants to know about my lifestyle, character, purchasing habits, and above all, beliefs. They ask for "all aliases or nicknames," as well as all previous addresses for the past five years. Then they ask me to describe in detail my "conversion experience." They request references from pastors or church leaders, and leave four spaces for separate individuals to fill out.

I skip to a page that includes a ten-point National Background Check Authorization. It states that the applicant understands the CEF will conduct a check of his or her "character," work habits, and other details. The application bears the heavy print of lawyerly fingers.

"By signing below, you hereby release Child Evangelism Fellowship and its agents, officials, representatives, or assigned agencies, including officers, employees, or related personnel both individually and collectively, from any liability for damages of whatever kind, which may at any time result to you, your heirs, family, or associates because of compliance with this authorization."

"I hereby authorize, without reservation, any law enforcement agency, institution, information service bureau, school, employer, church or nonprofit organization, reference, or insurance company contacted by CEF or its consumer reporting agency or its agents, to furnish the information described above."

"I hereby release any individual, church, youth organization, employer, charity, reference, or any other person or organization, both individually or collectively, from any and all liability for damages of whatever kind or nature which may at any time result to me, my heirs, or my family on account of compliance or any attempts to comply with this authorization, excepting only the communication of knowingly false information."

I also am required to refrain from "unscriptural conduct." What might that be? One is expected to know the answer. I'm guessing from previous contact with the organization that the CEF is more concerned with the passage in Leviticus that frowns on same-sex intimacy than the prohibitions, also in found in Leviticus, against eating pork, wearing mixed-fiber fabrics, or trimming one's beard.

Section Three offers a CEF Worker's Compliance Agreement, separate from the Doctrinal Protection Policy—though it really reads like a doctrinal purity vow. Applicants must "agree not to propagate or practice in CEF ministries any distinctive or controversial doctrines, methods and practices that would go beyond the CEF Statement of Faith and the approved CEF curriculum." These would include but not be limited to such things as "modes of baptism, alteration of the Gospel message, speaking in tongues, interpretation of scripture by experience, healing on demand, etc."

The application also calls for complete submission to the authority of the CEF on matters of conscience. I am required to agree that "should any problems arise between CEF and me that cannot be fully reconciled, I will quietly withdraw to preserve harmony essential to having an effective Christian witness."

The meat of the application clearly hangs on the applicant's complete and unquestioning support of the CEF's Statement of Faith. I have seen a number of such statements, mainly on the websites of churches and other religious organizations, but this is the most specific and detailed one I've ever come across. Most Statements of Faith for evangelical entities consist of eight or ten points; the CEF Statement of Faith has fifteen.

Therein are found a rigorous version of many typical fundamentalist bullet points: the conviction that scripture is the "inspirited" word of God, belief in the deity of Jesus, the idea that man was created in God's image, faith that Jesus will return, and the salvation of believers. There is some detail about what will happen to nonbelievers: they will "remain after death in misery until the final judgment of the great white throne." After that, they'll be "cast 'into the lake of fire' which is 'the second death,' to be 'punished with everlasting destruction.'" The coda is the belief "in the reality and personality of Satan, 'that old serpent, called the devil, and Satan, which deceiveth the whole world.'"

Interestingly, I find some other points that are less frequently spelled out in such statements:

"There is no degree of reformation however great, no attainment in morality however high, no culture however attractive, no humanitarian and philanthropic schemes and societies however useful, no baptism or other ordinance however administered, [that] can help the sinner to take even one step toward Heaven." In other words, loving your neighbor or being a kind, ethical human being don't matter after all.

To drive the point home, it is reiterated that "no feeling, no faith, no good resolutions, no sincere efforts, no submission to the rules and regulations of any church can add in the very least to the value of the precious blood" of Jesus.

We learn that believers should abstain from "worldly and sinful practices." They are exhorted to "good works," but advised that it is more important to do good works for fellow believers—"especially unto them who are of the household of faith"—than unbelievers.

We also learn that the "supreme mission of the people of God in this age is to preach the Gospel to every creature. That special emphasis should be placed on the evangelization of children."

The document mandates that "Applicants should be in agreement with the CEF Statement of Faith/Doctrinal Protection Policy/Workers Compliance Agreement" and should sign the documents where indicated to signify agreement." One signature works for all four sections of this application.

I know I can't sign this document.

I tell the woman at the Countryside Bible Church who is handing out the forms that I'd like to participate as an observer for the time being. And I quietly leave the building, with a promise to return to Countryside for the upcoming CEF training session.

HOME OF THE "Shot Heard Round the World" and the opening battle of the American Revolution, Lexington, Massachusetts, is regarded by many as the birthplace of our democracy. It boasts the Minute Man National Park as well as one of the nation's first Unitarian Universalist churches, a magnificent structure dating from 1692. Lexington today has sizeable communities of Catholics, all the mainline Protestant denominations, evangelicals, Jews, Buddhists, and free-thinkers among others. It is home to several Baptist churches, including Countryside, an unassuming wood-and-brick structure with a low, peaked roof located about a mile from the Lexington Battle Green. The church, founded in 1958, has a homey, if anachronistic feel. Recent debates at the church have centered on whether women ought to wear hats, and whether dancing is permissible.

Membership at Countryside has declined in recent years, and a typical Sunday morning service attracts only a few dozen worshippers. Countryside, like other churches that partner with the CEF, hopes the alliance will inject a sense of mission and purpose among existing members, and perhaps attract the kind of young families that will revitalize their church community.

On a rainy Saturday morning, I travel from my mother's house in Brookline to Countryside to attend the CEF teacher training session. About twenty congregants show up. About half are adult men; the rest are a mix of adult women and adolescent girls. Because I have not completed the requirements necessary to qualify as a CEF missionary, I am participating as a newbie who is "drawn to children and education" and "want to learn more about the CEF." I find my way into the church's rectory and introduce myself to Pastor Jack Fish.

Jack, a husky man in his mid thirties, and his wife, Amy, a tall, friendly woman with dark hair and an efficient manner, relocated from Dallas, Texas, just a year earlier. With four children under the age of five, they are naturally focused on kids and families, which I sense is a factor prompting them to partner with the CEF.

For the training, CEF brings in education specialist Carolyn Pinter from the state headquarters in Douglas, Massachusetts. A mature, energetic woman who wears her dark grey hair in tight curls, Pinter, or "Miss Carolyn" as she calls herself, taught at a Christian school some years ago. Now she dedicates herself full time to CEF, leading teacher-training sessions for adults and adolescents all around the state.

Over coffee, prior to the training, Amy quietly expresses some reservations about conducting Good News Clubs in Lexington public schools.

"We're definitely going to run some kids' clubs this summer," she says somewhat nervously, referring to the 5-Day Clubs that CEF is organizing at public parks throughout the city. "But," she confides, "I'm not sure about going into the public schools. I'm not sure we're ready."

Overhearing the exchange, Miss Carolyn reminds her that starting a Good News Club in the public school in the fall is "part of CEF's contract with each church." "How else are we going to reach children except to go where they are?" she asks us later, standing near the podium of the main chapel as we, the prospective CEF volunteers, fill the first pews.

"Those kids from the 5-Day Club will become the core kids of the school ministry in the fall," Miss Carolyn explains. "It's tough getting into schools in Massachusetts," she confides gravely. "Very tough. People don't want it," she says, than catches herself, adding, "Not everybody. . . . You need to use leverage, like a lawyer. Schools *will* open their doors."

"Folks, public schools are where we meet unsaved children!" Miss Carolyn says passionately. "Do you want them to go to hell?"

Miss Carolyn wants us to know she understands how nervous we might feel about presenting ourselves as authorities on religion, or public speaking of any sort. "Even if you are shaking in your boots, don't worry about it," she assures us. "We will be right there for you." She also directs us to additional CEF-produced teaching aids, such as *Evangelizing Today's Child* magazine and the Children's Ministry Resource Bible.

She reminds us of our purpose: "Boston 2010 is to give the children the chance to say, 'I want Jesus.' The boys and girls don't *understand* salvation!"

The seminar, which runs from nine in the morning until about two thirty in the afternoon, is split into parts: Preparing the Heart for Teaching, which is largely about prayer and meditation; a class on Teaching the Gospel; Life-Changing Bible Lessons; and finally, Music with a Message: How to Teach a Bible Song.

I have to admire Miss Carolyn's style. Energetic and expressive, she seems to revel in her work, projecting warmth and creativity.

"Don't just say, 'Now I'm going to tell you a story,'" she instructs us, mimicking the heavy monotone of a bored babysitter. "If you say it like that, you've already lost 'em. Instead, say 'Heeeeyyyy! That reminds me of a *greeeeaaat* story I once heard.'" Her voice rises an octave as she spreads out her arms and twirls around, eyes popping in delight.

I begin to feel that the public schools could really benefit from people like Miss Carolyn. She would make a great math teacher, I think to myself. But for Miss Carolyn and those like her, the quiet satisfactions of teaching academic subjects to children can't compare with the instantaneous emotional drama of conveying their sin-and-salvation beliefs.

Exhorting us to be more devout in our own Bible readings, Miss Carolyn offers an example of the kinds of lessons she teaches to children in the public schools. "Last fall, a boy in Dorchester asked what would happen if Jesus had never come. He said to me, 'Does that mean that everyone would go to hell?'"

She looks at us and blinks. "And I said, 'Yes! That's exactly what it would mean!'" she chortled.

With that, she instructs us on how to "counsel" an unsaved child. "Give the boys and girls an invitation (to salvation) every week. For the enemy," she reminds us, "that is the *last* thing he wants us to tell anyone else about!"

Next is a demonstration and explanation of the CEF's most popular classroom accessory: the Wordless Book. "Each page stands for a part of the gospel," she explains. "It's in logical order, to help you to explain it to others."

It's the same book I've seen everywhere else in the country, with its gold, black, red, white, and green pages offering a child-sized version of the story of original sin and redemption through Jesus.

"The Bible says our hearts are dark with sin," she says in a singsong voice, demonstrating how we might grab and hold the attention of a young audience. "Anything you can think or say or do that goes against the laws of God that makes him unhappy. Even a little baby is a sinner. Within a few minutes of being born, he's squalling and crying, because he wants it his way. Punishment for sin is to be separated from God forever."

I've heard all this before, in exactly the same words—the squalling baby, the "separation from God forever" —from Deborah Rowe, the auburn-haired mother teaching a CEF class at the Missions Fest in Seattle. It's like hearing a comedy routine for a second time. There isn't an ounce of spontaneity in the program's curriculum. Everything is scripted, down to the last punch line. This is religion on an industrial scale, streamlined and codified into a tight set of procedures crafted by experts for maximum ease of use by middle-aged volunteers and maximum impact on the six-year-old mind. It's the spiritual equivalent of two slices of pickle and 4.1 ounces of special sauce and 48 sesame seeds on a five-inch bun.

"I'd like to offer a warning," Miss Carolyn says gravely. "If a child comes in to be counseled, and does not realize that he or she is a sinner, then do not go ahead with the rest of the invitation. If they are not willing to admit that they are a sinner, then they can't be saved."

To help the child truly grasp his or her fundamentally sullied nature, she advises us to pray aloud with the child in question. "Dear God," she offers a sample prayer, "Help Johnny to understand how punishment means he has done something wrong. Help him to understand what sin is."

Carolyn shares an anecdote about a mother who sent her child to the Good News Club with a mistaken impression of its mission.

"The mother got mad," Miss Carolyn says incredulously. "She grabbed him by the arm and yanked him away from us, saying to him, 'You're not a sinner! You've never sinned in your life! And as she was dragging him away, he was saying, 'But mom, I *do* sin!'"

The group titters. "The *mom* needs to understand what sin is!" Miss Carolyn says.

To help children grasp the concept of sin, she advises us to show children the verses in the Bible. "Say, 'Those aren't my words, they're God's words!' Teach them 'The ABC's.' A is that they have to admit they have sinned. They MUST admit that they are sinners! B is they need to Believe Jesus died for you. His blood cleans you, cleans the darkness of your heart. And C is the assurance of salvation."

Although the message about salvation is the centerpiece of CEF programs such as Good News Clubs and 5-Day Clubs, Miss Carolyn says we should be careful about promising a child that he or she won't go to hell.

"We don't want to give false assurance to a child that just by raising their hand or praying with us that they are saved. You also need to impress that Jesus is *the only way* to heaven. Not *a* way. The *only* way! We need to teach this in *every* class!"

Her voice turns despairing. "Some of those children who are there in your class that week will never come back. And," she pauses for dramatic effect, "you know who doesn't want you to give an invitation?"

"*Satan*," the group replies darkly.

"Look for the part of the story where you can teach the dark heart, about sin," she instructs us, as we read a handout about Naaman, a story from the book of 2 Kings. "Teach the dark page. Say to the children, 'Naaman had big problems. He had leprosy! But boys and girls, you and I have an *even more* serious problem than Naaman.' Then tell them about sin and punishment. Now you have taught the whole dark page!"

"Make it personal," she adds. "Use the child's name. 'God wants *you*, Johnny,'" she says, stooping to child's level and sounding as reassuringly child-centered as Mr. Rogers. "Have *you* sinned?"

But there is no need to segregate classes by salvation status, Miss Carolyn generously assures us. "Saved" and "unsaved" children may be taught side by side. "They *are* two different groups," she tells us. "But we want *all* of them to be His children."

The lesson for the saved child in the story of Naaman is obedience, as personified by an Israelite slave: "She had been captured and taken away from her family, but she wasn't angry or bitter or rebellious," says Miss Carolyn approvingly. "She *loved* her masters! She wanted to help them!" Other lessons for the saved child include telling their peers about God's word. "If you know God is your savior," she counseled the imaginary "saved" child in the room, "You should tell others about God's *one way*."

I realize Miss Carolyn hasn't delivered anything I could remotely call "Bible study." What I have received, with an astounding degree of fidelity in repetition, is the CEF gospel of the ABC.

As the group breaks for a lunch of deli sandwiches and potato chips, some of the church volunteers anticipate the reaction of local public school authorities to their arrival. "Lexington public schools are gonna go crazy!" delights John Hall, a middle-aged consultant who attends the training with his teenaged daughter, a watchful young woman in faded blue jeans. Although Hall and his kids live some distance from Lexington, he seems energized by the possibility of injecting religious conflict into this particular public school community. "There is so much darkness here, and nobody's challenging 'em. Their kids *need* the Gospel!"

After lunch, Miss Carolyn resumes with the final segment of the seminar: Music with a Message. She opens the session by slapping her hands twice on her thighs and clapping twice, leading a rousing, call-and-response rendition of the well-known Christian hymn:

"Jesus loves me this I know

For the Bible tells me so."

Breaking her song, she looks at us conspiratorially.

"Folks, this may be a loaded question," she says. "But can you teach spiritual truths through music that is a little . . . jazzy?" She cocks her head, inviting us to consider the radical possibilities.

"Or . . . *has drums?*"

A warning expression crosses her face. Then, bravely, she raises her chin. "Yes," she says resolutely. "You can."

"Folks, I teach in housing projects. Where there are children of . . . all nationalities," she continues, giving us a significant look. "What kinds of music do you think they listen to in those places? Jazzy music! Rock music! Rap!

"I do believe some kinds of music are irreverent," she continues. "I don't like that. But we need to be careful. We want music to be reverent *and* teach Biblical doctrine. But you have to know where your audience is at. Some people who are not walking with God don't get it. They wouldn't get a hymn.

"We don't want to wallow in the things we have broken away from because of the Holy Spirit. But to reach out a hand, you need to find a balance. Not to be pulled into the kind of life they're living, but to help them to mature.

"Music can be a touchy subject," Miss Carolyn says. "CEF is very conservative. And for a long time they would never have done that song," she says, referring to the thigh-slapping "Jesus Loves Me."

"I don't want them to go too far," she says, referring to her employers, "but they realize that they need to be in the present age."

In fact, CEF already realizes that they are in the present age; every year they produce fresh new music and eye-catching graphics to appeal to a generation of visually and technologically savvy children. Miss Carolyn plays us one of them: "The Countdown Song," which has a large picture book to accompany it. The song assures us that there is a fine place "somewhere in outer space" for those who "trust . . . and obey," and that "Jesus will come again." The "countdown," it says, is "getting lower every day." The words that struck me came from the catchy chorus:

> *Ten and nine, eight and seven,*
> *Six and five and four,*
> *Call upon the Savior while you may;*
> *Three and two, coming through the clouds in a bright array,*
> *The countdown's getting lower every day.*

"Sometimes I assign kids numbers from ten to one, and as we count backwards, they sit down one by one," Miss Carolyn says. "This is a good tool for teaching children about the Rapture."

As I hear talk of the utter annihilation of life on Earth, I'm hit with another flash of déjà vu. I remember Joan, the CEF teacher I met in Alabama, taking refuge from the anxieties of her life in a calming fantasy about the end of the world. It reminds me of a scene from my own teen years, when a friend's mother took us to a screening of the 1981 film *Eight Minutes to Midnight*, Helen Caldicott's documentary about nuclear proliferation. I remember an eerie sense of tranquility I experienced upon learning that we were all about to die—a nihilistic reverie that faded as I realized we weren't all about to die after all. What is the effect, I wondered, of such a massive effort to teach a generation of children that we are one beat away from the end of the world? And is this why the adults in the program seem to have only passing concern, if any, for the conflict and hostility that their work arouses in the communities where they insert themselves?

Miss Carolyn returns to the pressing task of preparing us newbies for CEF summer training. Showing us some of the materials that the central CEF office has produced for all of this year's 5-Day Clubs, she pulls out what appears to be a large traffic sign with an arrow and bold black letters spelling out the words: One Way. This is one of the props we'll be showing random children in public parks. It will surely look familiar to all children. But in this context, the sign will have a different meaning, one it is hoped that they will forever call to mind every time they see the identical signs on their streets and in their neighborhoods. It strikes me as an apt metaphor for the Good News Club's entire modus operandi: co-opting symbols of government authority—traffic signs, public school buildings—to create an impression in the minds of children that theirs is an "approved" mission.

Miss Carolyn plays the corresponding song for us on her sound system.

"God said to get to heaven, Jesus is the only way," we hear children singing in unison to the jaunty tune. "One way to reach the pearly mansions. Jesus is the only way / No other way / No other way / No other way to go."

"This is what we're teaching this year," says Miss Carolyn. "Because what do children hear in the world?" Her voice drops. "There *are* other ways," she intones with a dire expression. "We need to say, 'No.'"

"Folks, people may not like what you are doing," she concludes. "But don't be afraid to stand up for Jesus! Are you going to help other people know Jesus too? You can do it!" She flashes us all a wide, reassuring smile. "Folks," she says, beaming, "you are going to be ready. Ready to take on *those* children in *this* neighborhood!"

AT THE END of the training period, the volunteers, together with the CEF adult missionaries and members of Christian Youth in Action— the CEF's youth missionaries—hold 5-Day Clubs—so-called because they take place for five days over the course of a week—in public parks and playgrounds where children are plentiful. The 5-Day Clubs are essentially Good News Clubs in the open air—a form of street preaching targeting children, complete with props, stories, songs, balloons, and treats. They are dry runs for the newbie missionaries, before the serious business of starting a public school Good News Club begins.

After the training at Countryside, I attend numerous 5-Day Clubs in those parks–in Dorchester, Newton, and Weymouth. Only a small number of attending children are accompanied by parents or relatives. In the poorer areas like Dorchester, several children are dropped off by single mothers, presumably grateful for a few hours of free childcare. In the middle-class and wealthier areas, many participating children are being supervised by babysitters, who seem relieved to have someone else entertaining the kids for a while. Whether the babysitters allow the kids to attend out of boredom, curiosity, or religious conviction is hard to determine.

In many instances, it is nearly certain that the parents would not approve. A boy who wanders over while his babysitter chats with her friends on a park bench tells me his family belongs to the Sacred Heart Catholic church. An Asian grandmother who speaks almost no English brings her English-speaking grandson over—and yanks him away angrily fifteen minutes later, when it dawns on her what the club is really about. A charming four-year-old, brought to a 5-Day Club in Newton, Massachusetts, by her babysitter, proudly announces to the club's leaders, "I have two daddies! I also have a birth mother."

As a side note, Miss Carolyn has suggested that those of us who are interested in pursuing a position with the CEF might want to look into the CEF's Children's Ministry Institute (CMI), with a home campus in Warrenton, Missouri, and more than a dozen satellite campuses worldwide.

When I get home, I look at the requirements for enrolling at CMI, which offers both online and on-campus courses. They are even more specific—and stringent—than those required by church workers wishing to volunteer at Good News Clubs. There are four pages of information to be filled out by the applicant, two pages of detailed information for the pastor or church leader, and an additional two pages for the CEF Worker or Ministry Supervisor to fill out.

In the CMI handbook, a section on Christian Character stipulates that applicants "must give evidence of a lifestyle that is consistent with Christian principles. Students of CMI are required to refrain from moral laxity and the use of tobacco, alcoholic beverages, and illegal drugs."

On a separate sheet, applicants are asked to state their age of conversion, to write a testimony of their conversion experience, and to describe their process of spiritual development.

The really key items appear to have been saved for the pastoral reference form.

"What are the applicant's weaknesses?"

"When asked to follow direction from God-ordained authorities, this applicant generally responds with: (circle one) respectful obedience; outward compliance with negative attitude; willful noncompliance."

"How teachable is the applicant?"

"How would you rate the applicant's standards for Christian living?"

"If you were asked to have this applicant as a co-worker for several years, how would you respond?"

"How do you rate this applicant's potential in ministry?"

On the following page, the pastor is asked to rate the applicant on 21 different character traits on a six-point scale, from "poor" to "excellent." Traits include: Attitude toward confrontation; Submission to authority; Sense of call or mission; Self-image (self-esteem); Freedom from worry; Relationship with opposite sex; and Servant's attitude. There is room beside each category for additional comments.

THE AXIS ON which this application turns, I realize, is almost entirely contained in a single question, one that appears about halfway down the list:

"What is the applicant's attitude toward authority?"

The CEF wants followers. Even by the very form of its grueling applications, it seeks out those who are eager to submit. What it offers in return for such submission seems equally clear. It promises all those who embrace their servitude with a kind of mastery of their own. They will gain control over themselves and, more to the point, they will get the chance to exercise authority over the minds of the children of strangers. And everyone in this chain of command will be happy.

ON MY LAST day in Brookline, I pass by the old school. Banners announce a forthcoming science fair and a recent victory at some sporting event. It still has the feel of progress and high spirits, but now there's something clouding my thoughts. I always believed that because we all want the best for our kids, and would recognize the link between education and national excellence, public education would progress and improve. Our kids would be smarter and better informed than we were. Now I wonder if it's just that I was lucky enough to have been born in a generation that put less stock in the anxious need to indoctrinate than in the hope that open minds will find the truth. Maybe my generation got the best years of American education after all. Maybe my kids will have to deal with something compromised and inferior, a place where the aspiration to teach children takes a back seat to the desire to recruit them.

Throughout the writing of this book, I saw this sad diminishment occur over and over again. In Loyal Heights, Washington; in the Permian Basin, Texas; in Santa Barbara, California; and in New York City, the dynamic was repeated, with results that are not dramatically tragic, but look more like a slow bleed. When a religious group that sets itself at odds with much of the community uses the school to pursue its sectarian agenda, the community naturally responds by withdrawing from the school in an emotional if not necessarily a literal sense. The school moves farther and farther from the heart of the community. Families start to look at their school as a building where they send their kids for a certain number of hours each day. They may even see it as an alien presence. One day, it might prove easy to give up on altogether.

12

IF YOU CAN'T OWN IT, BREAK IT

The Plan to Undermine Public Education

WHEN LEADERS OF the Christian Right talk about their goals for public education, they often get caught up in a paradox. On the one hand, they want to be as actively involved in the public schools as possible. On the other hand, they want to withdraw from the schools and dismantle them.

One might imagine that reforming the schools is their main goal, and that pulling out of the schools is Plan B. But the likely story is more complicated. In a society as diverse as ours, the attempt to turn America's public schools into Christian academies is bound to fail, after all, except in sowing intense divisions within communities and undermining support for public schools. Why pursue a policy that is certain to fail? Maybe failure is the point.

In failing, the plan weakens the schools, diverting school personnel's energies from the task of educating students in academic subjects and compromising a sense of loyalty to the schools among the communities they serve. It also undermines support for the schools among religious conservatives, who will continue to blame them for the failings and complexities of a modern society. Plan A, therefore, may very well be just the first step towards Plan B—to get rid of the schools altogether. This may not be the conscious goal of many on the Religious Right, but it is what they are actually doing. In fact, the national groups supporting initiatives to increase involvement with the public schools are the same ones behind initiatives to defund and ultimately eliminate those same schools.

If you can't own it, break it.

PUBLIC SCHOOLS HAVE always been convenient targets of criticism. Pretty much everybody has something bad to say about some aspect of the school system some of the time. And yet most people send their own kids to public schools, and in spite of the system's perceived imperfections, those parents express admiration and gratitude for the talent and hard work that teachers and administrators show in educating their children.

On the Christian Right, however, the vitriol directed at the public education system often achieves an unparalleled degree of ferocity and bitterness. When many leaders of the Christian Right talk about public schools, it is hard to believe that they are actually talking about the same places where our own kids are learning their multiplication tables, memorizing state capitols, and playing jump rope with their friends at recess. The complaints are often so extreme that it seems doubtful that they could ever be addressed by any school system in the real world. Indeed, the fury from Christian Nationalists is so total and uncompromising that it is hard to imagine it could be satisfied by anything short of destruction of the system.

The hostility to public education among conservative Christians goes back a long way. A. A. Hodge, a nineteenth-century theologian and principal at Princeton Seminary, predicted in 1890 that a system of public education would become an "efficient and wide instrument for the propagation of Atheism." "I am as sure as I am of Christ's reign," he said, "that a comprehensive and centralized system of national education, as is now commonly proposed, will prove the most appalling enginery for the propagation of anti-Christian and atheistic unbelief, and of anti-social nihilistic ethics, individual, social, and political, which this sin-rent world has ever seen."[1] Christian Reconstructionists, led by Rousas J. Rushdoony, continued the attack. The goal of "statist" education, according to Rushdoony, is "chaos," "primitivism," and "a vast integration into the void."[2] In the 1960s and 1970s, when Jerry Falwell and other leaders of the new Christian Right emerged, they borrowed from the Reconstructionists the same hostile attitude toward public education and made it a recurring theme of the movement.

In recent years, the rhetoric is as hot as it has ever been. "The infusion of an atheistic, amoral, evolutionary, socialistic, one-world, anti-American system of education in our public schools has indeed become such that if it had been done by an enemy, it would be considered an act of war," D. James Kennedy said in 1986.[3] In 2010, Dr. Gregory Thompson, a frequent contributor to Christian News-Wire, echoed the claim: "The government schools are anti-Christian, atheistic and pagan, and they are against God, family, and country. To know this truth, and to not do anything about it in your area of influence is sin."[4] In 2011, Dr. Robert Simonds, founder and president of the National Association of Christian Educators, said: "We don't have to be very bright to know: if we send our Christian Church children to an atheist, immoral school for 12 straight years—6 hours a day, for over 300 days a year, they will almost all (88% right now) give up their strong faith in God and leave the church."[5]

The voices decrying the godlessness of public education are not confined to the fringes of conservative Christianity. In 2009 Dr. Morris H. Chapman, president and chief executive officer of the Southern Baptist Convention's Executive Committee, joined the chorus. In a widely discussed article in the *Baptist Messenger*, "A Case for Christian Elementary and Secondary Schools," Chapman asserted that in far too many public schools throughout the country our children are being "bombarded with secular reasoning, situational ethics and moral erosion."[6] For religious conservatives, the idea was not new; but the fact that the most powerful Baptist leader was willing to express it drew a lot of attention.

"All Christians should note this sea-change in sentiment within the SBC," exulted Bruce Shortt, author of the 2004 book *The Harsh Truth About Public Schools.*[7] E. Ray Moore, another vocal critic of the public schools, also reveled in Chapman's assertion. "Dr. Morris Chapman's clarion call . . . could not have come at a more opportune moment when families are crying out for assistance with their children and churches are losing the next generation of youth to worldliness, humanism and post modernism due to public schooling."[8] Grady Arnold, a Texas pastor who directs an organization called the Alliance for the Separation of School and State, also welcomed Chapman's move. "Southern Baptists have been playing the 'ostrich with its head in the sand' routine long enough," he said. "The time is way overdue that we acknowledge the devastating effects public school is having on the faith of our children."[9]

At the Southern Baptist Convention meetings, the signatures that now adorn resolutions damning the public school system are increasingly weighty. They include presidential candidate Ron Paul, Dominos Pizza founder Tom Monaghan, Ed Crane of the Cato Institute, and educator and lecturer John Taylor Gatto. The enemies of the public school system are growing, and though many of them base their opposition on the rhetoric of free markets and choice, the effect of their advocacy converges exactly with that of the Christian Right.

IF THE PUBLIC schools are so bad, one line of thought on the Christian Right goes, then the thing to do is get involved and change them to our liking. In the 1970s and 1980s, Jerry Falwell urged his constituents to run for school boards across America. D. James Kennedy, the late leader of the Coral Ridge Ministries, endorsed the plan. "The Christian community has a golden opportunity to train an army of dedicated teachers who can invade the public school classrooms and use them to influence the nation for Christ," he enthused in a 1993 publication, *Education: Public Problems and Private Solutions.*[10]

As former director of the Christian Coalition Ralph Reed explained it, "We are focused on where the real power is, in the states and in the precincts and in the neighborhoods where people live and work."[11] Reed's organization and others, such as Citizens for Excellence in Education, worked with coalitions of church groups to train Christian candidates for school boards. Often, candidates would run while keeping their conservative religious agenda hidden, only opposing the teaching of science and anatomy, or advocating for abstinence-until-marriage programs, once on the board.

Dr. Robert Simonds set up his organization with the intention of getting Christian activists elected to school boards. "There are 15,700 school districts in America," he explained. "When we get an active Christian parents' committee in operation in all districts, we can take complete control of all local school boards. This would allow us to determine all local policy; select good textbooks; good curriculum programs; superintendents and principals. Our time has come!"

The Southern Baptist Convention (SBC) has traditionally favored this kind of active involvement in the schools over a strategy of withdrawal. In 2004, when Bruce Shortt introduced a resolution at the SBC's annual meeting calling for an "exit strategy" from public schools, the resolution was voted down on recommendation of the Executive Committee. "The church does not wish to interfere with the authority of parents to decide what is in the best interest of their children," the committee said. The underlying reality is that the vast majority of Baptists send their children to public schools; most of them like their schools; and a surprisingly large proportion are employed by those schools.

"School exit proponents are right to decry the moral chaos that is being sanctioned by the California public school system," said Dr. Tony Beam, a member of the SBC's Resolution Committee. "But calling for an exodus from the public school is not the answer. The solution is not retreat but a recommitment to retake the public schools for Christ." "Instead of withdrawing from public schools," evangelist Franklin Graham added, "Christians should train their children to share the Gospel with their non-Christian classmates." Dr. Chapman, the leader of the SBC executives, appeared to repeat the message in his widely discussed article on Christian schools of 2009. "Kingdom education should not be a reaction to public education," he said. "The focus should not be to abandon public schools, but to be certain not to abandon our biblical responsibility to come alongside parents in training up a child in the way he should go."[12]

The strategy of involvement, however, is often hamstrung by its entirely unrealistic ambitions. If the problem with public education is that it is inherently secular, as Chapman indicates, then the only way to reform it to the satisfaction of the Christian Right is to make it something other than what it is. The problem is evident in the writings of Dominionists, who also advocate active involvement in the schools—but only so that those schools can be completely transformed. "[I]f Christians are charged with exercising dominion in all spheres of life (Gen. 2:26–28), to abandon public education to Satan is to compromise our calling," wrote Reverend Andrew Sandlin in 1994 in the Chalcedon Report, a publication of Rushdoony's influential foundation. "The attitude and approach of Christians should be that they never expose their children to public education, but that they should work increasingly to expose public education to the claims of Christ. Certain specially suited Christians, in fact, should pray and work tirelessly to obtain teaching and school board and even administrative posts within public education. The penultimate goal of these Christians should be the privatization of these larcenous institutions, and the ultimate aim the bringing of them under the authority of Christ and His word."[13]

WHEN ACTIVE INVOLVEMENT fails, many leaders of the Christian Right have advocated withdrawal. Jerry Falwell had moved into this position by the time he gave a talk at Regent University on "Trends in Christian Higher Education" in 1993. "The public school system is damned," he announced. "Let me tell you how radical I am. Christian students should be in Christian schools. If you have to sell your car, live in a smaller house, or work a night job, put your child in Christian schools. If you can't afford it, homeschool."

Dr. Robert Simonds underwent a similar evolution. In 2010, his group, Citizens for Excellence in Education (CEE), flipped from advocating active involvement in the schools through school boards to promoting complete withdrawal from the schools. In an open letter to the group's 185 chapters and nearly 200,000 members, he wrote that "God has given CEE incredible victories in our efforts to save our Christian children in public schools—and thereby guiding CEE to save America's public school children from atheism, homosexuality, the occult, drugs, children having children, abortion, brainwashing, and crippling psychology. . . . Yet, with all the positive changes we've seen because of each of you, that together we have accomplished for God, the system of public education has refused to bend . . . Therefore . . . CHRISTIANS MUST EXIT THE PUBLIC SCHOOLS as soon as it is feasible and possible."

Bruce Shortt advocated the same policy in his 2004 book, in which he declared that the "spiritual, moral and intellectual pathologies of the government school system are now obvious even to casual observers. Christian parents and pastors need to ask themselves just how much longer they intend to render our children to Caesar's spiritually dark, morally decaying, and physically dangerous government schools."[14] The stated goal of E. Ray Moore's Exodus Mandate group, likewise, is "to encourage and assist Christian families to leave government schools for the Promised Land of Christian schools or home schooling."[15] A video posted on the Exodus Mandate website likens the proposed abandonment of public schools to the evacuation of allied forces at Dunkirk in World War II.

The campaign to remove children from public schools is quickly gathering steam. A substantial number of fundamentalist parents have already cast their votes silently, by bringing their children home. Between 1999 and 2007, homeschooling shot up by 74 percent, to over 1.5 million children, representing approximately 3 percent of all school-age children in the United States—a figure that is undoubtedly higher today. The largest part of that growth came from parents moti-vated by religious concerns. Many homeschooled Christian children use textbooks provided by Christian Nationalists, which teach that dinosaurs and humans walked the earth at the same time, minimum wage and progressive taxes are contrary to the Bible, and Biblical Christians have a duty to assume absolute power over government in preparation for the second coming of Christ.

A STILL BETTER option than to simply withdraw from the schools, as many of the more far-sighted strategists on the Christian Right have come to understand, is to take the money with you when you go. That, in essence, is the point of the voucher policies that many of the most powerful groups of the movement now favor. School vouchers allow parents to take a portion of the tax money that funds public education and divert it to the private school of their choice. Since many parents will choose to use the vouchers for religious schools, the proposed policy amounts to a means of using taxpayer money to fund religious education.

The voucher strategy comes complete with its own double-talk. The preferred euphemism among voucher advocates today is "school choice." Aside from being a word that liberals and moderates tend to like, "choice" helps voucher proponents conflate their agenda with the creation of magnet and charter schools. In fact, charter schools and school vouchers are essentially separate issues. Charter and mag-net schools are publicly funded, and therefore governed by constitu-tional law concerning the separation of church and state. School vouchers, on the other hand, allow parents to remove money from the funding sources of public schools and use it to fund religious schools.

The school choice concept has found a home among free-market-oriented think tanks such as the Heritage Foundation and Cato In-stitute, which now spend millions of dollars promoting the idea. The pitch is all about the miracle of the market: let schools compete, they say; the best ones will prevail, and inferior schools will improve themselves to meet the competition. The voucher movement is especially appealing to fiscal conservatives. Milton Friedman was a proponent of vouchers, as was Ronald Reagan, who was influenced by Friedman's ideas.

The idea of "school choice," however, did not originate with advocates of the free market. It first came into use in the 1950s and 1960s, when some white families in some southern states wished to avoid sending their children to integrated schools. Public officials began promoting "schools of choice," encouraging the creation of private schools that were, in effect, white-only. Such "choice" schools were also known as "segregation academies." In Virginia, where there was enormous resistance to racial integration, the state gave tuition grants to students so that they could enroll in private schools of their own choosing.

At the same time that the school choice movement was taking root, Catholics who wished to receive federal money for their parochial schools were making a fresh round of pleas for a share of federal funds. They were roundly opposed by Protestant and Jewish groups who argued against state support of religious schools. Now that conservative evangelicals feel that they no longer have a grip on the public schools, they have switched sides, and now they too endorse state subsidies for private, religious education.

In the states, the voucher movement is being led by the group of Republican governors who support educational privatization. Voucher supporters, seizing the moment, are pooling their resources. A voucher front group called Citizens for Educational Freedom reported in November 2010 that the previous summer, representatives from over 300 pro-voucher organizations met in San Francisco to strategize.

Academics, policy makers, and others have put forth numerous arguments and studies over whether or not voucher programs improve educational outcomes. But among the most important supporters of the idea, such arguments are irrelevant. The underlying motive, for them, is not to improve public education, but to eliminate secular public education at its root. Mae Duggan, who founded the voucher front group that met in San Francisco, Citizens for Educational Freedom, said disparagingly, "We don't want people teaching humanism. Secular humanism is the basis of the public schools."

Another pro-voucher initiative, National School Choice Week, was chaired by Michigan activist Kyle Olson, who runs websites attacking teachers' unions and public education. Although his group, Education Action Group, which he founded in 2007, appears to be a small outfit, he receives funding from the Gleason Family Foundation, a multi-million-dollar foundation that also distributes large sums to, among others, the Cato Institute, the Heritage Foundation, the Center for Education Reform, and Alliance for School Choice.

In a recent column for Townhall.com titled "Jesus Isn't in Michigan," Olson wrote, "I would like to think that, yes, Jesus would destroy the public education temple and save the children from despair and a hopeless future. And he would smash a temple that has been perverted to meet the needs of administrators, teachers, school board members, unions, bureaucrats, and contractors."[16]

Although the voucher movement comes cloaked in the rhetoric of choice and free markets, its real agenda is to eliminate the system of public education. "We think the public schools should go away," said Teri Adams, president of the Independence Hall Tea Party, an influential group running a PAC operating in Pennsylvania, Delaware, and New Jersey. "Our ultimate goal is to shut down public schools and have private schools only, eventually returning responsibility for payment to parents and private charities. It's going to happen piecemeal and not overnight, as it took years to get into this mess."[17]

COMPLEMENTING THE VOUCHER strategy is a push to remove the federal government as much as possible from education. In recent years, growing numbers of Republican Party platforms, including those of Maine, Minnesota, and Texas, state their support for dismantling the Department of Education—an idea endorsed by Tea Parties around the country. In October 2010, for instance, the California Tea Party's David Harmer advocated the elimination of public schools and a return to "the way things worked through the first century of American nationhood"—a time when an inconsistent patchwork of educational schemes left the majority of our nation's children without any formal schooling at all. In January 2011, Kentucky's Rand Paul, another Tea Party darling, stated his goal to abolish the Department of Education, calling it an "overreach of power by the federal government." Within the week, he was rewarded by Senate Republicans with an appointment to the Senate Education Committee. Even Focus on the Family has weighed in. Senior vice president of the Family Research Council, Rob Schwarzwalder, wrote in 2010, "The department [of Education] is unconstitutional, ineffective, and wasteful. In short, it should be abolished . . . aim carefully and slay the dragon for once and for all."[18] In theory, removing the federal government from public education might be a way of getting states more involved; in practice, the people militating for the elimination of the federal Department of Education almost never offer corresponding proposals to improve state-level administration.

THE SAME GROUPS that have masterminded the success of the Good News Club and other initiatives to introduce religion into the public schools are also leading the charge to deprive the public education system of funding and support by means of voucher programs. The Alliance Defense Fund, for example, is a leader in the effort to promote school voucher systems. So, too, is the Richard and Helen DeVos Foundation, which was built on the Amway fortune. The DeVos Foundation is a major supporter of the ADF, the Foundation for Traditional Values, and other groups actively seeking to influence public schools. It is now also a principal mover in the voucher debate, having created in 2010 an organization called the American Federation for Children to promote school vouchers.

The Bradley Foundation, another ADF funder, is a big supporter of the school voucher movement. The Edgar and Elsa Prince Foundation, with ties to the private military company Blackwater Worldwide (now Xe Services), is a major funder of religious conservative organizations such as the Alliance Defense Fund, Focus on the Family, the Family Research Council, and the secretive Council for National Policy. The Foundation also supports various "educational reform" initiatives.

Listening to the debates about public schools on the Christian Right, one hears plenty of opposing opinions and a great deal of confusion. Some want to change the schools, others want to leave them. But the smart money seems to know what it is doing. It provides support for programs like the Good News Club, which slowly erode the support for public education in the country at large and in their own constituency in particular. And then it lays the groundwork for dismantling public education in favor of a private system of religious education funded by the state.

Not all activists have adopted this endgame as a conscious part of their various religious initiatives around public schools. But it is the predictable consequence of their actions. Most schools are nowhere near as bad as the rhetoric of the Christian Right makes them out to be; the charges against them are ridiculously overblown. But if the Christian Right keeps up its efforts to weaken the schools, the schools may soon live down to the religionists' fantasies of decadence and decay. And then it will be much easier to "solve" the problem of public education once and for all.

CONCLUSION

IN THE COURSE of researching this book, I have had the privilege of getting to know many caring and generous individuals who shared moments of their lives and taught me a great deal. I think of Bob, a CEF teacher from Maine who gave me his well-worn Bible; Audrey, a CEF volunteer from Florida whose face shines with affection when she speaks about her Good News Club kids; and Evelyn, a gentle and elegant woman who welcomed me to her Texas church and shared her joy in prayer. I believe that these people mean well for the children over whom they are given charge and for the communities in which they work. I have concluded, however, that all of their good intentions have been harnessed in service of a national agenda that will ultimately erode our communities and undermine our public schools.

The goal of the national movement behind the assault on public education is to turn America into a "Christian Nation." I am not worried that they might succeed. I am worried about the damage that they will cause when they fail, as I suspect they will in a society as inherently open and pluralistic as ours. And I am alarmed that we have allowed them to get so far so fast.

How did we let this happen?

One reason why we haven't seen what is happening right in front of us is that the leaders of the religious assault on public education have learned to cloak their agenda in the language of liberalism and relativism. We are all children of the civil rights era now. We all agree that discrimination is bad. We all want to respect one another's worldviews, and we all cherish the right to freedom of speech. We are so used to the idea that the First Amendment is for liberals, and that it is our bulwark against fascist movements, that we fail to notice when it has been turned around and used as a wedge instead.

The judicial strategists of the Christian Right claim that all they want is "equal access" and "toleration." But that isn't in fact all they want. They don't want equality; they want control. They don't want toleration; they want the opportunity to practice their intolerance. They don't want their religion to be included in the schools; they want the schools to be absorbed within their religion.

Sometimes our legitimate concerns with individual rights so dominate our thinking that we deceive ourselves about the nature of the problems that we face. We have become very adept at measuring harm to individuals; but we are not so good at measuring harm to communities. We imagine that our legal rights and our ballot boxes are all we need for our democracy, and therefore we fail to appreciate the vital contributions made by other institutions. We suppose for legal purposes that a school is just a building, when it is not. We suppose that education is just another transaction, when it is much more than that. We have grown so used to the idea that collective action is never more than an infringement on individual rights—that government is always the problem—that we easily overlook one of the largest and most successful collective efforts in our history: the public school system. And we may well find, in a future world—where the rich have their own system of education, the religious have theirs, the poor don't get educated at all, and everyone is schooled in contempt for those who are different—that we have kept all of our rights, yet lost everything but the pretense of democracy.

Sometimes it is our deeply ingrained belief in American exceptionalism that prevents us from taking these problems seriously. Fundamentalism—politically aggressive fundamentalism in particular—is a growing global phenomenon. But it can't happen here, we tell ourselves. When fundamentalists elsewhere in the world insist on toleration for the oppression of women, for instance, we recognize the injustice of their demands. When fundamentalists talk about basing their laws on their sacred scriptures or making their state a theocracy, we have no trouble seeing that their ideas are deeply incompatible with modern liberal democracy. Yet when Christian Nationalists demonize gay men and lesbians and declare their intention to govern the country in the name of Christ, we imagine that, because this is America, it is somehow different. It isn't.

Maybe the main reason that we have let this happen is that we don't listen very well. We pay attention to Christian Nationalism when it runs for public office or makes pronouncements about federal policy. We don't notice when it shows up across the street or quietly takes up residence in our classrooms. And we just don't take its proponents at their word. Jerry Falwell, D. James Kennedy, Pat Robertson, James Dobson, and any number of other leaders of the Christian Right have told us that they abhor our public schools, and that they pray for the day when such schools cease to exist. Jay Sekulow, Mathew Staver, and other leaders of the Christian Right's judicial strategy have told us that they want to break down the "so-called" wall of separation between church and state. They have told us that the time has come to return our schools to the Lord. Maybe they are telling us what they really think. Maybe we should listen to them now, before it's too late.

ACKNOWLEDGMENTS

THIS PROJECT BEGAN with an article published in the *Santa Barbara Independent* on the appearance of a Good News Club in my daughter's public school. I'd like to thank *Independent* editor Marianne Partridge for embracing the story.

The project would not have been possible without the stories of many individuals whose lives have been affected by religious initiatives in their public schools. Many people invested their time and tested their patience in relating their experiences to me. I have acknowledged some of these people directly in the text. Many, however, prefer to remain anonymous, so I would like to thank them all anonymously.

The book benefitted from numerous interviews with people with in-depth knowledge of fields related to my topic. (The following list should not be taken to suggest that any of the individuals listed endorse the views expressed in the book.) They include Dan Mach, director of the program on Freedom of Religion and Belief at the American Civil Liberties Union; Rob Boston, senior policy analyst at Americans United for the Separation of Church and State; Richard Katskee, deputy director of the Program Legal Group, Office for Civil Rights at the US Department of Education; Charles C. Haynes, senior scholar at the First Amendment Center; Esther Kaplan, investigative editor at The Nation Institute; Chip Berlet, senior analyst at Political Research Associates; Mark Potok, director of the Intelligence Project at the Southern Poverty Law Center; Rev. Jennifer Butler, executive director of Faith in Public Life; Steven Newton, Public Information Project director at the National Center for Science Education; and the folks at the Texas Freedom Network.

Writers who have generously offered their insight into various aspects of my research include Sarah Posner, Kathryn Joyce, Chris Rodda, Jeff Sharlet, Bruce Wilson, and Tom Krattenmaker.

This project has also benefitted from the direction of professional academic researchers and experts. (I'd like to reiterate that the opinions expressed in this book should be blamed on me, not on those who have been generous enough to assist me.) They include Ira C. Lupu, professor of Law at George Washington University; Mark Chancey, associate professor in the Department of Religious Studies at Southern Methodist University; Professor Steven K. Green, the Fred H. Paulus Professor of Law and director of the Center for Religion, Law and Democracy at Willamette University; Professor Stephen Solomon, associate professor and the director of Graduate Studies in Journalism at New York University; R. Jonathan Moore, assistant professor of American Religious Pluralism at Denison University; David Sikkink, associate professor of Sociology at Notre Dame; Richard A. Layton, book review editor at the Journal of Early Christian Studies and associate professor for the Department of Religion at the University of Illinois at Urbana-Champaign; and David N. Figlio, professor of Education and Social Policy at Northwestern University;

I am so grateful to the many friends who have supported me in various ways: providing personal and professional encouragement, challenging me with different perspectives, and generously hosting me during my travels.

I'd like to thank Degen Pener for reading early drafts of several chapters, Sebastian Jones for some research assistance, and the folks at Media Matters for media research.

I am especially grateful to the staff at PublicAffairs for supporting the project so forcefully and improving the work. A special thanks to my brilliant editor, Lisa Kaufman, and my indefatigable publicist, Emily Lavelle. I am much indebted to my agent Andrew Stuart for his literary acumen and friendship. And finally, I'd like to thank my husband, Matthew Stewart, who made it possible.

NOTES

INTRODUCTION

1. Frank Schaeffer, *Sex, Mom, and God: How the Bible's Strange Take on Sex Led to Crazy Politics and How I Learned to Love Women (and Jesus) Anyway* (New York: Da Capo, 2011).

2. Jerry Falwell, *America Can Be Saved* (Murfreesboro, TN: Sword of the Lord, 1979), 52–53.

3. Robert L. Thoburn, *The Children Trap* (Ft. Worth, TX: Dominion Press, 1986).

4. D. James Kennedy, from a sermon titled "A Godly Education: A Sermon delivered on April 27, 1986" (Fort Lauderdale, FL: Coral Ridge Ministries, undated reprint), 5.

CHAPTER 1

1. See, for instance, Lauren Sandler, *Righteous: Dispatches from the Evangelical Youth Movement* (New York: Viking Penguin, 2006).

2. Karin Fleegal, "Rice Bowl Communication," *Evangelizing Today's Child* (Warrenton, MS: Child Evangelism Fellowship, 2000), November/December, 14–16.

CHAPTER 2

1. "Around the World in 80 Years," CEF online, www.cefonline.com /index.php?option=comcontent&view=article&id=517:around-the-world -in-80-years&catid=136:evangelism-and-discipleship-projects&Itemid =100175.

2. Ken Ham and Dr. A. Charles Ware, *Darwin's Plantation: Evolution's Racist Roots* (Green Forest, AZ: Master Books, 2007).

3. This and other quotes from Ken Ham and A. Charles Ware, ibid.

CHAPTER 3

1. Pat Robertson, *The New World Order* (Nashville, TN: W. Pub Group, 1991).

2. David Barton, "Early Education Laws Part 1," Davidbarton.net, April 23, 2010, www.davidbarton.net/2010/04/23/early-education-laws-by-david -barton/.

3. R. Freeman Butts and Lawrence A. Cremin, *A History of Education in American Culture* (St. Louis, MS: Holt, Rinehart & Winston, 1953).

4. David Nasaw, *Schooled to Order: A Social History of Public Schooling in America* (New York: Oxford University Press, 1979).

5. Rev. Walter Colton, "The Bible in public schools, A Reply to the allegations and complaints contained in the letter of Bishop Kenrick, to the Board of Controllers of Public Schools" (Philadelphia : T. K. & P. G. Collins, 1844). This and other details concerning the Philadelphia riots come from Bruce Dorsey, chair of the Department of History at Swarthmore College, who authored the report for the Historical Society of Pennsylvania, www.hsp.org.

6. Ibid.

7. Ibid.

8. Clarence Darrow, *The Story of My Life* (New York: Charles Scribner's Sons, 1932).

9. Jerry Falwell, *America Can Be Saved! Jerry Falwell Preaches on Revival* (Murfreesboro, TN: Sword of the Lord, 1979).

10. Quoted in Frank S. Ravitch, *School Prayer and Discrimination: The Civil Rights of Religious Minorities and Dissenters* (Boston: Northeastern, 2001).

CHAPTER 4

1. See Tony Mauro, "The Secrets of Jay Sekulow," *Legal Times*, November 1, 2005.

2. Alan Sears, *The Homosexual Agenda: Exposing the Principal Threat to Religious Freedom Today* (Nashville, TN: B&H Books, 2003).

3. Mathew Staver, *Same-Sex Marriage: Putting Every Household at Risk* (Nashville: B & H Publishing Group, 2004).

4. Jeffrey Toobin, *The Nine: Inside the Secret World of the Supreme Court* (New York: Doubleday, 2007).

5. Ibid.

6. Ibid.

7. Adam Liptak, "Reticent Justice Opens Up to a Group of Students," *New York Times*, April 13, 2009.

8. Posted on Jews for Jesus website, January 1, 2005, http://jewsforjesus .org/answers/lifestories/jay_sekulow.

9. *CASEBulletin*, July 1990, as cited in e-mail to the author from Rob Boston, Americans United for Separation of Church and State, July 22, 2011.

10. Marci A. Hamilton, *God vs. the Gavel: Religion and the Rule of Law* (New York: Cambridge University Press, 2005).

11. Quoted in Catherine Crier, *Contempt: How the Right Is Wronging American Justice* (New York: Rugged Land, 2005).

CHAPTER 5

1. Jim Laffoon, with Rice Broocks, "To Reach and To Rule," Morning Star International/Every Nation Churches and Ministries 2004 World Conference: Every Leader—Every Church—Every Nation, Anaheim, CA, July 15, 2004 (Victory Christian Fellowship).

2. Jim Brown, "Families Claim Religious Club's Cult-like Practices Injured Teens," News from Agape Press, July 25, 2005, www.agapepress.com.

3. See John Fialka, "Fervent Faction: Maranatha Christians, Backing Rightist Ideas, Draw Fire over Tactics," *Wall Street Journal*, August 16, 1985.

4. C. Peter Wagner, *Dominion: How Kingdom Action Can Change the World* (Ada, MI: Chosen, 2008).

5. Rousas John Rushdoony, *The Messianic Character of American Education* (Vallecito, CA: Chaldecon, 1963).

6. Gary North, *Political Polytheism: The Myth of Pluralism* (Tyler, TX: Institute for Christian Economics, 1989), 601.

7. George Grant, *The Changing of the Guard: Biblical Principles for Political Action* (Ft. Worth, TX: Dominion Press, 1987), 3.

8. Tape of first service held in P.S. 15 on August 18, 2002, cited in *Bronx Household of Faith v. Board of Education,* U.S. Court of Appeals, 2nd Circuit, Case 07-5291, reference number 2590203_1.

9. Ryan Abernathy, Comment posted May 13, 2010, on "Messenger Insight Vidcast Special Report—Dr. Ronnie Floyd," www.baptistmessenger.com, May 10, 2010, http://baptistmessenger.com/messenger-insight-vidcast-special-report-dr-ronnie-floyd.

10. Dan Wooding, "How a Salvadoran came to America, changed his name, and became a husband, father, writer, futurist, activist, artist and spiritual and cultural leader," ASSIST News Service, Lake Forest, CA, www.assistnews.net/stories/2008/s08010207.htm.

11. Jason T. Christy, *The Church Report* (Scottsdale, AZ) January 2007. See also www.thechurchreport.com for later issues.

12. "The Strategic Focus Cities Initiative/New Hope New York." The original website has been taken down as of August 21, 2011, but references to it may be found in: James Dotson, "New Hope New York," SBC Life, October 2003, www.sbclife.org/Articles/2003/10/Sla4.asp; and James Dotson, "Major SBC effort to focus on New York City in 2004," *The Christian Index,* January 29, 2004, www.christianindex.org/9.article.

13. As reported in "Dominionism: The Seven Mountains," posted by *Living Journey,* December 10, 2007, http://livingjourney.wordpress.com/2007/12/10/dominionism-the-seven-mountains/. See also the letter from C. Peter Wagner, dated May 31, 2007, posted at www.erwm.com/ApostolicLetter.htm.

14. "2000 to the present day," www.orchardgroup.org/about-us/history/2000-to-the-present-day/.

15. "Statement on Homosexuality," www.villagechurchnyc.com/homosexuality/.

16. Timothy J. Keller and J. Alan Thompson, *Redeemer Church Planting Manual* (New York: Redeemer Presbyterian Church, 2002).

17. Cited in discovery, *Bronx Household of Faith v. Board of Education*, U.S. Court of Appeals, 2nd Circuit, Case 07-5291.

CHAPTER 6

1. Dan Brewster, "The 4/14 Window: Child Ministries and Mission Strategy." In *Children in Crisis: A New Commitment*, Phyllis Kilbourn, ed. (Monrovia, CA: MARC Publications, 1996).

2. Ibid. See also Luis Bush, *The 4/14 Window: Raising Up a New Generation to Transform the World* (Colorado Springs, CO: Compassion International, 2009).

3. Bush, *The 4/14 Window*.

4. Ibid., 22.

5. Kilbourn, *Children in Crisis*, p. 126. The graph appears to have first been presented by Bryant L. Myers, "The State of the World's Children: A Cultural Challenge to the Christian Mission in the 1990s," paper presented to the Evangelical Fellowship of Mission Agencies Executive Retreat, Glen Eyrie, Colorado, September 1992, www.themissionexchange.org.

CHAPTER 7

1. Transcript of a portion of a radio debate on KEOS 89.1 FM from February 2010 that took place in Bryan, Texas, between State Board of Education candidates Don McLeroy, the incumbent, and Thomas Ratliff in the Republican primary race for SBOE district 9, posted by Paul Burka in *Texas Monthly*, February 17, 2010, at www.texasmonthly.com/blog/burkablog.

2. Adam Blaylock, *North Texas Daily*, September 20, 2010.

3. Cynthia Noland Dunbar, *One Nation Under God* (Oveido, FL: Onward, 2008), 17.

4. Ibid., 101.

5. Susan Jacoby, "One Classroom, From Sea to Shining Sea," *New York Times*, March 18, 2010.

6. Reproduced in Lester J. Cappon, ed., *The Adams-Jefferson Letters* (Chapel Hill: University of North Carolina Press, 1988), 592.

7. From the Peter Marshall website, http://petermarshallministries.com /about/index.cfm.

8. Letter from President Thomas Jefferson to the Danbury Baptist Association, January 1, 1802, available, among other places, at the Library of Congress website, http://www.loc.gov/loc/lcib/9806/danpre.html.

CHAPTER 8

1. "Is This Legal?" on the NCBCPS website, www.bibleinschools.net /Is-this-Legal.

2. Matthew McGowan, "Trustees Examine Local Teen Pregnancy Rate," *Odessa American Online*, September 3, 2009, http://www.oaoa.com/articles /rate-36292-county-teen.html.

3. www.bibleinschools.net.

4. www.afa.net.

5. Mark A. Chancey, for the Texas Freedom Network Education Fund, *The Bible in Public Schools: Report on the National Council on Bible Curriculum in Public Schools* (Austin, TX: TFN, 2005). See also Terrence Stutz, "Texas Education Board Members Back Bible Curriculum," *Dallas Morning News*, September 27, 2008; and Suzanne Sataline, "Bible Curriculum Dispute Heats Up in Texas Town," *Wall Street Journal*, May 16, 2007.

6. Kathy Miller, "Clergy, Parents Voice Concerns about Public School Bible School Classes: New Report Reveals Poor Quality, Bias, Religious Agenda in Texas Courses," TFN Press Release, September 13, 2006.

CHAPTER 9

1. Harriet Ryan, "The Kabbalah Center of Los Angeles is the Focus of an IRS Investigation into Tax Evasion," *Los Angeles Times*, May 6, 2011.

2. Janice M. Irvine, *Talk About Sex: The Battles of Sex Education in the United States* (Berkeley: University of California Press, 2004).

3. "Jimmy Swaggart Camp Meeting Hour," weekly radio broadcast, August 19, 1984.

4. Phyllis Schlafly, "The Consequences of Sex Education," *The Phyllis Schlafly Report, 1999*. Published in *The Eagle Forum* by Phyllis Schlafly, www .eagleforum.org/column/1999/july99/99-07-21.html.

5. Doug Herman, *Come Clean* (Carol Stream, IL: Thirsty/Tyndale House Publishers, 2004), 66.

6. Cited in Barry Lynn, *Piety & Politics: The Right-Wing Assault on Religious Freedom* (New York: Harmony 2006), 187–188.

7. Michelle Goldberg, *Kingdom Coming: The Rise of Christian Nationalism* (New York: Norton, 2006).

8. Max Blumenthal, *Republican Gomorrah* (New York: Nation Books, 2009), 159. See also Sexuality Information and Education Council of the United States, www.siecus.org/index.cfm?fuseaction=Page.ViewPage&PageID=1142.

9. Dr. David Wiley and Dr. Kelly Wilson, *Just Say Don't Know: Sexuality Education in Texas Public Schools* (Austin, TX: Texas Freedom Network, 2009), 21.

10. "Condoms & STDs," Austin LifeGuard, www.austinlifeguard.com/condoms.htm. Accessed December 22, 2008. Not available as of August 22, 2011.

11. www.powerteamschools.com/principals.html.

12. http://answeringthecries.org/.

13. www.gotellministries.com/about.html.

14. The citation originally appeared in the Becker website, accessed in September 2010, but has since been removed. For further information, see "Group says Becker Foundation violating Constitution," *Kearney Hub*, May 4, 2010. www.kearneyhub.com/news/local/article_e01117ba-57a4-11df-af74-001cc4c002e0.html.

CHAPTER 10

1. Details from John Stossel, Sylvia Johnson, and Lynn Redmond, "The Black Sheep of Hardesty," *ABC News–20/20*, May 11, 2007, and "Atheists file civil rights suit in 'Oklahoma Outrage,'" www.atheists.org.

2. In the U.S. District Court for the Western District of Oklahoma, *Chester and Nadia Smalkowski & American Atheists, Inc. v Hardesty Public School*, filed 8/11/2006, case 5:06-cv-00845-M, page 7.

3. Brad and Suzanne Dacus, *Reclaim Your School* (Sacramento, CA: Pacific Justice Institute, May 2002), 32.

4. Ibid., 24.

5. www.kfcusa.org/our-vision/. The citation comes from a version of the website accessed on May 5, 2010. As of August 22, 2011, the language has changed somewhat, but the substance is largely unchanged.

6. ADF news release, January 14, 2011, http://adfmedia.org/News/PR Detail/4534.

7. "Help your children and grandchildren go through school with their faith and values intact," from the website of Gateways to Education: Keeping the Faith in Public Schools, www.gtbe.org/news/index.php/5/95/96.html.

8. www.thelifebook.com/index.php. The citations come from a version of the website accessed on May 5, 2010. As of August 22, 2011, the language on the website has changed. Blunt's quotes as reported in: "There is a way to spread the gospel in schools legally," *The Cypress Times*, November 26, 2010, www.thecypresstimes.com/article/Books_Reviews/Authors_News /THERE_IS_A_WAY_TO_SPREAD_THE_GOSPEL_IN_SCHOOLS _LEGALLY/36344.

9. http://everyschool.com/campus-alliance-the-vision.

CHAPTER 11

1. www.cefonline.com/index.php?option=com_content&view=article& id=513:good-news-across-america&catid=136:evangelism-and-discipleship -projects&Itemid=100175.

CHAPTER 12

1. A. A. Hodge, *Popular Lectures on Theological Themes* (Philadelphia: Presbyterian Board of Publications, 1887), 283f.

2. Rousas John Rushdoony, *The Messianic Character of American Education: Studies in the History of the Philosophy of Education* (Vallecito, CA: Ross House Books, 1963), 339.

3. D. James Kennedy, "A Godly Education," sermon as delivered on April 27, 1986 (Ft. Lauderdale, FL: Coral Ridge Ministries, undated).

4. Gregory Thompson, "Are you going to Hell and taking someone with you?" *Christian NewsWire*, April 20, 2010, www.christiannewswire.com /news/1127513671.html.

5. Robert Simonds, *News Letter*, Citizens for Excellence in Education, April 2011.

6. Morris Chapman, "A Case for Christian Elementary and Secondary Education," *Baptist Messenger*, April 24, 2009. The article appeared on the

Baptist Messenger website and was accessed in June 2010. It was also available on morrischapman.com at the same time. As of August 2011, it appears to have been taken down on both sites. See also: "The Southern Baptist Convention is finally throwing in the towel on government schools," *Christian NewsWire*, June 2, 2010, www.christiannewswire.com/news/9859810513.html.

7. Bruce Shortt, *The Harsh Truth About Public Schools* (Vallecito, CA: Chaldecon Foundation, 2004).

8. "The Southern Baptist Convention is finally throwing in the towel on government schools," *Christian NewsWire*, June 2, 2010.

9. "Baptists revive anti-public-school resolution," WorldNetDaily.com, June 1, 2005, http://wwrn.org/articles/17084/?&section=home-schooling.

10. D. James Kennedy, *Education: Public Problems and Private Solutions* (Fort Lauderdale, FL: Coral Ridge Ministries, 1993).

11. *New York Times*, November 21, 1992.

12. Morris Chapman, "A case for Christian elementary and secondary education," *Baptist Messenger*, April 24, 2009.

13. Rev. Andrew Sandlin, *Chalcedon Report* (Vallecito, CA: Chalcedon, March, 1994). Cited in *Church & State*, a publication of Americans United for the Separation of Church and State 47:4 (April 1994), 4–5.

14. Robert Parham, "Southern Baptist Convention Top Exec Boosts Anti-Public School Agenda," ethicsdaily.com, June 10, 2009, www.ethicsdaily.com/news.php?viewStory=14356.

15. www.exodusmandate.org/.

16. Kyle Olson, "Jesus isn't in Michigan," Townhall.com, March 18, 2011. http://townhall.com/columnists/kyleolson/2011/03/18/jesus_isnt_in_michigan.

17. Rob Braun, *New Jersey Star-Ledger*, July 11, 2011.

18. Rob Schwarzwalder, "To Save Children, Cut Education," *Washington Times*, January 21, 2010.

INDEX

Katherine Stewart is a journalist whose work has appeared in *Newsweek International*, *Marie Claire*, the *Times* (London), the *New York Times*, the *Village Voice*, *Rolling Stone*, and many other publica-  tions. She has published two novels and was the coauthor of *Rent by Jonathan Larsen*, the book about the musical *Rent*. She and her family recently moved from Santa Barbara, California, to New York City.

For more information, please visit her website: www.thegood newsclub.com.

PublicAffairs is a publishing house founded in 1997. It is a tribute to the standards, values, and flair of three persons who have served as mentors to countless reporters, writers, editors, and book people of all kinds, including me.

I. F. STONE, proprietor of *I. F. Stone's Weekly*, combined a commitment to the First Amendment with entrepreneurial zeal and reporting skill and became one of the great independent journalists in American history. At the age of eighty, Izzy published *The Trial of Socrates*, which was a national bestseller. He wrote the book after he taught himself ancient Greek.

BENJAMIN C. BRADLEE was for nearly thirty years the charismatic editorial leader of *The Washington Post*. It was Ben who gave the *Post* the range and courage to pursue such historic issues as Watergate. He supported his reporters with a tenacity that made them fearless and it is no accident that so many became authors of influential, best-selling books.

ROBERT L. BERNSTEIN, the chief executive of Random House for more than a quarter century, guided one of the nation's premier publishing houses. Bob was personally responsible for many books of political dissent and argument that challenged tyranny around the globe. He is also the founder and longtime chair of Human Rights Watch, one of the most respected human rights organizations in the world.

. . .

For fifty years, the banner of Public Affairs Press was carried by its owner Morris B. Schnapper, who published Gandhi, Nasser, Toynbee, Truman, and about 1,500 other authors. In 1983, Schnapper was described by *The Washington Post* as "a redoubtable gadfly." His legacy will endure in the books to come.

Peter Osnos, *Founder and Editor-at-Large*